Machiavelli's *The Prince*
Available On Amazon.com and other bookstores

The Prince isn't just for princes who thirst for, or are forcibly thrown into, advancement. It is a raw and bloody field manual for upper- and mid-level managers on predatorial ethics and power: what it is, how to obtain it, and what to do with it once you have found, stumbled across, or been granted it.

Edited by William Dean A. Garner
New York Times bestselling ghostwriter/editor

Sun Tzu *The Art of War*
Available On Amazon.com and other bookstores

This contemporary edition of Sun Tzu's timeless masterpiece has been edited down to its bare essence. It is just as, if not more, relevant today as it was 2,500 years ago, and is wholly effective on the battlefield, and in the boardroom and bedroom. The wisdom of *The Art of War* teaches us that war is unnecessary. Peace is always the goal.

Edited by William Dean A. Garner
New York Times bestselling ghostwriter/editor

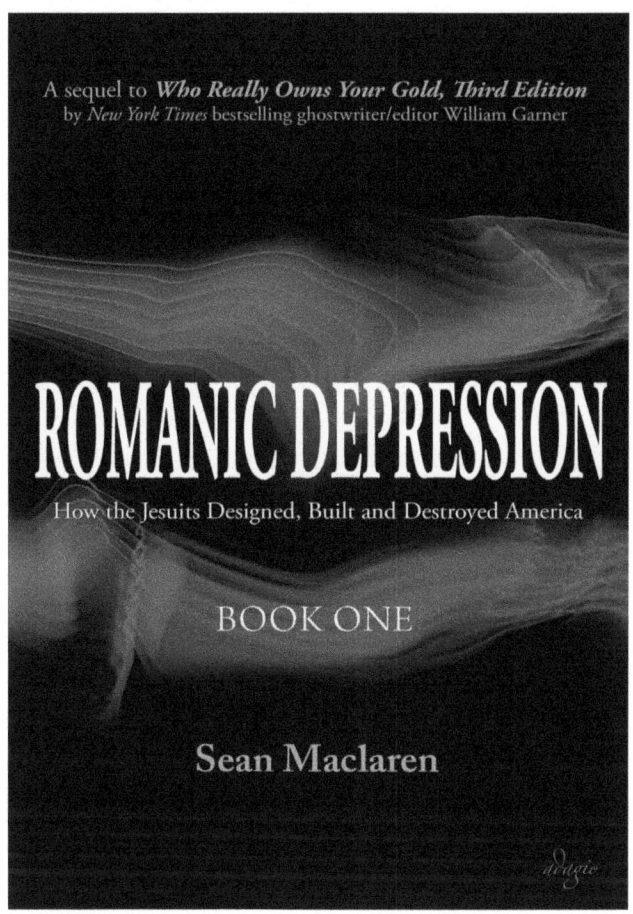

A sequel to *Who Really Owns Your Gold, Third Edition*
by *New York Times* bestselling ghostwriter/editor William Garner

ROMANIC DEPRESSION
How the Jesuits Designed, Built and Destroyed America

BOOK ONE

Sean Maclaren

Romanic Depression
Available On Amazon.com and
other bookstores

The first book in a four-part series that reveals how the Jesuits have designed, built and destroyed every sector of American society, from Law and Government to Politics to Healthcare to Education. Also with more than 200 excellent references.

Edited by William Dean A. Garner
New York Times bestselling ghostwriter/editor

"The Jesuits are so expert in their deeds of blood, that Henry IV said it was impossible to escape them, and he became their victim, though he did all he could to protect himself. My escape from their hands, since the letter of the Pope to Jeff. Davis has sharpened a million of daggers, is more than a miracle."

—Abraham Lincoln

Burke McCarty

The Suppressed Truth About The Assassination of Abraham Lincoln

adagio

AN INDEPENDENT PUBLISHING CRUISE
est. January 1, 2001

Katharine L. Petersen
Publisher / Senior Editor
William Dean A. Garner
Editor

Copyright © 2016 Adagio Press

Published in America by Adagio Press

Adagio and colophon are Trademarks of Adagio Press

Library of Congress Control Number: 2015956701

ISBN: 978-0-9967677-1-2

Adagio website: AdagioPress.com
Email: 69@adagiopress.com

Cover design: Dean Garner

B20161117
Second Print Edition

for Abraham Lincoln
Who knew the Jesuits would murder him,
yet kept moving forward and doing the right thing

and for You, dear Reader

Contents

Preface

America was doomed before her inception, a well-planned takeover by the Society of Jesus, the Jesuits, whose dark plan was hatched more than 100 years before America declared independence from the British Crown. The so-called "Founding Fathers" of America knew about the Jesuits and did absolutely nothing to oppose them. Does this mean they were in league with the Jesuits, or were they simply too afraid to speak out or act against this powerful secret society?

We do know that the Rothschild bastard Alexander Hamilton actively plotted against America, her government and her people by creating the country's first central bank, which plunged the country into immediate debt, from which she has yet to recover.

The author cites several Congressional records that show definitively that members of Congress knew about the Jesuits and their danger to America. There is absolutely no question about this fact.

President Abraham Lincoln was one of the few American politicians who acknowledged that the Jesuits were a menace to our society, but he felt powerless to do anything about the threat. It appears the most he did was discuss them and their ugly deeds in letters to, and discussions with, close friends, in particular Reverend Charles Chiniquy, whom he ably defended against the Jesuits years before his presidency.

Reverend Chiniquy documented his talks and letters with the president in his book, *Fifty Years in the Church of Rome*. In it, he shares openly his experience with the Jesuits over decades, and confirms for us that the Jesuits continue to be a great threat to American society and the world. Adagio Press will soon be releasing the newly updated edition of *Fifty Years in the Church of Rome*.

In *The Suppressed Truth About the Assassination of Abraham Lincoln,* former member of the Catholic Church, Burke McCarty, documented her well-researched nature of the murder. She deftly uncovered the history of the secret European society that actively plotted against America and her people for many years, among numerous other conspiracies that eventually led to the assassination of President Lincoln.

Ms. McCarty said: "The masses of any people cannot be corrupted. The strong sense of justice and right and fairness which God has implanted in each human heart at birth, unless destroyed by some evil influence, or system, will invariably spring into action at a crisis, if they are permitted to have a clear understanding of the issue. As a matter of fact, their very instinct of self-preservation sharpens their judgment and strengthens their resolutions. The only instances of wrong decisions, or actions at such times, comes from false, wicked leaders."

Outstanding as Ms. McCarty's work was, she did not uncover the true nature of assassin John Wilkes Booth's apparent death, which is the subject of an upcoming book by Adagio Press, *The Escape and Suicide of John Wilkes Booth: The Jesuit Assassin of Abraham Lincoln*. Booth was not shot shortly after he assassinated President Lincoln. As the book shows, he lived quite a long life. Please read the book to learn the details. They are indeed fascinating.

A note on how we edited and produced this book: we corrected obvious errors in grammar, spelling and syntax, while leaving Ms. McCarty's text intact, including her heavy use of emphasis (bold text, upper case words and sentences, etc.). We chose to reproduce the general layout of her original book, including the often-sensational chapter subheadings, because, everything taken together, it demonstrates Ms. McCarty's deep passion and concern about the subject and keen diligence in presenting it as accurately as possible. We also used the original photographs from her book.

Whatever you choose to believe about these horrendous conspiracies that plague America to this day, please take the time to do your own research, as Ms. McCarty did, and learn the basic history of our country, and not the typical revisionist history we are taught in schools, colleges and universities, and exposed to in mainstream media and entertainment. The more you understand who runs America and the planet, the better you can adjust your life to make the most of it without your rights being subjugated to the point that you remain a slave to a despotic system.

William Garner

Introduction

The Conspiracy of Silence on the Death of Abraham Lincoln

In all the bloody history of the Papacy, perhaps in no one man, as in Abraham Lincoln, was there concentrated such a multitude of reasons for his annihilation by that system.

In all the history of the political assassination plots by the enemies of freedom, which for cold calculation, malicious methods, relentless pursuit, subtle cunning, and cowardly execution, nothing can exceed the cruel murder of this greatest of all Americans, for President Lincoln was the living, breathing type in which was fulfilled the triumph of the New Concept of Popular Government, the central postulate of which is, the consent of the governed. It was the life of Abraham Lincoln that placed this form of government forever outside an "experiment" where its enemies persisted in endeavoring to keep it.

That a barefoot, nameless boy on poverty's path could, by his own efforts, reach the highest office in the gift of the American people, gave the lie to the "Divine Right" croakers, and merited their most unceasing hatred.

Barring the martyrdoms of Jesus Christ and Joan D'Arc, the methods used in Abraham Lincoln's assassination will stand pre-eminent in point of malice and cruelty, and strange as it may seem, the same diabolical cunning that nerved the hand of the assassin has pursued Lincoln beyond the grave, and has been largely successful in hiding from the public all details of his physical destruction. This crime, in the eyes of the writer, almost outstrips the first, for by this conspiracy of silence on his death, the youth of America are being deprived of the knowledge of the details of the greatest tragedy in their country's history.

This appalling fact has been the one big urge that inspired the writing of this book, the contents of which represent only a part of the result of leisure hours spent in public and private libraries in the various cities, covering a period of the past seven years, gathering a fact here and one there, from books, magazines, newspapers and court records, filing them away, and finally condensing the salient points between the covers you now hold in your hand.

I feel safe in stating that nowhere else can be found in one book the connected presentation of the story leading up to the death of Abraham Lincoln, which was instigated by the Black Pope, the General of the Jesuit Order, camouflaged by the White Pope, Pius IX, aided, abetted and financed by other "Divine Righters" of Europe, and finally consummated by the Roman Hierarchy and their paid agents in this country and Canada on Good Friday night, April 14, 1865 at Ford's Theatre, Washington, DC.

I am convinced that if this knowledge can be given adequate distribution and placed in possession of the boys and girls of the public elementary schools, for whom it is especially designed to reach, that the wicked boast of the Jesuits and their lay agents, the Knights of Columbus, to make America Catholic can never be accomplished.

The great spirit of the martyred Lincoln will rise up and defeat his slayers and their successors!

In closing, I only ask each reader whose heart beats in unison with those of us who love our country and all that it represents, to assist in the sale of this little book, by giving it all the publicity possible, thereby joining in President Lincoln's expression of loyalty, "If ever my country is destroyed, it shall be my proudest plume, not that I was the last to desert her, but that I never deserted her!"

Yours Truly,
Burke McCarty

I

Destruction Of This Republic
Plotted By European Monarchists

The death of President Lincoln was the culmination of but one step in the attempt to carry out the Secret Treaty of Verona of October 1822, a pact entered into by the "high contracting parties" of the former Congress of Vienna, Austria, which had held its sessions secretly, covering the whole year of 1814-15.

Simultaneously with the calling of the Congress of Vienna in 1814, Pope Pius VII restored the Society of Jesus (Jesuit Order) which had been abolished by Pope Clement IV July 21, 1773 on the grounds that it was immoral, dangerous, and was a menace to the very life of the papacy. Clement was promptly poisoned for his act. With the restoration of this order, the execution of the Secret Treaty of Verona was placed in their keeping.

The Congress of Vienna was a black conspiracy against popular governments at which the "high contracting parties" announced at its close that they had formed a "holy alliance." This was a cloak under which they masked to deceive the people.

The particular business of the Congress of Verona was the ratification of Article Six of the Congress of Vienna, a promise to prevent or destroy popular governments wherever found, and to re-establish monarchy where it had been set aside.

The "high contracting parties" of this compact, Russia, Prussia, Austria and Pope Pius VII, king of the Papal States, entered into a secret treaty to do so. That the reader may get some idea of the villainy of these two Congresses and their relation to our government, and to the death of Abraham Lincoln, I quote excerpts from that document below, as it appears in the US *Congressional Record* of April 25, 1916, placed there by Senator Robert L. Owen and as it is recorded in the *Diplomatic Code* by Elliott, page 179:

SECRET TREATY OF VERONA

The undersigned specially authorized to make some additions to the treaty of the Holy Alliance, after having exchanged their respective credentials, have agreed as follows:

ARTICLE 1. The high contracting powers being convinced that the system of representative government is equally as incompatible with the monarchial principals as the maxim of the sovereignty of the people with the divine right, engage mutually, in the most solemn manner to use all their efforts to put an end to the system of representative governments, in whatever country it may exist in Europe, and to prevent its being introduced in those countries where it is not yet known.

ARTICLE 2. As it cannot be doubted that the liberty of the press is the most powerful means used by the pretended supporters of the rights of nations to the detriment of those of princes, the high contracting parties promise reciprocally to adopt all proper measures to suppress it, not only in their own state but also in the rest of Europe.

ARTICLE 3. Convinced that the principles of religion contribute most powerfully to keep nations in the state of passive obedience which they owe to their princes, the high contracting parties declare it to be their intention to sustain in their respective states, those measures which the clergy may adopt with the aim of ameliorating their own interests, so intimately connected with the preservation of the authority of the princes; and the contracting powers join in offering their thanks to the pope for what he has already done for them, and solicit his constant cooperation in their views of submitting the nations.

ARTICLE 4. The situation of Spain and Portugal unite unhappily all the circumstances to which this treaty has particular reference. The high contracting parties, in confiding to France the care of putting an end to them, engaged to assist her in the manner which may at least compromise them with their own people and the people of France by means of a subsidy on the part of the two empires of 20,000,000 of francs every year from the date of signature of this treaty to the end of the war.

ARTICLE 5. In order to establish in the peninsula the order of things which existed before the revolution of Cadiz, and to insure the entire execution of the articles of the present treaty, the high contracting parties give to each other the reciprocal assurance that as long as their views are not fulfilled, rejecting all other ideas of futility or other measure to be taken, they will address themselves with the shortest possible delay to all the authorities existing in their states and to all their agents in foreign countries, with the view to establish connections tending toward the accomplishment of the objects proposed by this treaty.

ARTICLE 6. This treaty shall be renewed with such changes as new circumstances may give occasion for, either at a new congress, or at the court of one of the contracting parties, as soon as the war with Spain shall be terminated.

ARTICLE 7. The present treaty shall be ratified and the ratifications exchanged at Paris within the space of six months.

Made at Verona the 22nd of November, 1822.
For Austria: Metternich.
For France: Chateaubriand.
For Russia: Bernstet.
For Russia: Nesselrode.

When Senator Owen was questioned by members of Congress upon the meaning of the Treaty, the *Record* shows his reply in part:

> "This Holy Alliance, having put a Bourbon prince upon the throne of France by force, then used France to suppress the condition of Spain, immediately afterwards, and by this very treaty gave her a subsidy of 20,000,000 francs annually to enable her to wage war upon the people of Spain and prevent their exercise of any measure of the right of self-government. The Holy Alliance immediately did the same thing in Italy, by sending Austrian troops to Italy, where the people there attempted to exercise a like measure of liberal constitutional self-government; and it was not until the printing press, which the Holy Alliance so stoutly opposed, taught the people of Europe the value of liberty that finally one country after another seized a greater and greater right of self-government, until now it may be fairly said that nearly all the nations of Europe have a very large measure of self-government.
>
> However, I wished to call the attention of the Senate to this important history in the growth of constitutional popular self-government. The Holy Alliance made its powers felt by the wholesale drastic suppression of the press in Europe, by universal censorship, by killing free speech and all ideas of popular rights, and by the complete suppression of popular government. The Holy Alliance having destroyed popular government in Spain, and in Italy, had well-laid plans also to destroy popular government in the American Colonies which had revolted from Spain and Portugal in Central and South America under the influence of the successful example of the United States.
>
> It was because of this conspiracy against the American Republics by the European monarchies that the great English statesman, Canning, called the attention of our government to it, and our statesmen then, including Thomas Jefferson, who was still living at that time, took an active part to bring about the declaration by President Monroe in his next annual message to the Congress of the

United States that the United States would regard it as an act of hostility to the government of the United States and an unfriendly act, if this coalition, or if any power of Europe ever undertook to establish upon the American continent any control of any American republic, or to acquire any territorial rights.

This is the so-called Monroe Doctrine. The threat under the Secret Treaty of Verona to suppress popular government in the American republics is the basis of the Monroe Doctrine. This secret treaty sets forth clearly the conflict between monarchial government and popular government, and the government of the few as against the government of the many."

The above comments of our United States Senator before Congress in 1916, clearly defines the object and intent of these "Divine Righters" in Europe.

It will be well for the reader to understand that the Church of Rome with its sixteen centuries of intrigue, plans fifty or a hundred years ahead. The ultimate goal of the great scheme is to throw the lever of time back by restoring the pope as the "universal arbiter" from whom all the rulers of the earth must receive their authority to rule, as during the Dark Ages.

The big idea of democracy, taught by Jesus Christ when he proclaimed the spiritual equality of all men, has always been hated and feared by the Jesuit system, and made the target of their venom, despite all their protestations of Christianity.

The idea of spiritual equality, logically and inevitably leads to social equality, which has been made practical by popular governments.

The central idea of popular government is "consent of the governed."

The first real social freedom resulted from the Protestant Reformation, led by the little German monk, Martin Luther, in 1517. This was an unpardonable sin. It was the death blow of the Papacy.

Protestant Germany, Protestant England, and of course, Protestant United States, have been from the beginning marked by them for destruction. Ex-Catholic Italy and Ex-Catholic France are next in this "rule or ruin" policy. In Protestant Denmark, Sweden and Holland, the same process of "working from within" is being pursued as it is in this country and Canada.

The seeds of hate between Germany and England were planted in those two glorious Protestant countries by the Jesuits so that they might develop in time to block the celebration of the Protestant Reformation on its four hundredth anniversary, an event planned to surpass anything of the kind the world has ever seen, a celebration that would have set Protestantism fifty years ahead.

The Jesuits, anticipating this, staged the World War, which completely sidetracked this epic celebration.

For over sixty years the Great Scheme the Vatican and its Jesuits have been working on is, in a nutshell, to form an ecclesiastical empire, uniting French Canada with our Atlantic States, Maine, New Hampshire, Vermont, Massachusetts, Rhode Island and Connecticut. This is to be done by annexation, manipulated through corrupt politicians at Washington, D.C, in much the same method as the annexation of Texas was accomplished over sixty years ago.

The next big card being played by Rome is the unification of the French Canadian and Irish-Catholic vote in the New England States where the influx of Catholic Canadians is of such proportion as to cause serious consideration of loyal Americans right now.

The Church is meeting with some difficulty, owing to the deep-seated dislike between the French and Irish Catholics. This, however, is being rapidly overcome by two methods: intermarriage and through the work of the Knights of Columbus, which is by far the most dangerous lay organization in this country.

The *Tragedy of Quebec*, a book written by a Protestant Canadian, exposes the plan in detail, and the facts and figures given by this writer who has been a close student of the subject for many years are startling.

It would be illuminating to the reader who is not familiar with this book to read it. The full plan of extending the Pope's empire on the Atlantic coast will be done by Latinizing our Southern States, a process begun very early in our history, prior to the Civil War.

The big efforts of the Catholic Church to papalize the negro in the South should not be overlooked where great strides have been taken in that direction.

The next step in the Vatican's Great Scheme is to make war between this country and Japan after the latter country has been placed under full dominance of the Jesuits. The priests, monks and nuns of the Roman Church have been pouring into Japan from all over the world now for many years with that purpose in view. The writer was told by a Christian Japanese minister in charge of a Protestant mission in Los Angeles in reply to the question as to why the Jesuits, who had been barred for years from Japan, had now been permitted to enter.

He answered that the Roman Church had gotten into his country under the guise of Mohammedanism, and that after it was well entrenched threw off its disguise, and his country learned to its astonishment that it was to the Roman Church and its monastic orders it had opened its doors.

That the Roman Catholic-controlled trade unions in California are at the bottom of most of the agitation against the Japanese in that State is a fact; that the Roman Catholic politician, James Phelan, was sent to the United States Senate in 1913 by the solid Roman vote, and has been the prime mover in the anti-Jap agitation, is also a fact.

There are many Californians, of course, outside the Roman church, who fear the Japanese menace on account of their prolific propagation, and their nonassimilative proclivities, but it is only since I have realized the activity of the Jesuits to papalize Japan, that the real horror of the "yellow peril" has impressed itself upon me. Add Romanism to Japan, and it certainly becomes terrifying in its aspect.

I am not presenting these things as a calamity howler, but I believe with careful consideration and immediate intelligent activity, the danger can be averted. We must be alert and doing. And now we will take up the Roman question which is the big, overshadowing world question today, and it will continue to be until the Papacy is finally uprooted.

We will have to take cognizance of it in Europe frequently through these pages to get a clear view of the impending danger to ourselves. I ask the reader to be patient and follow me closely in my hurdling of the Atlantic, back and forth, at various times which I have been obliged to do. It is a big and perplexing question to try to simplify sufficiently for the busy non-Romanist who is so absorbed in his own affairs and who so little understands that pernicious system.

The great mistake that the American non-Catholic people make is that they judge the papacy by the Roman Church as they find it in this country. One cannot gauge it from this standpoint, for we must remember that it is operating where more than five-sixths of the people are non-Romanists—in a Protestant country. To get an accurate estimate, one must survey it in its native state, so to speak, in Catholic countries where it has held sway for centuries. On this side of the Atlantic, for instance, we will have to contemplate it as it is in Mexico or Central and South America to get a true estimate.

I shall quote through these pages copiously from several books, some of which are out of print, so that their messages may not be entirely lost.

II

The Society Of Jesus:
The Engine Of Destruction

The Society of Jesus, the members of which are referred to as the Jesuits, has absorbed the papacy. This Society was founded by a fanatic, Ignatius Loyola, in 1541, its object being to combat the Protestant Reformation of Martin Luther, of 1517.

Loyola was the son of a prominent Spanish family who had distinguished himself as a soldier, and by the immoral excesses of his private life, but who, owing to an accident that maimed him, was supposed to have become "converted," and during the illness that followed, the Society of Jesus was conceived in his brain, fertile with deviltry.

The Society of Jesus is under the strictest military discipline, due to the military training and psychology of its founder. It is absolutely commanded by the General, its head, also known as the Black Pope. The garb is always a plain black cassock. But here permit me to present the definition of one of its eminent Generals of the 17th century. The definition aptly describes it today:

> "The members of the Society are dispersed in every corner of the world, and divided into as many nations and kingdoms as the earth has limits: divisions, however, marked only by distance of places, not of sentiment; by the differences of languages, not of affections; by the dissemblance of faces, not of manners. In that family the Latin thinks as the Greek, the Portuguese as the Brazilian,

the Hibernian as the Sumatran, the Spanish as the French, the English as the Flemish; and amongst so many different geniuses, no controversy, no contention, nothing which gives you a hint, to perceive that they have more than one. Their birthplace offers them no motive of personal interest. The same aim, same conduct, same vow, which like a conjugal knot, has tied them together. At the least sign, one man, the General, turns and returns the entire society and shapes the revolution of so large a body.

It is easy to move, but difficult to shape." (*Imago Primsaeculi Societas Jesu*, published by the authorization of Mutto Vittelschi, General in 1640.)

With the above authentic illumination, you will be able to somewhat grasp the reason that the execution of the mandate of the Holy Alliance and Secret Treaty of Verona was entrusted to the members of the Society of Jesus. God save the mark!

THE JESUIT OATH

As a further item of interest, we quote the following excerpts of this oath-bound organization. It is the oath taken now by practically all priests of the Church of Rome, and has been charged as the one taken by the members of the Fourth Degree in the Knights of Columbus. (See *Congressional Record*, House Bill 1523, Contested election case of Eugene C. Bonniwell, against Thomas S. Butler, Feb. 15, 1913, pages 3215-16.)

"I ...., now in the presence of Almighty God, the Blessed Virgin Mary, the Blessed Michael the Archangel, the Blessed St. John the Baptist, the Holy Apostles, Peter and Paul, and all the Saints, sacred hosts of Heaven, and to you, my ghostly Father, the Superior General of the Society of Jesus, founded by St. Ignatius Loyola, in the Pontification of Paul the Third, and continued to the present, do by the womb of the Virgin, the matrix of God, and the rod of Jesus Christ, declare and swear that his holiness, the Pope, is Christ's Vice-regent, and is the true and only head of the Catholic or Universal Church throughout the earth; and that by the virtue of the keys of binding and loosing, given to his Holiness by my Savior, Jesus Christ, he hath power to depose heretical kings, princes, states, commonwealths and governments, all being illegal without his sacred confirmation, and that they may be safely destroyed.

Therefore, to the utmost of my power, I shall and will defend this doctrine and his Holiness' right and customs against all usurpers of the heretical or Protestant authority, whatever, especially the Lutheran Church of Germany, Holland, Denmark, Sweden and Norway, and the now pretended authority of the Church of England and Scotland, the branches of the same, now established in Ireland, and on the continent of America and elsewhere.

I do now renounce and disown any allegiance as due to any heretical king, prince or state named Protestant or Liberals, or obedience to any of their laws, magistrates or officers.

I do further declare that I will help and assist and advise all or any of his Holiness' agents in any place wherever I shall be, and do my utmost to extirpate the heretical Protestant or Liberal doctrines and to destroy all their pretended powers, legal or otherwise.

I do further promise and declare, that notwithstanding I am dispensed with to assume any religion heretical for the propagating of the Mother Church's interest to keep secret and private all her agents' counsels from time to time as they may instruct me, and not to divulge directly or indirectly, by word, writing, or circumstances whatever, but to execute all that shall be proposed, given in charge or discovered unto me by you, my ghostly father.

I do further promise and declare that I will have no opinion or will of my own, or any mental reservation whatever, even as a corpse or cadaver (*perinde ac cadaver*) but unhesitatingly obey each and every command that I may receive from my superiors in the Militia of the Pope and Jesus Christ.

That I will go to any part of the world whatsoever without murmuring and will be submissive in all things whatsoever communicated to me. I do further promise and declare that I will, when opportunity presents, make and wage relentless war, secretly or openly, against all heretics, Protestants and Liberals, as I am directed to do to extirpate and exterminate them from the face of the whole earth, and that I will spare neither sex, age nor condition; and that I will hang, waste, boil, flay, strangle and bury alive these infamous heretics; rip up the stomachs and wombs of their women and crush their infants' heads against the wall, in order to annihilate forever their execrable race.

That when the same cannot be done openly, I will secretly use the poison cup, the strangulation cord, the steel of the poniard, or the leaden bullet, regardless of the honor, rank, dignity or authority of the person or persons whatsoever may be their condition in life, either public or private, as I at any time may be directed so to do by any agent of the pope or superior of the brotherhood of the holy faith of the Society of Jesus."

The late Edwin A. Sherman, a 33rd Degree Mason of Oakland, CA, in his book, *The Engineer Corps of Hell*, quotes Charles Sauvestre, whose work he translated from the Spanish:

"Such are the Jesuits. Always expelled, forever returning, and little by little, clandestinely, and in the darkness, throwing out its vigorous roots. Its wealth may be confiscated, its losses cannot be detained for they are covered.

"Confessors, negotiators, brokers, lenders, peddlers of pious gew gaws, inventors of new devotions to make merchandise. At times, mixing in politics, agitating states, and making princes tremble upon their thrones, for they are terrible in their hate.

"Woe unto him when they turn upon him as an enemy! Its society grows and increases in riches and influence by all sorts of means; and no one can attack them, for everywhere we find men prompt to serve them, to obtain from them some advantage of position or pride.

"For themselves, they are nothing, not having pompous titles, no croziers, no mitres, no capes of the prebendaries, but pertain to that one order, everywhere governing and directing . . . In whatever place of the Catholic world a Jesuit is insulted or resisted, no matter how insignificant he may be, he is sure to be avenged, and this we know."

"The General is always surrounded by counselors, professors, novices and graduates," says Michelet, "prescribing friendship in the seminaries and being prohibited to walk two by two, it is necessary to be alone or three together, but not less, for it is well known that the Jesuits never establish any intimacy before a third, for the third is a spy; for when there are three, which is indispensable, there cannot be found a traitor."

THE JESUIT OATH TAKEN BY THE FIRST ARCHBISHOP OF BALTIMORE (1769) LEAVES ITS IMPRESS

The papal church, when expedient, follows the rule of pagan Rome to hold a conquered country in leash, and make it yield its pound of flesh, by placing over it native rulers, which is the easy way to approach the people on their blind side.

In 1753, an American-born boy of eighteen, John Carroll, from Upper Marlboro, Maryland, entered the College of the Society of Jesuits at Watteau, Flanders, to study for the Romish priesthood in that Order.

The time required ordinarily for the training in that Society is fourteen years and, as John Carroll was not ordained until he had served sixteen years in preparation, it is safe to conclude that this American-born youth was an especially well-grounded "cadaver" upon his return to the Colonies in 1769, and that his Society was justified in feeling that its interests would be competently administered.

John Carroll had taken the oath from which we quoted some pages back to "When opportunity presents, make and wage relentless war, secretly or openly, against all heretics, Protestants and Liberals."

It is interesting to note that John Carroll was a first cousin to Charles Carroll of Carrollton, the only Romanist who signed the Declaration of Independence.

The officials of Maryland Colony sent a committee, of which Benjamin

Franklin was a member, to visit French Canada to see if help could be had from that source in the interest of the Colonies in the coming conflict with England.

It was recommended by Congress that Charles Carroll ask his cousin, John Carroll, the Jesuit priest, to accompany them, hoping that he would use his influence in securing the assistance of the French priests in the cause of the Colonies, an act that showed the lack of understanding of the fundamentals and discipline of the Jesuit society by the Colonists.

Of course, the expedition utterly failed, owing to the influence of the French priests and the people of French Canada, over whom Father John Carroll was supposed to have had the power of persuasion. Though England was a heretical country, the exceedingly liberal and the independent spirit of defiance in the American Colonies was far more menacing, in the eyes of the priests, to the interests of the church and the "Divine Righters," and Jesuit Priest Carroll's Jesuit Oath precluded the possibility of his having any interest in his native country.

Consequently, he had to think in the same channel as his French compatriots in religion. That he, a few years later, merited the distinction from his church to be made the first Archbishop of Baltimore and was permitted to live to the ripe old age of four score years is proof positive that he served his church faithfully by strictly adhering to his Jesuit Oath.

The first Archbishop of Baltimore left his indelible stamp on that diocese as clearly demonstrated during the Civil War, for every plot to assassinate President Lincoln—and there were many—was hatched in Baltimore. In fact, Baltimore is the "Vienna of America."

The fact also must not be overlooked that there were less than 30,000 Romanists and 25 priests in the Colonies at the start of the American Revolution. This, of course, was a handicap to the Reverend Carroll.

The first Archbishop of Baltimore must have been, however, thoroughly conversant with the rumblings of the Revolution in Europe, for his Society was having some "rough sledding" during the early 18th century when he arrived in Flanders, and its members were being driven out of first one country and then another.

The great battle for political freedom was being bitterly waged between the Jesuits on one hand and Freemasonry on the other, just as in the final analysis of the present irrepressible conflict in the United States today, these two forces are lining up, a fact that is becoming more obvious as time goes on.

They stand today as they have always stood, these Jesuits, against every principle upon which Freemasonry is founded—upon which Americanism is based.

A group of French cyclopedists, led by Jean Jacques Rousseau, had embodied a new concept of government, in which the central postulate was that the only authority to govern should come from the consent of the governed. This was whipped into shape and published early in the 18th century and boldly proclaimed to the world by Rousseau in his *Social Contract*—a contract of society.

Eleven years after, Thomas Jefferson, Thomas Paine and other framers of our Declaration of Independence, incorporated it in that great chart of liberty, and when the silver tones of our old Liberty Bell in Philadelphia rang it out on July 4th, 1776, it reverberated around the world and stirred the red blood of every divine-right hater to its depths:

> "Gravely plain the good pen lined it,
> And the Fifty-Six all signed it;
> Pledged their lives to seal and bind it,
> True and well!
> Then sudden from the steeple,
> Clanged the tocsin of the people,
> Spoke the sum of history's pages,
> Pealed the thoughts of saints and sages,
> Rang the keynote of the ages, in the Bell."
> —*The Liberty Bell,* Howard S. Taylor

It is difficult now for us to realize the boldness and courage required of that little group of Colonial "Rebels" who gathered around the table in Independence Hall in Philadelphia to sign that document. It was a grim joke, indeed, that Benjamin Franklin sprung when he took up the pen to write in his name, and said: "Gentlemen, we must now all hang together, for if we don't, we will hang separately."

The success of the Revolution in the American Colonies gave the stimulation to the French to revolt in 1789. The triumphant conclusion of John Wilkes's battle for a free press in England, the rumblings of revolt in the papal states where the pope was king, all these held the cradle of popular government in this country in security until the infant had dropped its swaddling clothes and got a fair start to grow.

John Carroll was studying at the Jesuit College in Flanders when Rousseau's *Social Contract* set Europe ablaze with its message to the downtrodden masses. The sensation precipitated by that revolutionary proclamation can be but faintly imagined now. Certain it is that the pope of Rome with the rest of the crowned heads of Europe saw the handwriting on the wall, if the new idea of government were permitted to take root.

Four years later, John Carroll was a full-fledged Jesuit priest, and was returned to his native land where he had an opportunity to get a close-up of the working out of the first popular government where the people were the only source of authority.

In 1808, this Jesuit priest was made the first Archbishop of Baltimore by his "Lord-God," the pope. In receiving the pallium, he took a more disloyal oath of allegiance than that as a priest, to direct the work of his Jesuit Order and his church.

Verily, "The ways of God are wondrous strange." Who would have thought that a few months later an infant son would be born to a pioneer couple in the backwoods of Kentucky, in a rude log hut, who was destined to, fifty years later, with one blow, defeat the cautiously laid plans of the Vatican, its Jesuits, the Romanoffs of Russia, the Hapsburgs of Austria and the King of Prussia!

I have often pictured the baby Lincoln playing about the humble log cabin in the Kentucky woods, whose life was no different from the infant life of other children of the pioneers, except in the greater degree of poverty, and wondered if by chance in her day dreams, Nancy Hanks Lincoln could have glimpsed the perspective in which her baby boy was destined to become the savior of this popular government; if, when she gathered him to her proud motherly heart, quieting him to sleep with a crooning lullaby, which all mothers sing, the noble but storm-tossed future of the child she snuggled might by chance, like summer lightning, have flashed over her vision?

And, in my mind's eye, I pictured the meeting on the other side of the Great Divide of this mother and son on the morning of April 15, 1865, and the happy look of triumph in her glistening eyes as she beheld him in the immortal garb of martyrdom that his enemies had inadvertently placed upon him.

III

The Saint Leopoldine Foundation
Spy System

Owing to the combination of circumstances Europe just referred to, the autocrats did not dare to "wage open war" on the American government, since the warning enunciated in the Monroe Doctrine.

In 1828, an organization in Vienna was formed: the Saint Leopoldine Foundation. The plan was to operate under the mask of religion, which would ensure its safety from any governmental innuendo and what could not be done by bullets and bayonets.

The Hapsburg family of Austria was the most powerful Roman Catholic ruling family in Europe and consequently the most cruel, despotic and reactionary, and had the American people not been so absorbed in the new building of their republic, they would have detected the hypocrisy of this "holy" fraud, the Saint Leopoldine Foundation.

One of the Hapsburg brothers, Prince Rudolph, was a member of the Roman Curia, the Cardinal Rudolph Hapsburg of Olmutz. It was easy for the Jesuits of the Vatican to operate through him as the agent for the foundation funds, which poured into the United States in a stream of gold.

The Vatican did not furnish all the funds. They were most likely furnished by the "high contracting parties" of the Holy Alliance and the Secret Treaty of Verona.

In short, the immense sums distributed among the bishops and archbishops of the Catholic Church in this country, in establishing bishoprics in cities where none existed, were used solely as gigantic political slush funds to corrupt and ultimately destroy the government and set up a monarchial one instead.

One year after the Saint Leopoldine Foundation had been established, it received the recognition and blessing of the pope. The wonderful generosity of the Hapsburg family was called to his attention. The blessing was conveyed at a political high mass in Vienna, in January 1829, at which all of the royalty was in attendance, and the happy occasion was closed by a grand ball in the palace at night.

The scum of Catholic Europe, especially from Ireland, then began pouring into this country from every nook and cranny of that poverty-stricken continent, in many cases, their passages being advanced from this slush fund. The Roman bishops of every large city, from New York to San Francisco, then began massing this foreign Catholic vote.

Tammany Hall had years before been organized and, from its very inception, began a system of political corruption that dominates New York's politics to this very day. This situation should have staggered the world, but it failed to awaken the American people except in spots.

The massed Roman vote in the cities placed the balance of political power in the hands of the Roman bishops and priests. Intimidation has always been the "big stick" used when any man in public office presumed to oppose the advance of these ecclesiastical bosses.

With the rapidly increased foreign immigration, these agents of the "Divine Righters of Europe," operating through the Jesuits and their lay agents, have made progress beyond their wildest dreams. City councils, state legislatures and even Congress have been brow-beaten and bribed. It was boasted within a year that any seat in Congress can be bought for one hundred thousand dollars!

Not only so, but some years ago when the Chicago Congressman William Lorimer's seat was contested, it was made a matter of record that this sum was the purchase price. A forced resignation followed. It is interesting to note that Mr. Lorimer's chief witness was a Catholic priest of Chicago, who testified, according to the Associated Press reports, that a penitent of his had acknowledged in the confessional that he had libeled Mr. Lorimer. The said penitent was not named, of course.

A few months after Mr. Lorimer's resignation, the press dispatches notified us that he had been received into the Catholic Church with great acclaim. I cite this one case merely to emphasize my point.

The Saint Leopoldine Foundation is a great Jesuit Spy System that is not confined to the ecclesiastics of the Roman church, but embraces every element of society, from the private secretary of the president in the White House, to the Catholic servant girl employed in the Protestant-American families. Nor, indeed, is it restricted to Roman Catholics, for the Jesuits do not hesitate to use non-Catholic tools whenever it is possible. In fact, they prefer them, for in this way attention is distracted from them. In case of failure, it is always preferable to use non-Catholics.

The priest of every parish in this country is the kingpin in this web of spying, and reports regularly to his bishop every item of interest, directly or indirectly and, in turn, the bishop to his archbishop, the archbishop to the cardinal and the cardinal to the pope. The confessional box is the Roman clearing house, whereby the pope keeps his finger on the pulse of the world.

It is a strange thing to know that no matter how densely ignorant a Roman priest may be, that is on any subject outside the things bearing on his church, that priest knows perfectly the psychology of every non-Romanist of any prominence in his district. He knows his mental attitude toward the Romish church; he knows what the man will think and do under certain circumstances; he particularly knows if he is friendly or unfriendly to the Roman church; he knows the extent of his wealth, and if the party is of enough importance in the community, he knows the most intimate details and conduct of his private life.

The man, on the other hand, knows little or nothing of the parish priest. More than likely, if he was asked, he would say that he was the Catholic priest of such a parish. If it happened to be in a town where the Catholic population was small and of no social or political importance, this would express the limit of his knowledge. If, on the other hand, he was politically ambitious and alert, the priest would be one of the first with whom he would ingratiate himself, for most of the politicians have learned to realize the political advantage of an organized vote.

The sources of information the Roman priest can tap are almost unlimited and unknown to the ordinary layman outside that corporation. The Leopoldines are honeycombed in every avenue of civic, state and national life. There are, to begin with, the police departments of the various cities, ninety per cent of whom I may, I think, conservatively say, are Fourth Degree Knights of Columbus. They are always at the beck and call of the hierarchy. Their chief duty as Catholic citizens is to obey their bishops and the Holy See as God himself. (See *The Great Encyclical Letters of Pope Leo XIII*, page 192.)

Then there are their Jesuit college graduates in every state, who are especially trained as expert spies.

If any man holding a political position refuses to prostitute that position, by yielding to the demands of the Romish priests, and persists in his stand, they use their blackmail threats, if they cannot accomplish their purpose in any other way, for, "Any means to an end" is the Jesuit motto. If there is no such knowledge in their possession by which to discredit or frighten him, they do not hesitate to set their traps for him, and should this fail, they are fortified to resort to what is known in common parlance as a "frame-up," which is an easy matter through their "red-light" affiliations.

Many a good man has been driven from public life by this route. Many a man in politics this moment is a subservient tool of the Roman priests, because he fears the physical violence of their arson and murder gangs, or that they may drag out some family skeleton to discredit him.

I am aware that these are harsh sayings, but the truth is very often shocking.

The principal branches of the Leopoldines, still operating in this country under various titles, are: The German Catholic Central Verein, with headquarters in St. Louis and Detroit; The Third Order of St. Francis, which bids fair to supplant, outwardly at least, the original organization; The Catholic Laymen's Council, the League of the Sacred Heart, and the Catholic Women's Council. These organizations are all branches of the Leopoldines' Spy System.

To name one incident in which the ramification of this spy system may be seen, I call to the mind of those of my readers who read *The Menace*, published at Aurora, MO, some years ago, when the editor of the *Melting Pot*, Mr. Tichener, accompanied by Mr. Marvin Brown, editor of *The Menace*, located 50,000 cancelled envelopes the Menace Publishing Company had sold to a junk dealer—as is the custom of publishers—in the offices of the German Catholic Central Verein at St. Louis, MO.

The Menace ran a cut made from the snapshots they had taken of these editors, inside the offices of the SPY headquarters, surrounded by bales of *The Menace* envelopes Mr. Brown was about to appropriate, and succeeded in doing so, a fact demonstrating that the Jesuits have not a corner on the market when it comes to cleverness.

The Aurora paper had for months been receiving complaints from its subscribers, to the effect that they were being persecuted, and if in business, boycotted in their hometowns by Roman Catholics, and it had been puzzling the editors about the avalanche of complaints coming from all directions until the discovery of the big consignment of cancelled envelopes, a large proportion of which had the return addresses on them.

It was by this means that the list was procured. The publicity *The Menace* gave to this matter at the time put a stop to the inquisition, for the most part. This was an attack upon free press these Leopoldines were pledged to execute.

This great spy system penetrates every avenue of social life. The field of journalism has been invaded until a Roman Catholic sits at many important editorial desks of great newspapers, from coast to coast. They fill the reportorial staffs and other departments in the front offices, and it goes without saying that the presses, composing rooms and other mechanical departments are dominated by them.

These spies are members of all the important commissions, public works, school boards, library boards, housing commissions, naturalization departments, and are even active members of Americanization Committees.

Yes, I shall go further and say that I doubt if there is ever an assemblage of the ministers of any Protestant church in this country that meets without the presence of the Leopoldines. Our state universities and Protestant universities are honeycombed with them. Roman priests hold professorships in several state universities! On every textbook committee selected to pass on the books to be used in our public schools sits a Roman priest or his personal representative. He is there for the purpose of seeing to it that every truth derogatory to the Roman Catholic church is eliminated and everything that will in any way reflect credit upon that institution is incorporated.

This explains why it is that the extent of the knowledge of the facts leading up to the assassination of Abraham Lincoln has been carefully suppressed so that the extent of the knowledge about this greatest of all tragedies in the history of our country does not exceed these words:

"President Lincoln was assassinated in Ford's Theatre, April 14th, 1865, by an actor named John Wilkes Booth. Andrew Johnson was immediately sworn into office."

The one point upon which the Roman church is and has always been exceedingly broad is in regard to its members in the saloon and red-light districts of the cities.

Have you ever asked yourself how it comes that a large majority of the proprietors of the whiskey places and brothels are members of that church in good standing? Did you ever hear of a saloon keeper being excommunicated by the Church in Rome? Have you any knowledge of any female member of the underworld having had the anathemas of Rome hurled at her head? I think not. I will tell you some of the reasons why. A large part of the enormous income of the Catholic Church reaches it through these channels.

The Church of Rome has for centuries been a large manufacturer of wine, liquors and beers. The most expensive European wines are made by the monks and nuns of that church. The finest champagne, for instance, is manufactured by the Carthusian Monks. Benedictine, that beverage of hell, the sole purpose of which is intended to increase prostitution, was concocted by a monk of the Benedictine order eleven centuries ago. He was later created a cardinal by the Pope for the valuable service, which he thereby rendered his holy church.

The cross is blown in the glass of every bottle of Benedictine; the coat of arms of the order is impressed upon the wax that seals it, and the Latin motto dedicates it "To God, the purest and the best."

Fifty per cent of the wines manufactured in the United States was made in California and about 50% of this was manufactured by the Roman Catholic Church in its monasteries in that state. To illustrate: At Los Gatos, the Jesuit Fathers Novitiate of the Sacred Heart conducted a large winery in which three special brands of wine were made: Villa St. Joseph was described in their advertising as:

"A dry white wine, pleasant flavor, delicate taste."

"Novitiate, a heavy bodied, sweet, rich, mellow fragrance, does not need to be bottled. One hundred gallons at $39.00. New Revenue tax ten cents a gallon, or two cents per bottle."

"Retail store—Pure Altar Wine Company, East Dubuque, IL."

The above is from the advertisement that goes on to tell us that its purpose is to "supply Reverend clergy in the N.W. States and Mississippi Valley, Rev. Walter F. Thornton, S. J. (Society of Jesus, or Slick Jesuit) Rector of Novitiate of the Sacred Heart. Appointed F. M. Rhonberg, Agent on personal recommendation of His Grace, Archbishop of Dubuque, Iowa."

The following letter is official and will explain itself:

> St. Mary's Cathedral, 1100 Franklin St.
> San Francisco, California
>
> To whom it may concern:
> Having appointed the Rev. D.O. Crowley Superior of St. Joseph's Agricultural Institute, to superintend the making of altar wines, I commend the wine made under his supervision at the Beaulieu Vineyard, and vouch for its absolute purity.
>
> (Signed) Edward J. Hanna
> Archbishop of San Francisco

I wish to digress further by saying that the sale of these wines was not confined to the clergy. Their retail stores in all of the large cities were opened for anyone to purchase from.

At this St. Joseph's Agricultural Institute near Napa, California, a large part of the work was done by children—waifs, orphans and half-orphans. Priest D.O. Crowley, the big ecclesiastical boss of the politics of San Francisco, gathers in through the Juvenile Court and elsewhere to his institution known as the Catholic Youths' Directory, which occupies one of the highest knobs overlooking San Francisco in what is known as the Mission District. These boys, ranging from 10 to 18 years old are shipped every so often up to St. Joseph's Institute where they are supposed to spend their vacation helping to manufacture the wine.

Priest Crowley, bye the bye, has been for several years President of the Public School Playground Commission, appointed by Mayor James Rolph, who is not a Roman Catholic, but I am sorry to say, a member of the Masonic Fraternity. I cite this example to show how non-Romanists are utilized as Leopoldines.

Just one more instance of the connection between "Wets" and the Roman Catholic church. Twenty-one brewing, wineries and distilling companies of Chicago, IL contributed $20,250 as their last gift to the Roman Catholic charities in a drive that Archbishop Mundelein launched in 1918, just previous to the November election Political Slush Fund ("Charity" covers a multitude of sins.)

ROME'S REPRESENTATION IN THE UNDERWORLD

The courtesan has always securely held her position in the Roman church. In the 10th Century, two infamous courtesans, one the mother of a Pope, held sway in Rome where they helped to make and unmake popes. The two most eminent Catholic modern historians, the Rev. Doctors John Alzog and Ludwig Pastor, are authority for startling facts pertaining to these women and their influence with the papacy. Dr. Alzog said:

> "Marozia, who was one of the infamous daughters of the infamous courtesan, Theodora, the Elder. Marozia had Pope John X thrown into prison and put to death in order to have her son, who reigned as Pope John the XI, placed on the pontifical throne. Pope John the XI was throughout his whole reign subject to the baneful influence of either his mother or brother." (See Alzog's *Universal Church History*, Vol. 2, page 293 and 296.)

Vanozza, a married woman, the mistress of Pope Alexander VI, the occupant of the pontifical throne in 1492, when Columbus didn't discover America, was the mother of his four children, Caesar, Juan, Jofre and Lucrezia, who were afterward legitimatized by papal bulls. This documentary evidence found in the secret archives of the Vatican and quoted by the above Catholic historians. During the early years of the pontificate of Alexander VI, Vanozza occupied a palace close to the Latern palace—the first Vatican—which the pope had built for her, and in this residence the most brilliant social functions were held, presided over by his recognized affinity.

JENNIE DALY—MADAM

It is not exaggerating to say that there is not a city in the United States today in which the members of a large quota of its demimonde are faithful devotees of the Romish church who ply their profession every day in the week but who would not think of missing mass on Sunday.

One of the most notorious women in Indianapolis some years ago was Jennie Daly, the keeper of houses of ill repute within a gunshot of the courthouse in that city.

Her flagrant association with a prominent lumberman, a man of family for years, Warren Tate, whose business was close to the red-light district where this coarse-featured female held sway, and ultimately separated him from his family. In the early eighties, Tate, who was a bad tempered, abusive man was twitted about his affinity by a man named Love during the progress of some litigation in which they were engaged. The incident occurred in the court room. Tate told Love he would kill him for that remark. He hurried out, went to his mill nearby, got his revolver and shot Love to death as he was coming down the courthouse steps.

As the threat was made in the presence of witnesses, Tate, who was arrested for murder in the first degree, had to use the bulk of his fortune during the sensational trial that followed, to save his neck.

Public opinion, naturally, was highly in the favor of the prosecution and it was an open secret that Jennie Daly spent $90,000 of her money in Tate's defense, and that she finally threatened everyone connected with the case that if he was convicted she would, "tell all she knew." Strange as it may seem, the murderer was allowed to go free.

During all these years, Jennie Daly was a regular attendant at the Roman Catholic church and was a generous donor. She finally, after amassing a large fortune, retired from business, purchased a pretentious residence in a respectable part of the city, and she and Tate married and lived there. At this time, she was a pew-holder in St. Joseph's Catholic Church.

After some years, Tate was taken ill, and faithful daughter of the church that she was, she called in the parish priest who formally received this man into its folds. He was buried in a conspicuous place in the Catholic cemetery south of that city where his widow erected a beautiful monument to his memory. In a few years, she followed. She was given all the consolations within the gift of the Romish Church, and at the Requiem Mass at which she was buried, the great eulogy which the priest delivered over this notorious prostitute aroused the indignation of many of the decent, respectable parishioners.

The dust of the righteous mingles with that of these two scandalous characters, for were they not obedient children of the Holy Mother Church? The only unforgiveable sin in the Romish corporation is to

MONUMENT OF NOTORIOUS
JENNIE DALY

Keeper of "resorts" in Indianapolis in the early 1880s. "Faithful daughter of the Holy Church."

tell the truth about it. Jennie Daly proved herself to have been a useful devotee, generous and faithful to the end, and was so rewarded.

In San Francisco, the "Jennie Daly" happens to be a Spanish woman in close proximity to one of the large churches there, who may be seen hurrying to early mass on almost any Sunday morning. In San Francisco, however, I might say there are hundreds of the demimonde devotees of this church. So I might go on, ad lib, ad nauseum.

I wish my readers to get a true estimate of the ramification of this wicked system responsible for the assassination of Abraham Lincoln. You must remember that some of the most valuable information is poured into the listening ear of the Romish priest in the confessional box by this route. You must know the real significance of what they mean when they tell you that they intend to "Make America Catholic."

You cannot defeat an enemy you do not understand. You can never have a conviction strong enough to stir you to fight this common enemy of ours unless you do, and this is the motive of the writer. The clean, pure, upright life, public and private, of Abraham Lincoln, was his protection from these Leopoldines. There never was an act of his that would have placed this great American in their power. This fact alone was sufficient to merit their implacable hatred, and it did.

And now let us hasten on and trace the soft footfalls of these Jesuits, step by step as they shadowed the public life of our beloved martyr.

IV

The Turning Point In Lincoln's Life

While the Society of Jesus was organizing its destructive forces in Vienna under the title of the St. Leopoldine Foundation, in 1828, two boys from the tall timbers of Spencer County, Indiana, in their teens, guided their flatboat which they had spent weeks in making toward the wharf in New Orleans, Louisiana.

One was a tall, awkward youth, with frank gray eyes, tanned skin, a mouth of generous proportions, a shock of rather coarse black hair on a well-shaped head, which was topped by a coonskin cap, commonly worn by the men and boys from the "backwoods" of the interior. When the boat holding its small cargo was within reach of the pier, the taller lad climbed to it with the agility of a cat, seized the rope, tied the boat to the pier, and helped his thick-set companion up. This done, the boys strode away, soon lost in the crowd.

They attracted no special attention from the pedestrians, for these pioneer young merchants frequently visited the great southern metropolis. They were busy taking in the sights of a real city for the first time and it is not difficult to fancy the impressions and wonderment at what they saw, and their exchange of ideas while making their rounds.

There was one incident, however, that made a lifelong impression and proved to be the turning point in the taller boy's life, this lad who measured six feet two. Their attention was directed to a large crowd by the loud voice of a man towering above it. He had long black hair, loose flowing tie, wore a large slouch hat, dressed in the garb of a city man, and was calling out in the language of an auctioneer, emphasizing his points with the crack of a black snake whip.

The boys moved over, pushing their way through the crowd, from the gentleman in broadcloth down to the street urchin, nor did they stop until they had reached the inside of the circle around the large block upon which stood a young negro, about the age of the two youths whose curiosity had drawn them there. The colored lad was ordered to display his teeth, the fitness of his muscles, which stood out like great brown cords, demonstrating his splendid physical strength.

The bidding was snappy, being worked up by the expert tactics of the auctioneer, whose facetious remarks brought many a coarse guffaw from the bystanders. Finally, the hammer banged down on the table, the signal that the lad had been sold to the highest bidder, and the deal was closed.

A shrill cry rang out, followed by the stifled sobs of a beautiful mulatto girl, whose refined features, glossy black hair, hanging carelessly to her waist, betokened the dominance of the white blood in her veins. She was one of the parcel of slaves who was to be auctioned off the following morning, and was the bride of the boy who had just been disposed of.

There was not the slightest attention paid to the incident, for the details of the business transaction in human souls were being completed by the parties of the first and second parts. The crowd quickly dispersed as the show was over for that day.

The two boys from the timbers quickly walked away. Finally, as they were nearing the place where their boat was secured, our tall friend turned quickly to his companion and said: "John, if I ever get a chance to hit that thing, by God. I'll hit it, and I'll hit it hard." He kept his oath, but no one but God and the angels, as they looked down that night, knew the time nor the place, but God knew then that the deft brown hand that tossed the rope lightly into that old flatboat, would one day sign the emancipation of three million slaves!

Permit me here to give a close-up of our boy-hero twenty-six years later, a pen picture dispatched by a reporter for the *Boston Journal* who covered the debates between Abraham Lincoln and Stephen Douglas, which made both of these men famous.

The State Convention had nominated Mr. Lincoln for the United States Senate. The report was as follows:

"The men are entirely dissimilar. Mr. Douglas is a thickset, finely built, courageous man and has the air of self-confidence that does not a little to inspire his supporters with hope. Mr. Lincoln is a tall, lank man, awkward, apparently diffident, and when not speaking, has neither firmness nor fire in his eye. He has a rich, silvery voice, enunciates with great distinctness, and has a fine command of language. He commenced by a review of the points Mr. Douglas had made. In this he shows great tact and his retorts though gentlemanly, were sharp and reached to the core of the subject in dispute. (Lincoln) 'My distinguished friend says it is an insult to the emigrants of Kansas and Nebraska to suppose that they are not able to govern themselves. We must not slur over an argument of this kind because it happens to tickle the ear. It must be met and answered. I admit that the emigrants of Kansas and Nebraska are competent to govern themselves, but (the speaker rising to his full height) I deny the right to govern any other person, without that person's consent.'

The vast throng was as silent as death; every eye was fixed upon the speaker. He then charged Mr. Douglas with doing nothing for freedom: with disregarding the rights and interests of the colored man, and for about forty minutes he spoke with a power we have seldom heard equaled. There was grandeur in his thoughts, a comprehensiveness in his arguments, and binding force in his conclusions, which were perfectly irresistible . . . He was the tall man eloquent; his countenance glowed with animation, and his eye glistened with an intelligence that made it lustrous. He was no longer awkward and ungainly, but graceful, bold, commanding. Mr. Douglas had been quietly smoking up to this time, but here he forgot his cigar and listened with anxious attention. When he arose to reply, he appeared excited, disturbed and his second effort seemed to us vastly inferior to his first. Mr. Lincoln had given him a great task, and Mr. Douglas had not time to answer him, even if he had the ability."

Thus we see that Mr. Lincoln made good on his boyhood promise, "to hit that thing hard."

As early as 1856, Mr. Lincoln availed himself of his opportunity to "hit that thing hard" when he entered the political campaign, after an absence of several years, which he had been devoting to his law practice in Springfield, Illinois, with the intention of never leaving it again. He was drawn into the field by the infamous Dred Scott Decision rendered by the fanatical Romanist, Judge Taney, Chief Justice of the United States Supreme bench. The Taney decision in a nutshell was that the "Negro had no rights which the white man had to respect." This virtually placed the government endorsement on black slavery, and aroused Mr. Lincoln to action.

In November, 1855, Abraham Lincoln drew down upon him the fire of Rome when he answered a wire from the Reverend Charles Chiniquy, Catholic priest of Kankakee, IL, asking his professional services. The reverend had been engaged in a series of court suits with the bishop of the Chicago diocese, of which he was a "subject." Within twenty minutes the reply came to Chiniquy: "Yes, I will defend your life and your honor at the next May term of the court at Urbana. A. Lincoln."

Promptly on May 19, 1856, Mr. Lincoln appeared at Urbana and consulted with Father Chiniquy, but I will let him tell you of their meeting:

> "He was a giant in stature, but I found him still more a giant in the noble qualities of his mind and heart. It was impossible to converse with him five minutes without loving him. There was such an expression of kindness and honesty in his face, such an attractive magnetism in the man, that after a few minutes' conversation, one felt as tied to him by all of the noblest affections of the heart.
> When pressing my hand, he told me: 'You were mistaken when you telegraphed that you were unknown to me. I know you by reputation, as the stern opponent of the tyranny of your bishop, and the fearless protector of your countrymen in Illinois. I have heard much of you from two friends, and last night your lawyers, Messrs. Osgood and Paddock, acquainted me with the fact that your bishop employs some of his tools to get rid of you. I hope it will be an easy thing to defeat his projects, and protect you against his machinations.' He then asked me

how I had been induced to desire his services. I answered by giving the story of that unknown friend, a lawyer, who had advised me to have Mr. Lincoln—for the reason that he was the best and most honest man in Illinois. He smiled at my answer with that inimitable and unique smile which we may call the 'Lincoln smile' and replied: 'That unknown friend would have been more correct had he told you that Abraham Lincoln was the ugliest lawyer in the country,' and he laughed outright." (Chiniquy's *Fifty Years in the Church of Rome.*)

The defeat of Rome in this celebrated case by Mr. Lincoln; his terrific arraignment of the "perjuring gang of priests" who had left no stone unturned to ruin Father Chiniquy by a false accusation against him, in which it was charged by the infamous priest La Bell that Mr. Chiniquy had made an attack upon the sister of the former. On the night before the case was to go to the jury, Mr. Lincoln himself had almost given up hope of an acquittal, notwithstanding the fact that he was convinced of Father Chiniquy's innocence. He frankly told Chiniquy of his fears and his last admonition to the distressed and persecuted man was:

> "My dear Mr. Chiniquy, though I hope tomorrow to destroy the testimony of La Bell against you, I must concede that I see great danger ahead. There is not the least doubt in my mind that every word he has said is a sworn lie, but my fear is, that the jury thinks differently. I am a pretty good judge of these matters: I fear that our jurymen think you are guilty. I have never seen two such skillful rogues as those two priests. There is really a diabolical skill in the plan they have concocted to ruin you—the only way to be sure of a favorable verdict tomorrow is that God Almighty would take our part and show your innocence! Go to Him and pray, for He alone can save you."

Surely a more direct answer to prayer was never received, for that very night Father Chiniquy spent almost the entire time on his knees interceding that his innocence might be exonerated, when at three o'clock in the morning he answered a knock on his door, and there stood Mr. Lincoln, "his face beaming with joy" as Chiniquy expressed it, "Cheer up, Mr. Chiniquy, I have the perjured priests in my hands. Their diabolical plot is known, and if they do not fly away before the dawn of day, they will surely be lynched. Bless the Lord, you are saved!"

The wide publicity given the case in Chicago through the press had brought out the fact that Chiniquy would probably be convicted. This was read by the French Catholics and brought to light two witnesses, two women who were present in priest La Bell's house when he offered his sister two sections of land if she would swear falsely against Father Chiniquy. La Bell allayed her scruples by assuring her he could forgive her sin if she would confess to him. (Priests' relatives rarely ever confess to them, if it can be avoided). One of these female witnesses whose conscience was aroused by the unjust position in which Father Chiniquy had been placed, came to Springfield that night and told the facts to Mr. Lincoln. The priests left town early in the morning, fearing the consequences as public opinion had been strongly against them, and La Bell's lawyer asked that the case be dismissed, which was granted.

Mr. Lincoln did not permit the priests to go unscathed, however, and in a most terrific scorching at their audacious attempt to corrupt the courts, he closed his rebuke as he towered above his auditors with these words:

"May it please your honor, gentlemen of the jury and American citizens, this conspiracy, I am aware, has failed in its efforts, but I have a few words which I wish to say." He then went on and depicted the career of Father Chiniquy, how he had been unjustly persecuted, and in conclusion said: "As long as God gives me a heart to feel, a brain to think, or a hand to execute my will, I shall devote it against that power which has attempted to use the machinery of the courts to destroy the rights and character of an American citizen." And this promise made by Abraham Lincoln in his maturer years he also kept. That same year when he entered the political field, tearing to tatters as no other man could, Taney's Dred Scott Decision, in favor of black slavery, he fully understood the motive power behind it was Rome. Whenever Lincoln "hit a thing," he "hit it hard."

From that time on, the black clouds of Jesuitism were fast gathering about the life of Abraham Lincoln. These enemies followed his path as a shadow follows sunshine. From that moment, his doom was written in letters of blood.

A remarkable thing transpired when, after the trial, Mr. Chiniquy asked Mr. Lincoln for his bill. While he was drawing up a note for $50.00, as his client had requested, Mr. Lincoln said to him: "Father Chiniquy, what are you crying for? You ought to be the happiest man alive. You have beaten your enemies and come out triumphant; they have fled in disgrace." To which the emotional Frenchman replied: "I am not weeping for myself, but for you, sir. They will kill you; and let me tell you this, if I were in their place and they in mine, it would be my sole, my sworn duty, to take your life myself, or to find a man to do it."

Chiniquy was right. They found their man.

LINCOLN: THE THIRD PRESIDENT ASSASSINATED

The murder of five presidents of this republic by these enemies of popular governments in less than sixty years is a toll that is worthy, it would seem to the writer, of the most serious consideration of the American people. Five presidents of this republic in 59 years were assassinated; two by the poison cup and three by the leaden bullet.

Abraham Lincoln was the third president assassinated; three before him had been given the "Poison Cup." Indeed, poison had been administered to President Lincoln, according to the Charles Selby letter to Booth, a conspicuous government exhibit in the trials of Mrs. Mary E. Surratt and the other conspirators, which stated:

"The cup failed us once, and might again."

There were two things the ultra-pro-slavery leaders of the South had been urging for years by which they expected to make the breach for their entering wedge. One was the invasion of Cuba; the other, the annexation of Texas. The fine Italian hand is easily discernible in both.

An invasion of Cuba would have meant war with Catholic Spain, Catholic France, Catholic Austria, Catholic Belgium, and, of course, Italy, where the pope was king of his dominion. What chance would our young Republic have had in case they succeeded? Disruption? Not only disruption but total annihilation of popular governments and the setting up of the monarchial institutions pledged at the Congress of Vienna in 1814, and ratified at Verona in 1822.

The plan of these imperialistic conspirators was to wipe out the little Republic of Mexico where the Liberals had succeeded, under the leadership of Juarez, the half-Indian, rebellious ex-priest, in throwing off the Spanish and papal yokes. Juarez had been elected president of Mexico when Civil War broke out in the United States.

During this time, the new popular government was progressing rapidly in Mexico. The first official act was the confiscation of all the Roman church property, which included over thirty-five per cent of the most valuable and choicest land and holdings.

There was a certain line of policy these monarchical plotters were pursuing in this country through the Leopoldines. The slave question was becoming more acute all the time. The Jesuit-controlled leaders only were aware of the plan. The masses of the Southern people had no real knowledge of it. They were not permitted to have, but their political leaders had. The masses of any people cannot be corrupted. The strong sense of justice and right and fairness that God has implanted in each human heart at birth, unless destroyed by some evil influence or system, will invariably spring into action at a crisis, if they are permitted to have a clear understanding of the issue. As a matter of fact, their very instinct of self-preservation sharpens their judgment and strengthens their resolutions. The only instances of wrong decisions, or actions at such times, comes from false, wicked leaders.

I say again, that it was the evil "Un-Christian, un-American influence of the Roman Church" that dominated and controlled the ultra-pro-slavery leaders, which led to its own destruction. They carried on a constant "rule or ruin" policy in state and national affairs. They were, in fact, the strong element in the beginning. But with the advent of the abolitionists of the North, a weakening of their hold began, for the slavery was thrust out in the open and could not be further obscured.

In 1841, General William Henry Harrison of Ohio was elected President by a large majority. The loyalty to the Union of General Harrison was above question, and it was out of the power of the Leopoldines to defeat him. It was with his election that the "Big Stick" of intimidation was first raised when political intrigue had failed.

In his inaugural address, which was a masterpiece, President Harrison clearly, definitely and finally cut any ground for hope from under them, which these enemies to the Union of States might have had when he said:

> "We admit of no government by divine right, believing
> that so far as power is concerned, the beneficent Creator

has made no distinction among men; that all are upon an equality, and that the only legitimate right to govern, is upon the express grant of power from the governed."

With these unmistakable words, President Harrison made his position clear; he hurled defiance to the Divine Right enemies of our popular government. Aye, he did more—for those were the words that signed his death warrant. Just one month and five days from that day, President Harrison lay a corpse in the White House. He died from arsenic poisoning, administered by the tools of Rome. The Jesuit oath had been swiftly carried out:

> "I do further promise and declare that I will, when opportunity presents, make and wage, relentless war, secretly or openly, against all heretics, Protestants and Liberals, as I am directed to do, to extirpate them and exterminate them from the face of the earth. . . ."

JESUIT OATH FULFILLED
FIVE TIMES IN SIXTY YEARS

PRESIDENT
WILLIAM HENRY HARRISON
By the "Poison Cup"
April 4, 1841

PRESIDENT
ZACHARY TAYLOR
By the "Poison Cup"
July 5, 1850

PRESIDENT
JAMES A. GARFIELD
By the "Leaden Bullet"
July 2, 1881

PRESIDENT
WILLIAM MCKINLEY
By the "Leaden Bullet"
Sept. 6, 1901

"That when the same cannot be done openly, I will secretly use the poison cup . . . regardless of the honor, rank, dignity, or authority of the person or persons . . . whatsoever may be their condition in life, either public or private, as I at any time may be directed so to do by any agent of the pope or Superior of the Brotherhood of the Holy Faith of the Society of Jesus."

Allow me to quote for you from U.S. Senator Benton's *Thirty Years' View*, volume 11, page 21, regarding the death of President Harrison:

"There was no failure of health or strength to indicate such an event or to excite apprehension that he would not go through his term with the same vigor with which he commenced it. His attack was sudden and evidently fatal from the beginning."

And at the close of the chapter in Senator Benton's book, we read this significant bit of information which should be well pondered:

"That the deceased President had been closely preceded and was rapidly followed by the deaths of almost all of his numerous family, sons and daughters."

That is "extirpation" with a vengeance, is it not? Wholesale extirpation. In fact, there was but one of his eight children, a son, permitted to live.

Intimidation was the covert motive behind this wholesale assassination of the Harrison family of Liberal "heretics," whose distinguished father had been martyred for his belief in the popular government, of which he had been made the highest representative by the people.

THE ASSASSINATION OF THE TWELFTH PRESIDENT

As these plotters against the Union had tried President Harrison out on the annexation of Texas, they used the invasion of Cuba as the test for Zachary Taylor, and had their plans ready to launch their nefarious scheme in the early part of his administration, but from the very beginning President Taylor snuffed out all hope of its consummation during his term. In his first message to Congress, he said:

> "But attachment to the Union of States should be fostered in every American heart. For more than half a century, during which kingdoms and empires have fallen, this Union has stood unshaken . . . In my judgment its dissolution would be the greatest of calamities, and to avert that should be the steady aim of every American. Upon its preservation must depend our own happiness and that of generations to come. Whatever dangers may threaten it, I shall stand by it and maintain it in its integrity to the full extent of the obligations imposed, and power conferred on me by the Constitution."

There was no quibbling in this. The pro-slavery leaders had nothing to count on in Taylor, therefore they decided on his assassination. While these politicians were not influential enough to name the President, they were cunning enough to be able to control the nomination of the Vice President, and it goes without saying that they always chose a man who was in full sympathy with their plans. They pursued this as the next best thing. It had become practically a trade between the two groups of politicians.

John Tyler, a staunch pro-slavery man, strong for the things his party wanted, was chosen as Vice President for Taylor. The President, knowing the calibre of this running mate, had no sympathy, and as little to do with him as possible. The arch-plotters, fearing that suspicion might be aroused by the death of the President early in his administration, as in the case of President Harrison, permitted him to serve one year and four months, when on the Fourth of July, arsenic was administered to him during a celebration in Washington at which he was invited to deliver the address. He went in perfect health in the morning and was taken ill in the afternoon about five o'clock and died on the Monday following, having been sick the same number of days and with precisely the same symptoms as was his predecessor, President Harrison. I quote again from Senator Benton's *Thirty Years' View*:

> "He sat out all the speeches and omitted no attention which he believed the decorum of his station required. The violent attack began soon after his return to the Presidential mansion." (Vol. 11, P. 763.)

The Vice President, John Tyler, was immediately sworn in as President, after the death of "Old Rough and Ready," as Zachary Taylor's friends affectionately called him.

Tyler, who had been approached by these assassins previous to the death of President Taylor, had replied to their interrogations on the annexation of Texas question:

> "If I should ever become president, I would exert the entire influence of that office to accomplish it."

President Tyler made good his promise: the **annexation of Texas,** which was tricked through, caused the resignation of every member of President Taylor's Cabinet, with the exception of Daniel Webster, but let us again quote from Benton's *Thirty Years' View*:

> "He (Webster) had remained with Mr. Tyler until the Spring of 1843, when the progress of the Texas annexation scheme carried on privately, not to say clandestinely, had reached a point to take an official form, and to become the subject of government negotiation, **though still secret.** Mr. Webster, Secretary of State, was an obstacle to

that negotiation. He could not be trusted with the secret, much less conduct the negotiations. How to get rid of him was a question of some delicacy. Abrupt dismissal would have revolted his friends. Voluntary resignation was not to be expected . . . . A middle course was fallen upon—that of compelling a resignation. Mr. Tyler became reserved and indifferent to him. Mr. Gilmer and Mr. Upshur, with whom he had few affinities, took but little pains to conceal their distaste to him . . . Mr. Webster felt it and told some of his friends. They said "resign." He did and his resignation was accented with an alacrity which showed it was waited for. Mr. Upshur took his place and quickly the Texas negotiations became official, still secretly." (*Thirty Years' View*, P. 562.)

Circumstances pointed to the Messrs. Gilmer and Upshur, as being the actual assassins of Zachary Taylor. Thus, after years of effort, at last they accomplished one of their daring schemes—the annexation of Texas.

THE ATTEMPTED ASSASSINATION OF THE THIRTEENTH PRESIDENT

The Presidential election of 1856 was a hotly contested one, for the pro-slavery forces fully realized that they would never again be able to dominate or control the presidency. The newly awakened social conscience of the North had animated public sentiment to such an extent that this would be impossible. They were ready to take the most desperate chances to elect James Buchanan as the only presidential possibility, in whom they could have any hope. Not being absolutely certain of his dependableness, they resorted to their old policy of being doubly sure of his **running mate** and nominated John C. Breckenridge of Kentucky.

In order that the Dred Scott Decision should not in any way hazard the chances of Buchanan's election, these Jesuit schemers compelled Judge Roger E. Taney to withhold his decision until after the election. It was not published until two days after the Inauguration, March 6th, 1857.

The new President proved himself a decided "Trimmer." Although he was a Northern man, he had strongly courted the Southern leaders, and given them to understand that he was "with them heart and soul."

PRESIDENT JAMES BUCHANAN
Given "Poison Cup" at the National
Hotel, Washington, D. C, February,
1856, but escaped in a wholesale
poisoning in which fifty were affected
and thirty-eight died.

In short, he double-crossed them. He was invited to deliver an address on Washington's birthday, and made a reservation at the National Hotel (which, by the way, was the headquarters for the Jesuit traitors) for himself and friends. The Southern leaders immediately got in touch with him with the intention of testing him out and learning precisely whether he intended to make good on his pre-election promises.

The gentleman had put his ear to the ground and heard the rumble of the Abolitionists' wheels, and when the committee asked for a conference, he coolly informed them that he was **President of the North, as well as of the South**. This change of attitude was indicated by his very decided stand against Jefferson Davis and his party, and he made known his intention of settling the question of Slavery in the Free States to the satisfaction of the people in those States.

The following quotations from the *New York Herald* and the *Post* at the time chronicled what followed:

"The appointments favoring the North by the Jeff Davis faction will doubtless be accepted, and treated as a declaration of war, and a war of extermination on one side or the other." Feb. 25, 1857.

"On Washington's birthday, Buchanan's stand became known and the next day (Feruary 23) he was poisoned. The plot was deep and planned with skill. Mr. Buchanan, as was customary with men in his station, had a table and chairs reserved for himself and friends in the dining room at the National Hotel. The President was known to be an inveterate tea drinker. In fact, Northern people rarely drink anything else in the evening. Southern men prefer coffee. Thus, to make sure of Buchanan and his Northern friends, arsenic was sprinkled in the bowls containing the tea and lump sugar and set on the table where he was to sit. The pulverized sugar in the bowls used for coffee on the other tables was kept free from the poison. Not a single Southern man was affected or harmed. Fifty or sixty persons dined at the table that evening, and as nearly as can be learned, about thirty-eight died from the effects of the poison."

"President Buchanan was poisoned, and with great difficulty his life was saved. His physicians treated him understandingly from instructions given by himself as to the cause of his illness, for he understood well what was the matter."

"Since the appearance of the **epidemic**, the tables at the National Hotel have been almost empty. But more remarkable than the appearance of the epidemic itself, is the supineness of the authorities of Washington, in regard to it."

"Have the proprietors of the Hotel, or clerks, or servants, suffered from it? If not, in what respect did their diet and accommodations differ from those of the guests (Northern)?"

"There is more in this calamity than meets the eye. It is a matter that should not be trifled with." *New York Post*, March 18, 1857.

Thus again, we see the Jesuits "found their man" and kept their oath that:

"I do further promise and declare, that I will have no opinion or will of my own, or any mental reservation whatsoever, even as a corpse or cadaver, but I will unhesitatingly obey each and every command that I may receive from my superiors in the Militia of the Pope, and of Jesus Christ.

"That when the same cannot be done openly, I will secretly use the poison cup . . . the steel of the poinard, or the leaden bullet, regardless of honor, rank, dignity or authority, either public or private, as I at any time may be directed to do."

The close call to death frightened and made James Buchanan the most subservient tool the Jesuits ever had. An old friend who visited him in Washington a few months after, said he had "aged twenty-five years." He had been the picture of health, robust and straight as an arrow, when he arrived in Washington for his Inauguration. After he had gotten his dose he was emaciated and bent. An item from the *Newark News Advertiser* of March 18, 1857:

> "SYMPTOMS OF THE ATTACK AND NAMES OF SOME OF THE MURDERED DEAD."
> "A persistent diarrhea, in some cases accompanied by violent vomiting, and always with a most distressing loss of strength and spirits in the person. Sometimes the person for one day would be filled with the hopes of recovery, then relapse again to loss of spirits and illness."
> "Elliott Eskridge, the nephew of President Buchanan, died from the effects of the poisoning."

During the Buchanan administration seven States seceded, headed by South Carolina, taking seven forts, four arsenals and one Navy Yard, and the United States Mint at New Orleans, with five hundred and eleven thousand dollars. The total value of the government property stolen at this time was TWENTY-SEVEN MILLION DOLLARS AND EIGHT MILLIONS OF INDIAN TRUST BONDS!

Allow me here to give the following graphic picture of the situation in 1850-60, taken from a eulogy, delivered on Wendell Phillips in Boston, April 9, 1884, by the Rev. Dr. Archibald H. Grimke of Washington, DC, one of the most scholarly and eloquent thinkers of his race:

> "But when the year 1850 came and the slave power hung its Black bill over the Free States, non-resistance had no longer any place in the conflict. The time for argument had passed; the time for arms had arrived. On the first

wave of this momentous change Wendell Phillips
mounted to leadership. His speeches were the first billows
breaking in prophetic fury against the South. They were
the first blasts of the tempest; the first shock on the
utmost verge of the Civil War. Forcible resistance of the
Black bill was now obedience to God . . . The passage
of the Bill was the actual opening of hostilities between
two sections. The Union from that moment was in the
state of war. Of course there were not then any of the
visible signs of war—no opposite armies—two belligerent
governments. . . . It was nonetheless real, however . . .
The peacable surrender of a fugitive slave becomes now
treason to freedom. Wendell Phillips comprehended the
gravity of the situation. He refused to cry peace when
there was no peace. He answered the Southern manifesto
with the thunder of his great speech on the anniversary
of the rendition of Sims . . . He is in command and has
called for guns . . . He saw clearly that the danger of the
reform lay in the stupor and indifference which repeated
executions under the law would produce.

"The South was **united and highly organized**, impelled
by a single purpose, and in **possession of the whole
machinery of government**. He saw the North timid,
irresolute, sordid, drugged by Whigs and Democrats, and
frozen with the fear of disunion . . . Peace was slavery, and
sleep was death. The only hope of freedom lay now in the
finger that could pull the trigger. This might beat back the
advancing apathy and save the citadel of liberty. It is the
glory of Phillips that he saw this . . . He was an army in
himself. His eloquence poured out month after month,
and year after year, a kind of imminent presence . . . the
very air of the Free States vibrated with the disembodied
soul of his mighty invectives . . . Shock after shock has
loosened the ice from the conscience and courage of the
North. The Republican party is born, and then comes the
first political freedom. Abraham Lincoln has entered the
White House, and Jeff Davis has turned his back upon
Washington forever. The trial morning is rising gloomily

upon the republic. The gray light is haunted with strange voices, winged portents, bloody apparitions. Right and Wrong, Freedom and Slavery have reached the plains of '60!"

Thus we have been given a glimpse of the decade from the murder of Taylor to the Election of Lincoln.

V

When The Pope Was King

That Pope Pius IX conspired with Napoleon III to take advantage of the conflict between the North and the South in this country and to with one blow destroy both Popular Governments of Mexico and the United States, is beyond question.

During the years from 1864 to 1865, the activity of these Jesuits in Europe was redoubled. There is no doubt that they were not in close touch with every step and phase of the Rebellion in this country. In 1856 Prince Maximillian of Austria was called to Rome where a marriage had been arranged through ecclesiastical and royal intrigue between himself and the Princess Carlotta, daughter of King Leopold II of Belgium, thus uniting two of the strongest Catholic powers in Europe.

The next step was the marriage of this royal couple in the Cathedral at Vienna. In April 1864, by the orders of the pope, they were crowned Emperor and Empress of Mexico at Pontifical High Mass and amidst great rejoicing. On April 14, 1864, just one year to the day before Lincoln's assassination, this royal couple set sail in an Austrian ship of war for Mexico. They put in at Cevita Vecchia, the port in the Papal States, and were received at the Vatican by the most elaborate ceremonies that had ever been extended by a pope to royalty. After several days of these honors and being loaded down with the papal blessings, they again resumed their journey across the Atlantic.

During a previous visit to Napoleon III and his Empress Eugenia, Maximillian had been assured of the assistance of 30,000 French and

Belgium troops for his invasion into Mexico, the specific object of which was the destruction of the young Republic already established under Juarez. These troops were poured in and were being supported by the Mexican people. It had been impressed upon Maximillian at the Vatican that his first official act must be complete restoration of all the church property and ecclesiastical "rights" of the clergy that had been confiscated by the Liberal government.

After the conquest of Mexico, the plan was for this imperialistic commander "Emperor" Maximillian to join Jefferson Davis and Confederate troops at Richmond, where they would sweep north and capture Washington.

Davis had made a strong appeal in 1863, in a letter to the Pope, and after the reply he promptly received from "His Holiness" a wholesale desertion of the Irish Catholic troops of the North to the Confederacy followed. In fact, the government figures are that, out of 144,000 Irish Romanists, 44,000 remained loyal.

We have seen and heard how the Roman priesthood the world over, is bending every effort to restore the pope to the position he occupied during the Dark Ages. This is perhaps an opportune time for the reader to take a survey of the conditions that existed in the Papal States prior to and during the Civil War where the popes of Rome had been in supreme command for over 1,400 years. Certainly, 1,400 years ought to be sufficient for a thorough test of the merits of a system. Pius IX was elected in 1846. There had been three popes in the interim between him and Pius VII who had restored the Jesuits and called the Congress of Vienna in 1814. There was no change in policy, however, nor any laxness about the attitude of the church toward its obligations to the "high contracting parties" of the Holy Alliance and their Secret Treaty at Verona.

Of all of his predecessors, Pius IX was one of the most reactionary. His notorious Syllabus, which was proclaimed to a startled world in December 1864, he anathamatized every fundamental principle upon which this Republic is based. The historians are inclined to place all the blame of his mistakes, and they were many, upon his Secretary of State, Cardinal Antonelli, who was beyond doubt "the power behind the throne"—he was the agent for the Black Pope. Antonelli is far more interesting as a character study than the "White" pope, inasmuch as he was so deeply interested in the affairs of this country during the war, I am taking the liberty of reproducing some graphic pen pictures by the distinguished French journalist, M. About, who made a personal visit to the Papal States to learn firsthand if the astounding reports from the Italian Revolutionists that had been pouring into the European Dress for several years were correct. M. About's book, *The Roman Question*, is intensely interesting and written in the peculiarly piquant style of the brilliant Frenchman. It is long since out of print and difficult to secure, as the Leopoldines have bought up every copy that comes under their WATCHFUL EYE. It is a terrific arraignment, especially so, as the author himself was a Roman Catholic.

His visit to the Papal States was made in 1859, the same year you will remember that Abraham Lincoln was making his telling political campaigns for the presidency, and immortalizing himself by his debate with Judge Douglas, tearing to tatters the Dred Scott Decision and Judge Roger E. Taney.

The great Italian poet and patriot, Mazzini, was an exile, living in a London attic, pouring out his soul's most noble appeals to the Liberals of Europe. His large property holdings in Italy had been confiscated by the Pope's government. The Carlysles had visited him in his attic and through their friendship he was brought from the miserable surroundings and ensconsed in comfortable quarters, where the most distinguished literati of London and Paris visited him and were captivated by his remarkable talents and his sincere patriotism and completely won over by his irresistible arguments for a FREE AND UNITED ITALY.

The exile Garibaldi, with his "Redshirted Legion" had answered the call of his country after a sojourn in the United States where he had also lived in an attic in New York City, following the humble profession of a candlemaker, saving up his money.

One day he suddenly closed his attic door and disappeared as mysteriously as he had come. The great soldier patriot returned to Italy by the way of London and one of his most brilliant conquests was the capture of the hearts of the people of London. The red-blooded staunch Protestants not only of the city itself, but from all over England, came to welcome the man who had returned to offer his sword against the papal yoke. They went wild with delight. Garibaldi with his yellow flowing hair under his big slouch hat was lifted to the shoulders of the crowd, mad with joy which surged about him, and carried as though his great form was but a feather's weight.

This was an insult, aye, it was the unforgivable sin in the eyes of the black-robed Jesuits and the Vatican, which aroused the deadly hatred for the English Protestant nation, a hatred that has not abated up to today.

One might presume under the circumstances that the pope would have been too occupied with his own affairs to have meddled with the politics in the United States, at such a time.

The clever Frenchman, M. Dupin, has said:

> "Le Jesuitism est un epee dont la poingee est a Rome, et la point partout."—Jesuitism is a sword whose hilt is in Rome and its point everywhere.

Gladstone had visited the Papal States in 1850 and on his return to England, had reported to his government and the London Press that the Papal government was "**The negation of God.**"

In the preface of his book, M. About says:

> "It was in the Papal States that I studied the Roman Question. I travelled over every part of the country; I conversed with men of all opinions, examined things very closely, and collected my information on the spot."
>
> "The pressing condition of Italy has obliged me to write more rapidly than I could have wished; and this enforced haste has given me a certain air of warmth, perhaps of intemperance, even to the most carefully matured reflections . . . I fight fairly and in good faith. I do not pretend to have judged the foes of Italy without passion; but I have calumniated none of them."

He continues:

> "If I have sought a publisher in Brussels, while I had an excellent one in Paris, it is not because I feel any alarm on the score of the regulations of our press, or the severity of our tribunals. But as the Pope has a long arm that might reach me in France, I have gone a little out of the way to tell him the plain truths contained in these pages."

And now for the "plain truths" about his Secretary of State, the Cardinal Deacon Antonelli.

"He was born among thieves. His native place Sonnino, is more celebrated in the history of crime, than all Arcadia in the annals of virtue. This nest of vultures was hidden in the southern mountains, toward the Neapolitan frontier. Roads, impractical to mounted dragoons, winding through brakes and thickets; forests impenetrable to the stranger; deep ravines and gloomy caverns—all combine to form a most desirable landscape, for the convenience of crime.

The houses of Sonnino, old, ill built, flung pellmell, one upon another, and almost uninhabitable by human beings, were, in point of fact, little else than **depots of pillage** and magazines of rapine. The population, alert and vigorous, had for many centuries practiced armed robberies, and depredation had gained its livelihood at the point of the carbine."

"Newborn infants inhaled a contempt of the law with the mountain air, and drew in the love of others goods, with their mother's milk. Almost as soon as they could walk, they assumed cioccie, or moccasins of untanned leather, with which they learned to run fearlessly along the ledge of the giddiest mountain precipices. When they had acquired the art of pursuing and escaping, of taking without being taken, the knowledge of different coins, the arithmetic of the distribution of booty, and the principles of the Apaches or the Comanches, their education was rights of nations, as they are practiced among the deemed complete. . . .

"In the year of grace 1806, this sensual, brutal, impious, superstitious, ignorant and cunning race, endowed Italy with a little mountaineer, known as Giacomo Antonelli. **Hawks do not hatch doves**. This is an axiom in natural history, which has no need of demonstration. Had Giacomo Antonelli been gifted with simple virtues of an Arcadian shepherd, his village would instantly have disowned him. But the influence of certain events modified his conduct, although they failed to modify his nature."

"If he received his first lessons from successful brigandage, his **next teachers** were the gendarmerie. When he was hardly four years old, the discharge of a high moral lesson shook his ears; it was the French troops who were **shooting brigands** in the outskirts of Sonnino."

"After the return of Pius VII, he witnessed the decapitation of a few neighboring relatives who had dandled him on their knees. Under Leo XII, it was still worse. The wholesome correctives of the wooden horse were permanently established in village square . . . St. Peter's Gate, which adjoins the house of the Antonelli, was ornamented with a garland of **human heads, which** . . . grinned dogmatically enough in their iron cages. . . . Young Giacomo was enabled to reflect upon the inconveniences of brigandage, even before he had tasted its sweets . . . He hesitated for some time as to the choice of a calling. His natural vocation was that of the inhabitants of Sonnino . . . to live in plenty, to enjoy every sort of pleasure, to rule others, to frighten them if necessary, but above all, to violate laws with immunity."

"With the view of attaining so lofty an end, without endangering his life, for which he had ever a most particular regard, he entered the great seminary of Rome."

That's a beautiful picture of the next highest prelate to the Pope, is it not?

So much for the early years of Antonelli.

But permit me to quote again from the pen of the author of *The Roman Question*, who, as we know, was an eyewitness:

"No country in Europe is more richly gifted, or possesses greater advantages, whether for agriculture, manufacture or commerce. . . ."

Traversed by the Appenines, which divide it about equally, the Papal dominions incline gently on one side the Adriatic, on the other the Mediterranean. In each of the seas they possess an excellent port; to the east, Ancona; to the west, Civita Vecchia . . . If Panurge had had these ports in his kingdom, he would have infallibly built himself a

navy . . . The Phoenicians and Carthagenians were not so
well off.

A river tolerably well known under the name of the Tiber,
waters nearly the whole country to the west. In former
days it ministered to the wants of internal commerce.
Roman historians describe it as navigable up to Perugia.
At the present time it is hardly so far as Rome; but if
its bed were cleared out, and the filth not allowed to be
thrown in, it would render greater service and would not
overflow so often.

In 1847, the country lands subject to the Pope were
valued at about 34,800,000 pounds sterling . . . the
Minister of Public Works and Commerce admitted that
the property was not estimated at above a third of its real
value. If capital returned its proper interest, if activity and
industry caused trade and manufactures to increase, the
national income, as ought to be the case, it would be the
Rothschilds who would borrow money from the Pope at
six per cent interest."

As a matter of fact the Papacy was heavily indebted to the Rothschilds
upon which About throws a highlight further on. He continues:

"But stay! I have not yet completed the catalogue of
possessions. To the munificence of nature, must be added
the inheritance of the past. The poor Pagans of great Rome
left all their property to the Pope who damns them.

They left him gigantic aqueducts, prodigious sewers and
roads which we find still in use, after twenty centuries of
traffic. They left him the Coliseum, for his Capuchins to
preach in. They left him an example of an administration
without equal in history. But the heritage was accepted
without the responsibilities.

I will conceal from you no longer that this magnificent
territory appeared to me in the first place most unworthily
cultivated. From Civita Vecchia to Rome, a distance of
sixteen leagues, cultivation struck me in the light of very
rare accident . . . Some pasture fields, some land in fallow,

plenty of brambles, and, at long intervals, a field with oxen at the plow: that is what the traveler will see in April. He will not meet with the occasional forest which he finds in the desert regions of Turkey. It seems as if man had swept across the land to destroy everything, and the soil had been taken possession of by flocks and herds . . . I used to walk in every direction, and sometimes long distances . . . However, in proportion as I receded from the City of Rome, I found the land better cultivated. One would suppose that from a certain distance from St. Peter's, the peasants worked with greater relish . . .

I sometimes fancied that these honest laborers worked as if they were afraid to make a noise, lest by smiting the soil too hard, too deeply, too boldly, they should wake up the dead of the past ages.

St. Peter's is a noble church, but, in its way, a well cultivated field is a beautiful sight . . . . It seemed to me, that the activity and prosperity of the subjects of the Pope were in exact proportion to the square of the distance which separated them from Rome . . . in other words, that the shade of the monuments of the eternal city, was noxious to the cultivation of the country. Rabelais says, '**the shade of monasteries is fruitful**' but he speaks in another sense. I submitted my doubts to an old ecclesiastic, who hastened to undeceive me. 'The country is not uncultivated,' he said, 'or if it be so, the fault is with the subjects of the Pope. This people is indolent by nature, though 21,415 monks are always preaching activity and industry to them!'"

That is a birdseye view, dear reader, of the Papal States in the early 18th century when we were having our blind struggle with the Papacy for our national existence in this country.

In his chapter on PLEBEIANS, M. About has this to say:

"The subjects of the Holy Father are **divided by birth** and fortune into three very distinct classes—nobility, citizens, and people, or plebeians.

The Gospel has omitted to consecrate the **inequality** of men, but the law of the state—that is to say, the **will of**

the Popes—carefully maintains it. Benedict XIV declared it honorable and salutary in his Bull of January 4, 1746, and Pius IX expressed himself in the same terms at the beginning of his **Chirografo** of May 2nd, 1853."

Ponder these words well, dear reader, and add to them the following quotation I lifted from *The New World*, the Official Organ of the Roman Catholic Church in the Archdiocese of Chicago, Ill., which was a comment on the Federation of Catholic Societies held at New Orleans the previous November 1910:

"Human society has its origin from God and is constituted of two classes of people, rich and poor, which respectively represent Capital and Labor.

"Hence it follows that **according to the ordinance of God**, human society is composed of two classes, superiors and subjects, masters and servants, learned and unlettered, rich and poor, nobles and plebians." (*The New World*, Chicago, Ill., Dec. 20-1910.)

It is astounding to know that Diomede Falconio, the Pope's Legate to this country, who uttered the above divine right treason on that occasion was at the time a **naturalized citizen** of the United States!

That is what the oath of a Jesuit amounts to.

Falconio, who has since died, was instructing the subjects of the Pope in this country, and there were thousands of Catholics present at the New Orleans Convention, that a government based as our POPULAR Government is, is not worthy "favor or support." (See *The Great Encyclical Letters of Pope Leo XIII*, page 126).

In a nutshell, the Roman Church in America has always taught and **is still** teaching its subjects a separate citizenship inimical to our American citizenship that the sole authority to rule **must come from the consent of the ruled**.

This is the same divine right idea that rent this country from stem to stern in 1860, which gashed its fair face with the Mason and Dixon Line!

This is the same identical teaching that swept Abraham Lincoln from us at the most critical moment in our country's history.

This is the concentrated **treason** that is today being inculcated in the minds of 1,700,000 boys and girls who attend the Catholic parochial schools which we have wickedly permitted her to erect in direct opposition to the Public Schools where the fundamentals of POPULAR

GOVERNMENT is instilled.

This is the ROMAN QUESTION, the **irrepressible conflict**, the same old question the great Lincoln understood and defined so thoroughly in his campaign with Douglas—Douglas with the Roman Catholic wife—Douglas, the Leopoldine, the defender of slavery, who was chosen whether consciously or unconsciously, I cannot say, but chosen just the same to champion the doctrine of **class distinction** in this country with which they thought to destroy it.

> "That is the issue that will continue in this country when the poor tongues of Judge Douglas and myself shall be silent.
> It is the eternal struggle between these two principles—right and wrong—throughout the world.
> They are the two principles that have stood face to face from the beginning of time, and will ever continue to struggle.
> The one is the **common right of humanity** and the other, the divine right of kings . . . it is the same spirit that says: 'You work and toil and earn bread and I'll eat it.' no matter in what shape it comes, it is the same tyrannical principle." Lincoln's Speech at Alton, IL, October 15, 1858.

Abraham Lincoln was the living embodiment of "**the common right of humanity.**" In his life, the perfection of the NEW IDEA had been materialized, had become a living, breathing FACT which was unconquerable, yes, **unassailable**.

Lincoln knew the struggle would go on, after "these poor tongues of Judge Douglas and myself shall be silent."

I believe that the prophetic, inimitable, words that Charles Chiniquy attributes to him in his *Fifty Years In The Church of Rome* were said by him. They have the peculiar literary style of Lincoln, and could never be confused with the effusive, emotional manner of expression of the Frenchman that Chiniquy had than night with day.

The opening words, "**I do not pretend to be a prophet,**" ring with the modesty that distinguishes many of Mr. Lincoln's greatest sayings.

Listen:

"I do not pretend to be a prophet. But though not a prophet, I see a very dark cloud on our horizon. That dark cloud is coming from Rome. It will be filled with tears of blood. It will rise and increase, till its flanks will be torn by a flash of lightning, followed by a fearful peal of thunder. Then a cyclone such as the world has never seen will pass over this country, spreading ruin and desolation from north to south. After it is over, there will be long days of peace and prosperity; for popery with its Jesuitism and merciless Inquisition, will have been forever swept away from our country. Neither you, nor I, but our children will live to see these things."

—Reverend Charles Chiniquy *Fifty Years In The Church of Rome*, page 715

VI

Lincoln Takes Up The Burden

Certainly, no president of this Republic was ever beset with so many staggering problems as President Lincoln. The more we study those perilous years, the more we wonder at his great wisdom, firmness and boundless patience and charity.

The ultra pro-slavery leaders had sworn to prevent the seating of Abraham Lincoln in the presidential chair. So certain were they of the success of their plans that just as Buchanan was leaving the White House, before the arrival of Mr. Lincoln, he turned and said: "As George Washington was the first President, so James Buchanan will be the last President of the United States."

Mr. Lincoln had no idea of the rottenness and treason to face him in Washington. Almost every department in Washington was headed by a traitor to the Government, for the arch-plotters had been placing their trusted tools preparatory to the final blow.

The first months of his administration were spent in investigating these national assassins, and replacing them with men who were true. This, in itself, was a task that only the judgment of Lincoln could have accomplished.

Mr. Lincoln had no idea of the dimensions of the secession plot. He was later to find that his first call for 75,000 volunteers was inadequate and was amazed when the governors of three southern states refused to send their quota.

Another disillusionment was when he noted that as he increased his calls for troops, Jefferson Davis did not send out any call. From that on,

Lincoln began to realize something of the seriousness of the situation and his last call was for "three years or during the war." Southern leaders also realized the fact that they were up against the **real thing**.

When President Lincoln reached Philadelphia for his first inauguration, there was a plot discovered and disclosed to General John Hancock at Washington to assassinate Mr. Lincoln at Baltimore, where he was to have stopped to address the citizens on his way to the Capital. The full details had been planned. An Italian barber well known in Baltimore, a Romanist, was to have stabbed him while seated in his carriage, when he started from the depot.

The son of William H. Seward, who was at that time Senator and afterward Lincoln's Secretary of State, was sent post-haste to Philadelphia to warn Mr. Lincoln of his danger. It was a difficult matter at first to convince him of the seriousness of it. He flatly refused to go to Washington immediately, as was suggested by his friends, but promised that after he had raised the flag on Independence Hall in Philadelphia, and delivered an address to the members of the legislature at Harrisburg, he would take an earlier train to Washington, which he did, accompanied by only one friend, Wade C. Lammon, one of his law partners, and William. H. Pinkerton, head of the detective agency of that name in Chicago.

The party took the six o'clock train out of Philadelphia, quietly without attracting any publicity, and as Mr. Lincoln was soundly sleeping, the train whizzed through Baltimore, and got him to Washington early in the morning, where he was taken in charge by the largest military and Secret Service escort a president ever had been surrounded with. Thus was the first of Rome's assassination plot thwarted.

The awakening of the President and the North came on the morning of April 12, 1861 with the firing on Fort Sumpter. This opening shot of the rebellion was sent by General Beauregard, Jesuit leader of the military operations. Beauregard was a professed Romanist and sprung from a distinguished family of Jesuits.

The North was wholly unprepared for war. They seemed not to have been able to realize that there could ever be a conflict between the citizens of the United States. This delusion was shot to pieces on April 12, and amid the greatest consternation and excitement preparations began in earnest.

That President Lincoln fully realized it was not a Protestant South with which he was contending, is clearly evident from his own words

The Cabin home where the baby Lincoln played about while the "Holy Alliance" was entered into to destroy the Government he was to save.

The White House to which the People sent him Nov. 4, 1860, to "hit that thing hard."

The East Room where President Lincoln's body lay in state, slain by the "leaden bullet."
In this room the bodies of five slain Presidents have rested.

on this subject in his conversation with the Rev. Charles Chiniquy, ex-Catholic priest of Kankakee, IL, who called once each year during his administration at the White House to warn the President of his danger of assassination by these enemies of popular government and their agents, the Jesuits, through their Leopoldines.

> "THE COMMON PEOPLE HEAR AND SEE THE BIG NOISY WHEELS OF THE SOUTHERN CONFEDERACY CARS, AND THEY CALL HIM JEFF DAVIS, LEE, THOMPSON, BEAUREGARD, SEMMES, OR OTHERS. THEY HONESTLY THINK THAT THEY ARE THE MOTIVE POWER, THE FIRST CAUSE OF OUR TROUBLES, BUT IT IS A MISTAKE, THE TRUE MOTIVE POWER IS SECRETED BEHIND THE THICK WALLS OF THE VATICAN—THE COLLEGES AND SCHOOLS OF THE JESUITS; THE CONVENTS OF THE NUNS, THE CONFESSIONAL BOXES OF ROME."
>
> "THERE IS A FACT WHICH IS TOO MUCH IGNORED BY THE AMERICAN PEOPLE AND WITH WHICH I AM ACQUAINTED ONLY SINCE I BECAME PRESIDENT. IT IS, THAT THE BEST AND LEADING FAMILIES OF THE SOUTH HAVE RECEIVED THEIR EDUCATION IN GREAT PART, IF NOT ALL, FROM THE JESUITS AND THE NUNS— HENCE THE DEGRADING PRINCIPLE OF SLAVERY, PRIDE AND CRUELTY, WHICH ARE AS SECOND NATURE AMONG MANY OF THE PEOPLE."

And continuing Mr. Lincoln analyzed the Roman psychology that played its part in his own murder, when he said:

> "HENCE THAT STRANGE WANT OF FAIR PLAY FOR HUMANITY; THAT IMPLACABLE HATRED AGAINST IDEALS OF EQUALITY AND LIBERTY, AS WE FIND THEM IN THE GOSPEL. OF CHRIST—IT IS TRUE THAT WE BOUGHT

FLORIDA, LOUISIANA, SOUTH CAROLINA, NEW MEXICO AND MISSOURI FROM SPAIN, BUT ROME HAD PUT HER VIEWS OF HER ANTI-SOCIAL AND ANTI-CHRISTIAN MAXIMS INTO THE VEINS OF THE PEOPLE, BEFORE THEY BECAME AMERICANS."

Surely, no clearer conception of the masked enemy with which that great man was contending was ever glimpsed. While other men studied books, Lincoln STUDIED MEN, and the above interpretation of the terrible conflict in which he was the Commander-in-Chief is startling in its accuracy. It is very simple now for those of us who have the knowledge of an array of facts before us, to see what Lincoln then saw, but we must remember when he spoke those words, he was the very storm center and chief actor in the social upheaval without the advantage of retrospect. Mr. Lincoln had a prophetic sense almost uncanny, which alone made him superior to any of his contemporaries. More than once he told his close friends that he had a strong premonition that he would not outlast the Rebellion, that his work would be finished with it.

ROMAN CHURCH ALWAYS HAS ADVOCATED CHATTEL SLAVERY.

Disruption has always been the first motive of the Jesuits, and black slavery was the rock upon which they planned to rend this government. There was no other principle, no ethics involved, never is, so far as Jesuitism goes, except the **fundamental principles** of the divine right rule of the popes of Rome.

From the earliest times, the Roman Church advocated human slavery. In the Middle Ages, when feudal slavery nourished, the church fattened on the exploitation of the serfs who were bought and sold with the land. These serfs were supposed to have no souls, and were in precisely the same category as cattle. The great monasteries and nunneries were among the largest owners of serfs. For instance, had Joan D' Arc lived four hundred years before her time, she and her family would have been among the serfs attached to the Monastery of San Ramey. In short, **serfdom was the basis of the wealth of the papacy.**

It is true that in rare cases the church lifted out of serfdom, a boy in whom it recognized some peculiar native talent or personal trait that might be cultivated and turned to its own advantage, but the act was simply the removal from the thralldom of serfdom to that of ecclesiastical slavery for further and more useful exploitation by more exacting task masters, for the Roman church has always enslaved the minds of its victims. The Jesuit Oath exacts the obedience of "cadavers."

In the *Doctrine of the Jesuits* by Gury, translated into the French by that brilliant educator and statesman, Paul Bert, in 1879, we find the position of the church and the Jesuits on black slavery quoted as follows:

> "Slavery does not constitute a crime before any law, divine or human. What reasons can we have for undermining the foundations of slavery with the same zeal that ought always to animate us in overcoming evil? When one thinks of the state of degradation in which the hordes of Africa live, the **slave trade may be considered as a providential act**, and we almost repudiate the philanthropy which sees in a man but one thing—material liberty."

The above is the papal virus to which Lincoln referred and with which the youth of the best families of the Southern Confederacy were inoculated, and which made the leaders of the ultra pro-slavery forces an easy prey to the Roman hierarchy and its priesthood in the **great conspiracy or destruction that Lincoln envisioned**.

It was the virus that was let into the veins of Mary E. Surratt and was passed on by her to her son, the arch-conspirator John H. Surratt; it was the opiate that silenced the voice of conscience and kindness of heart of John Wilkes Booth, and nerved his hand to send the bullet into the great brain of Abraham Lincoln; it was the deadly drug that made Lewis Payne, the unfortunate, and the happy-go-lucky "Davy" Herold, the shiftless Edward Spangler, and the rest of the non-Catholic tools, wax, in the hands of the arch-Leopoldines in this wicked conspiracy to wreck this popular government.

This Jesuit virus that **"Slavery does not constitute a crime before any law, divine or human," was the deadly drug that set the BLOOD OF THE SLAVE OWNERS ON FIRE, JUSTIFIED THEIR "CAUSE" distorted their vision, controlled their ethics and appealed so strongly to their economic interests, and it was the one big urge underlying the whole progress of the treason of secession.**

In the *A Memoir* of Jefferson Davis, the leader of the Southern Confederacy, published by his wife after his demise, we find on page 445 this remark: "Mr. Davis's early education had always inclined in the Roman Catholics, friends who could not be alienated from the oppressed." In chapter 2, that gentleman is quoted as follows:

> "The Kentucky Catholic school called St. Thomas College, when I was there was connected with the church. The priests were Dominicans. They held large property; productive fields, slaves, flour mills, flocks and herds. As an association they were rich. Individually, they were vowed to poverty and self-abnegation. They were diligent, in the care, both spiritual and material, of their parishioners' wants. When I entered the school, a large majority of the boys belonged to the Roman Catholic church. After a short time I was the only Protestant boy remaining, and also the smallest boy in the school. From whatever reason, the priests were particularly kind to me. Father Wallace, afterwards bishop of Nashville, treated me with the fondness of a near relative."

It is very obvious from the above that the "kindness" shown to Jefferson Davis as a child clung to him and influenced his whole life. It bore fruit, and his friendliness to the Catholic church was well repaid by that institution which always, under such circumstances, rewards its tools.

When Mr. Davis had been arrested after the close of the Civil War and was to be tried for treason, it was the distinguished Catholic attorney, Charles O'Connor of New York City who offered his services, which were accepted in Mr. Davis's defense.

On Sept. 25, 1863, Davis addressed the following letter to Pius IX:

> "Richmond, VA, Sept. 25, 1863.
> Very Venerable Sovereign Pontiff:
> The letters which you have written to the clergy of New Orleans and New York have been committed to me, and I have read with emotion the deep grief therein expressed for the ruin and devastation caused by the war, which is

now being waged against the States and the people who have selected me as their president, and your orders to your clergy to exhort the people to peace and charity. I am deeply sensible of the christian charity which has impelled you to this reiterated appeal to the clergy. It is for this reason I feel it my duty to express personally and in the name of the Confederate States our gratitude for such sentiments of christian good feeling and love, and to assure Your Holiness, that the people threatened even on their own hearths, with the most cruel oppression and terrible carnage is desirous as it always has been, to see the end of this impious war; that we have ever addressed prayers to heaven for that issue which Your Holiness now desires; that we desire none of our enemies possessions, that we merely fight to resist the devastation of our country and the shedding of our best blood, and to force them to let us live in peace under the protection of our own institutions and under our laws, which not only insure to everyone the enjoyment of his temporal rights but also the free exercise of his religion.

I pray your Holiness to accept on the part of myself and the people of the Confederate States our sincere thanks for the efforts in favor of peace.

May the Lord preserve the days of Your Holiness and keep you under His divine protection.

(Signed) Jefferson Davis."

It occurs to me that after perusing the above bit of concentrated treason, any apologist for this leader of the Rebellion would be out of order.

Here is the Pope's reply:

"Bustrious and honorable President,
Salutation.
We have just received with all suitable welcome the persons sent by you to place in our hands your letter dated the 25th of Sept. last. Not slight was the pleasure we experienced when we learned from those persons

and the letter, with what feelings of joy and gratitude, illustrious and honorable President, as soon as you were informed of our letters to our venerable brother, John, Archbishop of New York and John, Archbishop of New Orleans, dated the 18th of October of last year, and in which we have with all our strength exerted and exhorted those venerable brothers that in their episcopal piety and solicitude they should endeavor with the most ardent zeal and in our name, to bring about the end of that fatal Civil War which has broken out in those countries in order that the American people may obtain peace and concord and dwell charitably together.

It is particularly agreeable to us to see that you, illustrious and honorable President, and your people, were animated with the same desires of peace and tranquility which we have in our letters inculcated upon our venerable brothers. May it please God at the same time to make other people of America and their rulers reflecting seriously how terrible is civil war and what calamities it engenders, listen to the inspirations of a calmer spirit and adopt resolutely the part of peace.

As for us, we shall not cease to offer up the most fervent prayers to God Almighty that He may pour out upon all its people of America the spirit of peace and charity, and that He will stop the great evils which afflict them. We at the same time beseech the God of Pity to shed abroad upon you, the light of His Grace and attach you to us by a perfect friendship.

Given at Rome, at St. Peters the 3rd day of December, 1863 of our Pontificate Eighteen.

(Signed) Pius IXth."

The reader will note the recognition by the pope of a divided country and also his recognition of Davis as the President. It was on the publication of this letter that the large desertions of Roman Catholics from the ranks of the North began.

Mrs. Davis tells us:

"During Mr. Davis' imprisonment, the Holy father sent

a likeness of himself and wrote underneath it, with his own hand, attested by the seal of the Cardinal Antonelli, 'Come unto me all ye who are weary and heavy laden, and I will give you rest.' "

The lady further opines that:

"The dignity and the man both illustrated the meek and lowly Lord of us all, whose Vice-Regent he was."

This remark leaves no doubt as to precisely where she stood on the question. The writer was amused to learn that Jeff Davis was a "Wet" which is also in keeping with his early education in the Roman Church, and that his explanation upon an occasion when he was pressed for his attitude upon the subject is almost identical with that of the late Jesuit Cardinal Gibbons. He says in part in his defense of the liquor traffic:

"To destroy individual liberty, and moral responsibility, [Get that, dear reader!] would be to eradicate one evil by the substitution of another, which it is submitted would be more fatal than that for which it was offered as a remedy. The abuse and not the use of stimulants, it must be confessed, is the evil to be remedied."

Upon the whole, surely no one can deny that Rome's fatal virus worked in the veins of this ultra pro-slavery leader in the late Rebellion, and that Lincoln was right when he recognized the "antisocial and anti-Christian views" of the foe with which he struggled. The fact that Jefferson

---

Author of infamous *Syllabus* proclaimed December 8, 1864 which anathematizes the fundamentals of representative governments and was aimed particularly at the United States which stands in authority today precisely as it did the day it was uttered as is attested by *The Great Encyclical Letters of Pope Leo XIII.*

Davis was not a professed Roman Catholic did not in the slightest curtail his usefulness as a Leopoldine.

A sense of justice and gratitude should compel every loyal American to remember the decisive and correct attitude of the English government at the psychological moment in our Civil War. It stands in sharp contrast with the meddlesome, treacherous letter of the pope, above quoted to the "Honorable and Illustrious President" of the Seceding States. On page 476 in the "Memoirs" by Mrs. Davis, quotes in full the ultimatum of England which was received by Davis at Richmond through the British Consul which says in part:

> "After consulting with the law officers of the Crown, Her Majesty's government have come to the decision that the agents of the authorities of the **so-called** Confederate States have been engaged in building vessels which would be at least partially equipped for war purposes on leaving the ports of this country; that these war vessels would undoubtedly be used against the United States, a country with which this government is at peace; that this would be a violation of the neutrality laws of the realm; and that the Government of the United States would have just grounds for serious complaint against her Majesty's Government, should they permit such an infraction of the friendly relations subsisting between the two countries. No matter what might be the difficulty of proving in a court of law that the parties procuring the building of these vessels are agents of the so-called Confederate States, it is universally understood throughout the world that they are so, and Her Majesty's Government are satisfied that Mr. Davis would not deny that they are so. Under these circumstances, Her Majesty's Government protests and remonstrates against any further efforts being made on the part of the so-called Confederate States, or the authorities or agents thereof to build or to cause to be built, to purchase or to cause to be purchased, any such vessels as those styled as "Rams," or any other vessels to be used for war purposes against the United States, or against any country with which the United Kingdom is at peace or on terms of amity; and Her Majesty's Government further protests against all acts in

violation of the neutrality laws of the realms.

I have the honor to be your Lordship's obedient servant,

(Signed) Russell"

Those are the words with the "bark on." No recognition of "Your Illustrious and Honorable President." Only recognition of a UNITED STATES— preservation of the Union—for which Abraham Lincoln was contending and gave his precious life.

The wobbly attitude of the past administrations in Washington on the dangerous interference of the Sinn Fein element in this country during the present unpleasant attempt at disruption in the British Empire on the so-called "Irish Question," which is not Irish at all, but Roman question, makes one ashamed and humiliated at the hemming and hawing of the politicians in high office at Washington.

On July 26, 1862 in a letter to Reverdy Johnson, who by the way was the attorney who afterwards gave his distinguished services to Mrs. Mary E. Surratt, Mr. Lincoln said:

> "I am a patient man, always willing to forgive on the Christian terms of repentance, and also to give ample time for repentance. Still, I must save the government if possible. What I cannot do, of course I will not do; but it may as well be understood, once for all, that I shall not surrender this game leaving any available card unplayed."

This was the same expression of sentiment which had caused the death of William Henry Harrison, the ninth president and Zachary Taylor, the twelfth President, the **preservation** of the UNION and that fact that Lincoln **did** it, was the grounds for his physical death, by these wreckers.

Nor did the great Lincoln stop pouring out his patriotic soul all during this trying four years. On August 15, 1863, he gave his opinion upon the Draft as follows:

> "Shall we shrink from the necessary means to maintain our free government, which our grandfathers employed to establish, and our own fathers have already employed once to maintain it? Are we degenerate? Has the manhood of our race run out?" (*Complete Works*, Vol 11, p. 391).

The President spent the first months of his administration feeling his way, so to speak. Delving into the condition in the various departments, finding traitors and carefully replacing them by those whom he knew to be true. The lesson he was learning would have staggered a man of less courage than Lincoln—the steadfast, **unyielding patriot**, when any principle of right was in the balance.

It was the sifting time with Lincoln. In his letter to Corning, June 1863 he writes:

> "The man who stands by and says nothing when the peril of his country government is discussed, cannot be misunderstood. If not hindered, he is sure to help the enemy; much more, if he talks ambiguously—talks for his country 'with buts and ifs and ands.' " (Barrett, p. 632)

In addressing the members of the general assembly Presbyterian Church, President Lincoln said:

> "As a pilot, I have used my best exertions to keep afloat our ship of state; and shall be glad to resign my trust at the appointed time to another pilot more skillful and successful than I may prove. In every case and at all hazards the government must be perpetuated." (*Complete Works*, Vol 2, Page 342.)

Thus almost daily was Lincoln telling of his American creed, adding fuel to the fires of hatred that were burning in the wicked hearts of his country's deadly enemies. Spurred on like a lot of demons, they rounded up their hell hounds in and about Washington for the final perfidious act.

It finally became manifest to President Lincoln that the presence of the foreign troops in Mexico was a menace to the safety of this country, and through our American Consul at Paris, this government served notice on Napoleon, that Jesuit tool of the Pope, that his troops must be removed from Mexico within the time indicated by this country.

That there could be no misunderstanding concerning the attitude of the Lincoln administration toward the Republic of Mexico was made plainly evident by the "note" sent through Secretary of State Seward to our Consul at Paris to be delivered to Napoleon III:

> "The United States government does not desire to suppress the fact that their sympathies are with Mexico, that is to say with the Republic of Mexico nor does United States government, in any sense, for any purpose, disapprove of the Republican government, then in force in Mexico, or distrust the administration. Neither was there any disposition apparently, to **deny the Liberals of Mexico financial assistance**."

When President Lincoln submitted to the Senate a Treaty granting a loan of $11,000,000 to the Republic of Mexico, although he made no recommendation upon the subject, it was a sufficient hint that expressed his sympathy.

The demand that the French troops be removed from Mexico was complied with to the letter, owing to complications in the situation, in which France at the time was involved in Europe, she feared war with the United States.

As can be imagined, this was a terrible blow to the CONSPIRATORS in Europe, Canada and Mexico, not to speak of their tools in this country. It served to practically break the morale of the Confederate army, and hastened the end of the war with a **Victory for the right**.

Meantime events were shaping up in Mexico in favor of the new Republic.

The Empress Carlotta, within a few months after their arrival in Mexico City, was sent to Rome by Maximillian to explain in person that the strength of Popular Government there had been underestimated; that it was impossible to restore the church property and the rights of the clergy. The important part of her mission, however, was to ask for more troops.

Her reception at the Vatican was simply "withering;" the Pope was so chagrined and angry at the failure of his designs and so severe in his reproach that the sensitive princess was carried out bodily in an unconscious state, upon which she recovered a mental wreck. She was incarcerated in the Castle of Bouchet near Brussels, Belgium, where she was placed under constant surveillance, and was unaware that on June 19, 1867, Maximilian, her husband, was shot at sunrise at Queretaro,

PRESIDENT LINCOLN AND HIS CABINET.
From left to right: Edwin M. Stanton, Secretary of War (seated); Salmon P. Chase, Secretary of the Treasury (standing); President Lincoln and Gideon Welles, Secretary of the Navy (seated); Caleb B. Smith, Secretary of the Interior (standing); William H. Seward, Secretary of State (seated); Montgomery Blair, Postmaster-General (standing); and Edward Bates, Attorney-General (seated).

Mexico, by the Revolutionists. This is the tragic termination of what has always been alluded to as one of the greatest love matches of the royalty of Europe.

A victory for the North was not indicated until the very last days of the War. The Leopoldines left no stone unturned to defeat Lincoln's renomination. They fully realized that if they did not, it meant their doom.

When the news of his re-election was flashed over the wires, they did not give up. Far from it, they redoubled their efforts. They saw more clearly than ever before that Abraham Lincoln was their Nemesis. They knew only too well that he would be the stumbling block to their future plans, for they felt that in Lincoln they would always encounter a powerful champion for the preservation of the Union and all its institutions.

They feared with a deadly fear the influence of his able pen and voice. They knew that to permit this calm, thorough, clear-visioned man who had such a complete estimate of their perfidious designs to serve at the helm during the RECONSTRUCTION PERIOD would mean their ultimate rout in America's political affairs.

M. Harris; August V. Kautz; J.A. Ekin; Hon. John. A. Bingham; Chas. H. Tompkins; R.S. Foster; D.R. Clendenin; D. Hunter; Lew Wallace; A.P. Howe; Hon. J. Holt; H.L. Burnett.

Military Commission that tried and convicted eight conspirators upon the evidence presented. It included probably more distinguished men than even were called upon to mete out justice in this country.

VII

Assembling The Chosen Assassins

One Sunday morning in November 1864, the congregation of the little Roman Catholic Church of St. Mary's, Charles County, Maryland, was filing out after high mass and stood about in groups on the lawn, talking in subdued voices about the news from the "front," which was not far distant.

A handsome young man with dark, glowing eyes, jet black curling hair, a swinging, graceful carriage, with the grooming of a city man of culture and refinement, sauntered out from the church and stood a moment scanning the crowd. He finally made his way to a group, the center of which was a Dr. Queen, a leading physician of that locality, and member of one of the prominent families. The stranger presented a card and the physician on glancing at it extended his hand and gave the gentleman a most cordial welcome. The contents of the card must have had a magic password that admitted him to the confidence and homes of these Romish devotees, every one of whom was a strong secessionist.

The doctor introduced the stranger, who was none other than John Wilkes Booth, son of the distinguished actor, Junius Brutus Booth. John Wilkes Booth was the most eminent young tragedian at the time in the country, by far the most talented of the Booth brothers. He had accumulated by his profession some $25,000, which was quite a fortune in those days for a young man still in his twenties to accumulate.

Booth was what is known as a "traveling star," having with great success played most of the big cities in this country and Canada. He was

ST. MARY'S ROMAN
CATHOLIC CHURCH, ON
BRYANTOWN ROAD

This is the Church where Booth
attended Mass the Sunday, middle
of November, 1864 when he
met Dr. S. A. Mudd and other
Knights of the Golden Circle and
tried to get in touch with Surratt.
This church marks the Catholic
community to which he fled and
received protection.

exceedingly popular with the members of his profession and up until
he was caught in the Jesuit web, his whole thought and ambition was
devoted to his art.

John Booth had chosen to work under the name Wilkes until he
gained recognition independent of the family name, desiring to win on
his own merits his theatrical laurels. This in itself showed a principle
somewhat out of the ordinary. After a pronounced success under the
name of John Wilkes, he allowed himself to be starred under his own
name. He assumed no airs, nor was he given to egotism as members of
this profession of lesser distinction and talent are prone to be.

There is no better way of estimating a man or woman's disposition
more surely than from the opinion of those with whom he comes in
daily contact in his vocation. I give the tribute paid to Booth before he
fell under the spell of the Jesuit psychology, at least before it had taken a
fatal hold of him. The witness is none other than that queen of tragedy
of two decades ago, Clara Morris. She is quoted thus:

> "In glancing back over two crowded and busy seasons,
> one figure stands out in clearness and beauty. In this case
> so far as my personal knowledge goes, there is nothing
> derogatory to dignity and manhood in being called
> 'beautiful' for he was that bud of splendid promise blasted
> to the core before its full triumphant blooming, known to
> the world as a madman and assassin, but to the profession
> as 'that unhappy boy, John Wilkes Booth.' He was so

young, so right, so kind.

"I could not have known him well? Of course, too, there are two or three different people in every man's skin. Yet when we remember that Stars are not in the habit of showing their brightest, best side at rehearsals, we cannot help feeling both respect and liking for the one who does.

"There are not many men who can receive a gash over the eye at a scene at night without at least a momentary outburst of temper, but when the combat between Richard and Richmond was being rehearsed, John Wilkes Booth had again and again urged McCullom—that six foot tall and handsome man who used to entrust me with the care of his watch during such encounters, 'Come on hard, come on hot, old fellow! Harder, faster!' that he would take the chances of a blow if only they could make a hot fight of it. Mr. McCullom, who was a cold man at night, became nervous in his efforts to act like a fiery one. He forgot that he had struck the full number of hard blows and when Booth was expecting a thrust, McCullom wielding his sword with both hands brought it down with an awful force fair across Booth's forehead. A cry of horror arose, for in one moment his face was marked in blood, one eyebrow was cut through. Then came simultaneously one deep groan from Richard (Booth) and an exclamation of 'Oh good God, good God!' from Richmond (McCullom) who stood trembling like a leaf and staring at his work. Booth, flinging the blood from his eyes with his left hand, said as gently as a man could speak: 'That is all right, old man. Never mind me, only come on hard, and save the fight,' which he resumed at once. And although he was perceptibly weakened, it required a sharp order from Mr. Ellsler to ring the first curtain bell to force him to bring the fight to a close a single blow shorter than usual. There was a running to and fro with ice and vinegar, raw steak and raw oysters, and when the doctor placed a few stitches where they were most required, Booth laughingly declared that there were provisions enough to start a restaurant.

"McCullom came to try to apologize, to explain, but

Booth would have none of it. He held out his hand saying, 'Why, old fellow, you look as if you lost the blood. Don't worry—now, if my eye had gone, that would have been bad.' So, with light words he turned to set the unfortunate man at ease, and though he must have suffered much mortification and pain from the eye, he never made a sign showing it.

"John Wilkes Booth, like his next elder brother was rather lacking in height, but his head and throat and the manner of their rising from his shoulders were truly beautiful. His coloring was unusual, the ivory pallor of his skin, the inky blackness of dusky curly hair, the heavy lids of his glowing eyes, were all oriental, and they gave a touch of mystery to his lace when it fell into gravity, but there was generally a flash of white teeth behind his black silky mustache.

"Now it is scarcely exaggerating to say that the fair sex was in love with John Wilkes Booth, or John Booth as he was called, the name Wilkes apparently being unknown to his family and close friends. I played with John Wilkes to my great joy, playing 'Player Queen' in the 'Marble Heart' I was one of the group of three statues in the first act, then a girl in my teens.

"With all my admiration for the person and genius of John Wilkes Booth, his crime I cannot condone. The killing of that homely, tender-hearted father, Abraham Lincoln, a rare combination of courage, justice, and humanity, whose death at the hands of an actor will be a grief of horror and shame to the profession forever. And I cannot believe that John Wilkes Booth was the leader of a band of bloody conspirators.

"Who shall draw the line and say, 'Here genius ends and madness begins'? There was that touch of strangeness, in Edwin it was a profound melancholy; in John it was an exaggeration of spirit, almost a madness. There was the natural vanity of the actor too who craves a dramatic selection in real life. There was also his passionate love and sympathy for the South, which was easier to play upon than a pipe.

"Undoubtedly he conspired to kidnap the President; that would appeal to him. But after that I truly believe he was a tool; certainly he was no leader. Those who led him knew his courage, his belief in fate, his loyalty to his friends, and because they knew these things **he drew the lot as it was meant he should from the first**. Then, half mad, he accepted the part fate cast him for and committed the murderous crime."

"God moves in a mysterious way
And His wonders to perform."

"And God shutteth not up his mercies forever in displeasure."

We can only shiver and turn our thoughts away from the bright light that went out in such utter darkness; poor guilty, unhappy, John Wilkes Booth."

John Wilkes was the only member of the Booth family whose sympathy was with the Confederacy. According to the *The Great Conspiracy*, a book published in 1866 by Barclay Company in Philadelphia, PA,

JOHN WILKES BOOTH
Horrible example of the degenerating effects of the Jesuit psychology.

John Wilkes Booth had been initiated into the Knights of the Golden Circle in Baltimore, in the fall of 1860, "in a residence opposite the Cathedral."

The same writer is authority for the following oath of the Knights of the Golden Circle, taken by John Wilkes Booth:

"I .... , do swear by the blood of Jesus Christ, by the wounds of the most Sacred Body; by the Dolors of His immaculate Mother, and in the name of the Holy and Undivided Trinity, that I will solemnly keep all secrets of the Golden Circle; that I will faithfully perform whatever I may be commanded, and that I shall always hold myself in readiness to obey the mandates of the said Circle whether at bed, or board, at the festive circle, or at the grave, and if I shall hesitate or divulge the secret may I incur the severest penalties to which flesh is heir.

"May I be cursed in all the relation of my life, in mind, body, and state, and may the pangs of hell be my eternal portion.

"I feel honored fellow knights and companions of the Golden Circle that you have deigned to admit me. No efforts shall be wanting on my part to advance the interests of the organization. . . .

"A distinguished Latin Author has justly remarked, that it is sweet and profitable to die tor one's country. I have but one life and am ready to give it should it be necessary . . ."

The President rises and says:

"Sir Knight you have just taken a most solemn adjuration and believe me that you are known to all members in every part of the country. The Order is extensive and though the government is zealous and would freely spend thousands to unveil our designs, all efforts have hitherto been fruitless. No traitor has yet appeared among us, and inevitable ruin awaits the individual who would play the part of a Benedict Arnold. No public steps would be taken. He would disappear and I leave it to you to judge his fate. '**Dead men tell no tales**.' Ponder well on these things, and remember you cannot escape us.

"Members, give the hand of fellowship to our new Knight."
The Great Conspiracy, published by Barclay in 1865.

The password to this organization was "Rome. Beware of the Negroes."

That the author of the book, *The Great Conspiracy* was thoroughly informed upon the details that could scarcely have come from anything short of actual membership in the organization is plainly evident. Also that he had knowledge of the assassination of the former President Harrison, and Taylor, we gather. The incident occurred just after the re-election of President Lincoln. Booth, sitting in a hotel lobby one day, appeared very dejected; he was aroused by the following remark, which evidently was part of the **secret phraseology** of the Knights of the Golden Circle:

"It would be a queer thing were Lincoln to die and Andy Johnson be President after all."

"What makes you think so?"

"Why, you know that Harrison and Taylor and that Fillmore and Tyler were presidents. Lincoln may take it into his head to follow their example."

"Perhaps," said the stranger at Booth's elbow and regarding him steadfastly, "neither Lincoln nor Johnson will serve their terms out."

"Do you mean that the President and the Vice-President both will die? Such a thing has never happened before in the United States."

"But it may occur nevertheless Lincoln and Johnson are both mortals. . . . I feel certain that ere another month Lincoln will die. . . . Yes, he **may** die of some disease."

Booth's suspicions were aroused and he turned suddenly around and asked: "You said I believe, sir, that the President might die of some disease?"

"Yes sir, of such diseases as commonly **prevail in Rome**."

"What diseases are they?" asked Booth. "All to which flesh is heir, the malaria from the Pantine marshes carries off hundreds; the plague of its day almost decimated the capitol of the Caesars. . . ."

"But I tell you again that the President will die of a disease from Rome."

Booth: "Sir, as you are well versed in history, perhaps you can answer me one question, which one of all the sovereigns of all Italy had the most fickle wife?"

"I am an indifferent guesser of conundrums, but I suppose the Doge."

Question: "Which Doge, he of Venice or Genoa?"

Answer: "He of Venice, because he wedded the sea with a golden circlet. You remember Byron's beautiful lines?"

After this "test," Booth was invited to the gentleman's room where they conferred privately.

That John Wilkes Booth was initiated in this Order as early as 1860, the same authority states. The following letter is quoted from Booth to a brother Sir Knight:

> "Dear Sir:
> The K. G. C. had a meeting; I was initiated. 'The die is cast and I have crossed the Rubicon and can never return. They tell me that Lincoln, the damn chicken-hearted nigger lover, will perhaps be inaugurated, but I most heartily wish, 'That never shall sun that morrow see.' I am devoted to the South, mind and body, so that she gains her independence, I don't care what becomes of me. If I am sacrificed, I know that my country will grant me immortality; if I escape, so much the better. I can serve her in other ways. One thing is very clear to my mind, the South must take some decisive step. She must throw a bomb-shell into the enemy's hand that shall spread terror and consternation wherever it goes. You know what I mean, so don't be surprised.
> Sincerely yours, John Wilkes Booth."
> *The Great Conspiracy*, page 26.

The same authority gives a letter signed "Veritas" (truth) to Booth, which one would be strongly inclined to believe might have been written by a priest, judging by the style and Latin quotations—possibly his ecclesiastical sponsor.

> "My dear Booth:
> Since you left us, the Circle has held another meeting. The members are all exceedingly dissatisfied and if something be not speedily done, the southern cause is lost forever. Important dispatches have been received from Canada. They spoke out almost too plainly to be sent by mail, but as there was no signature and addressed to a feigned name, I do not suppose there was any danger. There is to be a ball or party at the White House and the **Ape** I suppose will be there in all his glory retailing his filthy anecdotes and pointless jests till they fall on the ear, usque

ad naseum. Did you see what is the determination of the Lincoln Cabinet about confiscation? There is a clerk by the name of Charles Morton, who is employed in one of the government offices. He is gentlemanly but vain and exceedingly soft. I am told he drinks. Anyhow, make his acquaintance and see what can be got out of him. Handle him tenderly and you will be sure to catch your fish. Should you want any more money you will know where to send for it. An idea has struck me; you know in the correspondence between Sir Henry Clinton Arnold and Andre the whole matter was treated in a mercantile way. We for the sake of safety and to make assurance doubly sure, must do the same. I will not detain you any longer, but give you an opportunity to read about our friends in Canada. Whatever be the results, rely on me.

Sincerely your friend, Veritas."

The statements made by his professional friend, John McCullough, of a visit he paid Booth at the National Hotel, showed the deadly influence when he said:

GEORGE ATZERODT
Delegated to assassinate Vice-President. Always known as a Catholic prior to the assassination.

"At another time I came over suddenly from New York, and being in the habit of going right into Booth's room without knocking, I turned the knob and pushed right in. At the first wink I saw Booth sitting behind a table on which was a map, a knife and a pistol. He had gauntlets on his hands and spurs on his boots, and a military hat of a slouch character on his head. As the door opened he seized the knife and came for me. Said I, 'John, what in the name of sense is the matter with you—are you crazy?'

He heard my voice and arrested himself, and placed his hands before his eyes like a man dissipating a dream, and then said: 'Why, Johnny, how are you?' When I heard that it was he who killed Lincoln, I thought that he had been at the time I describe ready to carry out his purpose."

In answer to a request by the writer for a statement of his acquaintance with John Booth of Rear Admiral George W. Baird, US Army retired, of Washington, DC, who is probably the only living witness who helped to identify the body of John Booth, who was shot to death in the tobacco barn on the Garrett plantation, near Port Royal, Va., April 26, 1864, I received the following:

1505 Rhode Island Avenue,
Washington, DC, November 29, 1921.

Miss Burke McCarty,
Grace Dodge Hotel,
Washington, C.

My dear Miss McCarty:
Your letter of the 25th was received last night: I will try to answer it categorically, and, to avoid errors. I must go back to my diary.

My acquaintance with John Wilkes Booth was not at all intimate. I met him in New Orleans in the winter of '63 and '64, when he was playing in the theatre there in "Marble Hearts" and he was splendid in his part. My acquaintance was what may be called a bar-room acquaintance. Was introduced to him by a young officer of my ship the *Pensacola* whose name was Fitch and who afterwards married the eldest daughter of General Sherman. Booth seemed to be a congenial fellow with a sense of humor and I thought was very temperate in his habits, not like his father in that respect. The War was at its height and was freely discussed, but Booth did not seem to be much interested in it. He was from Maryland, whose population was divided, though men as a rule believed it proper to side with their state. My ship went north in the spring of 1864 and I was assigned to my duty in the navy department.

In 1850 when I was seven years of age, I went to school in Washington to two reverend gentlemen Cox and Marlot, who taught in the lower story of the Masonic Hall, Virginia Avenue and Fourth Street East. The boy who sat by me about my own age was David Herold, a little round headed, round eyed, round bodied boy, whose general rotundity was completed by a voice that rolled his R's. I envied David his disposition in that he got along with the big boys so well. When a big boy imposed on David, he would escape with a funny remark which was called witty, which generally got a laugh, and David was called popular. When a big boy imposed on me, I hated him; I hate him yet. David's father, Mr. George Herold, and my father were members of Naval Lodge of Masons. The Herolds were members of Christ Church Episcopal. My people were members of the Baptist Church.

When I left that school about a year later, I lost sight of David. I heard he became a drug clerk.

Now I quote from my records:

"On the night of the 14th of April 1865 I went to call on a young lady and about 10:30 her brother came in and said Abe Lincoln is dead. He had been to the theatre to see Laura Keene in "Our American Cousin" and during a play a man had got into the box where the President was, and had shot the President, jumped out of the box on to the stage, and escaped from the back of the stage. I left at once; saw policeman at the corner whom I interrogated and he confirmed the story. I inquired as to the appearance of the assassin and he not only gave a description that fitted but said he resembled me, and I thought that I had better hurry to my boarding house. On arriving at my boarding house Dr. Ludlam and Mr. Fitch inquired if I had heard the news and suggested that we go down town and get the latest "bricks" but nothing could induce me to appear on the streets again that night.

"The people were wild with excitement. I never heard such threats of vengeance. Before 10:00 o'clock the next morning almost every house was draped in mourning.

People had exhausted the stores here and wired Baltimore for black crepe and cambric. Dan Ballauf, the model maker, was standing leaning on the lower box in the theatre and saw it all. He denied the report that Booth had uttered the words "sic semper tyranis," but the newspapers had printed it. The newspapers had the story very early, that John Wilkes Booth was the assassin and David Herold was the accomplice."

"Though never intimate with John Wilkes Booth, I admired him, his voice, power of declaiming. I took drinks with him at the Franklin House, Custom House Street, a place frequented by army and navy officers. He seemed to me to have no interest in the war. It was hard to understand. I had not seen him but once in Washington and that about three weeks before the murder of the President. It was on Sunday when he was coming out of Saint Aloysius Catholic Church Vesper Service—great crowds of various creeds used to go to that vespers where the music was good. I think Mme. Kretzmayer was the attractive soprano."

A large reward was offered for Booth's arrest and conviction. The War had practically ended and our troops were at liberty to travel in any state without molestation.

I was detailed to make a series of experiments in the Navy Yard, and after Booth's body was brought to the Navy Yard and lay on board the "Montauk" this happened:

I was called on board the Montauk by Lieutenant W. W. Crowninshield, to identify the body of John Wilkes Booth, which I did. I noticed a piece of cord about the size of a cod line on his (Booth's) neck and invited Crowninshield's attention to it, who pulled it out and on it was a small Roman Catholic medal. Surgeon General Barnes arrived at that moment and probed the wound in Booth's neck.

I got a horse and buggy and drove down to Surrattville the following day. The house they said belonged to Mrs. Surratt and had been leased to John M. Lloyd whom I knew. He was a policeman at Washington during all of Buchanan's administration and bore an excellent

MRS. MARY E. SURRATT
Who "kept the nest that hatched the egg" — President Andrew Johnson.

reputation. I inquired of some boys whom I found very communicative. One boy said that Mr. Jenkins, brother of Mrs. Surratt, and Mr. Griffith and Mr. Wylie (or Wyville) and Mr. Lloyd were all out that night listening for the horses coming, that when the two men came, fresh horses were brought out of the stable, saddles transferred from the tired horses to the fresh, and the men rode on.

On May 22, 1865, I went to Baltimore on duty in connection with the *Pensacola*.

The *Washington Star* of May 12, 1865 gives Lloyd's testimony as follows:

"Sometime ago two carbines and some pistols were left at my house. The Friday before the assassination Mrs. Surratt came to my house and told me to have the carbines and pistols ready as two men would call for them. At the night of the assassination Booth and Herold rode up to the house; Herold dismounted, went in, and took a carbine and the pistols. Booth would not take his carbine on account of his lame ankle."

The *Washington Star* of the 15th said:

"Lloyd testified that it was John Surratt who brought the carbines. Watchman saw Mrs. Surratt, Booth, John Surratt, and Dr. Mudd together on Seventh Street, and that Booth was a frequent visitor at the house of Mrs. Surratt, and their interviews were always apart.

"I was retired from active duty by law in 1905 but continued on duty until 1906. The next year I passed some days at Poland Springs, Maine. Among other Washingtonians was Mr. Crosby Noyes, principal editor of the *Washington Star,* who told me he was the reporter for the *Star* at the trial of the conspirators, and he was satisfied that Mrs. Surratt and all the rest of them were guilty.

I was at sea when John Surratt was tried. My information on that trial was that printed in the *Washington Star.* Surratt was poor, but Mr. K. T. Merrick, a Roman Catholic Lawyer, was his principal counsel and it was commonly reported that he paid the entire expense of the trial. His associate counsel was Mr. Joseph Bradley, a famous criminal lawyer, who rarely, if ever, lost a case, and to whom the bad cases usually came.

Quoting from the *Evening Star* of September 23, 1868:

"Judge Wylie on the bench, Messrs. Merrick and Bradley argued on a demur to the plea of the amnesty proclamation which had been issued by the government in favor of the Confederates who had been in arms against the government. Their purpose was to make it apply to the case of John Surratt who had been tried for conspiracy to murder the President, and in whose case a year ago the jury had hung.

Merrick said the court was not technically a Court of the United States, wherein the judge held that the Court held that the Circuit Court of the District of Columbia was not on the same footing as the United States District Courts, though the judges of such Courts were vested with the same power.

He would submit in view of the double character of the Court that to except a person of some felony he must be indicted for felony in some Circuit Court of the United States. He referred to the Bankrupt Act.

Mr. Bradley referred the Court to several authorities. The Court suffered counsel to amend the plea.

From the *Evening Star* of September 24, 1868, page 4, Column 2, viz:

> "A NEW MOVE BY THE DEFENSE, STATUTE OF LIMITATION, DISCHARGE OF THE PRISONER.
>
> "Mr. Merrick stated that he had presented a new

plea. He claimed the indictment defective in that it did not aver that **Surratt had not fled from Justice**."

The paper stated that he walked out of the court unmolested.

I saw the medal when it was taken off Booth's neck and I saw it afterwards in the War Department. It was kept in a safe of the Judge Advocate General. It was in a little tin box which also contained a newspaper scrap referring to it with the bullet from Booth's neck, and I think the derringer also.

When I became superintendent of the S. W. and Navy Department in 1895, I asked the messenger at the Judge Advocate General's door if the relics were still on exhibition as I wanted to show them to some friends, and he said that they were all there but the medal, that the Secretary of War (Mr. Lamont) had sent for them to show some friends and forgot to return them, and they remained on his desk four months, and when returned the medal was missing.

John M. Lloyd, the Washington policeman in 1857-[9/1860] bore a good reputation. I think the claim that he was intemperate or a sot as Mr. Brophy called him was all propaganda. A policeman knows how to testify and he knows the penalty. I was reluctant to believe Lloyd a conspirator until the boys at Surrattville told me of the story of Lloyd, Jenkins, Wylie, et al listening for the coming of Booth that night, and his testimony confirmed it. One of the propaganda writers says that Lloyd had to be awakened from a drunken stupor that night when Booth arrived, when the boys, who had no purpose to serve, told me that Lloyd was wide awake on the road listening for horses. They said that when the horses were plainly heard, that Lloyd, et al, went into the stable and brought out the fresh horses as if in a hurry. Lloyd and his wife (whom I also knew) were Roman Catholics, and I believe members of St. Dominic's Congregation. The testimony shows Lloyd drunk but once; it was when he met Mrs. Surratt in Uniontown, now called Anacostia, and that was on the eve of the frightful tragedy and he might have needed "Dutch courage." My impression was that the effort to damage Lloyd's character was for the sole purpose of impeaching his testimony. I always thought he found himself in serious trouble and told the truth to save his neck.

Yours sincerely,
G. W. BAIRD."

U. S. troops under Lieutenant Baker, surrounded the barn and ordered Booth to surrender, which he refused to do. "Davy" Herold, however, asked to surrender and was allowed to come out. He was handcuffed and placed in charge of a squad of cavalrymen. The barn was finally fired by Colonel Conger.

Booth, who could be now plainly seen by the light of the flames was peering out, when a bullet from the revolver of Sergeant Boston Corbett whizzed by and Booth crumpled up on the barn floor. He was dragged out by the soldiers and lay on the grass, apparently dead, but was revived by a dash of cold water in the face. The bullet had entered almost at the same spot in which his own bullet had pierced President Lincoln's head. He was carried and laid upon the porch in front of the Garrett house where he suffered several hours of the most intense agony. Noting his lips moving, an officer stooped down and heard him whisper: "Tell

Post-mortem of Booth's body as it lay on the Monatuk, April 27, 1865.

my mother—tell my mother—I died for my country—and did what I thought best." Indicating a desire that his paralyzed arms be held up, which was done, contemplating them, he murmured, "Useless, useless." These were his last words.

The body was taken by wagon to the river and placed on board the Gunboat Montauk and brought to Washington, and Admiral Baird was one of the men who made positive identification.

From Admiral Baird's letter one would gather that as late as the winter of 1864, only a few months previous to Booth's coming to Washington, he was indifferent on the subject of the war. The fact that he was in New Orleans where he would have been very safe in expressing his opinion in favor of the South would seem to indicate he had no great feeling on the subject.

There is no doubt in the writer's mind but that Clara Morris was perfectly right in her statement that John Wilkes Booth was the victim chosen from the beginning and that he "**drew the lot**" after his New Orleans engagement where Admiral Baird had seen him. From the time he registered at the National Hotel in November 1864, it is plainly evident that he became obsessed with the idea, and the working of the **virus** is traceable in his every act from that time on. He lost all interest in his profession, a thing in itself most remarkable, for which we can only account in the one way.

John Harrison Surratt, the nineteen-year-old son of Mrs. Mary E. Surratt, who was chosen by the Jesuits as the arch-conspirator in the assassination of Abraham Lincoln, had studied three years in preparation for the Roman priesthood at the Sulpician Fathers monastery, in Charles County, Maryland, previous to the breaking out of the Civil war. The Sulpician Fathers is a branch of the Jesuit order.

In 1862 young Surratt was called to his home in Surrattville, a crossroads village 13 miles south of Washington, by the death of his father. The elder Surratt had been a railroad contractor, and had accumulated some money which was partly invested in slaves and in plantation and tavern at Surrattville where he served as postmaster at the time of his demise.

The family consisted of Isaac, the eldest son, a civil engineer, who enlisted in the Southern Cause at the very beginning of the war and who the last heard of him had joined Maximilian's forces in Mexico; Anna, the only daughter, a girl in her early twenties, and John H., the youngest.

The Surratts were all ardent secessionists and fanatical Roman Catholics. Mrs. Surratt was, early in life, perverted to Romanism from the Protestant faith. Her children were Romanists from birth.

That John Harrison Surratt, was cool, clever, calculating and crafty, far in advance of his years, is shown by the fact that at the very beginning of the Rebellion he was selected to do important work in the southern secret service, bearing the most important dispatches from Jefferson Davis at Richmond to his agents at Washington and to the members of his "kitchen cabinet" in Montreal, Canada. On his return home from the monastery near Baltimore, John Surratt was sworn in as postmaster in his father's place at Surrattville.

His Jesuit training enabled him to lift his hand and swear undivided allegiance to the United States. So much for a Jesuit's oath. To get a complete estimate of John Surratt's part in the diabolical conspiracy to murder President Lincoln and other heads of this government we must fully consider the preliminary training he received.

This boy (for we must remember that he was but in his teens, at his entrance into this plot), was never free from the espionage and evil influence of the Romish church, from his baptism in infancy to the day of his death at the age of seventy-two years. When he was but twelve years old he was placed in Gonzaga College, Washington, DC, a Catholic preparatory school, under the tutorage of Priest Wiget, who was the confessor for years of both himself and his mother.

After leaving Gonzaga College he spent two years at Georgetown in the Jesuit College before leaving for the Sulpician Fathers monastery. I am calling the attention of the reader to this fact when you come to pass judgment on this young man, that you may place the blame for his conduct where it belongs—on the Jesuit psychology inculcated by the priests of the Roman Church.

That he was a leader and a dependable one, in this conspiracy of wholesale assassination, is shown by the fact that the object of John Wilkes Booth's first visit to St. Mary's Catholic Church in Howard County, Maryland, was to learn the whereabouts in Washington of John Surratt.

Young Surratt, had then, never the slightest chance or desire to escape from the deadly **virus**. This virus stultified every noble aspiration, every natural affection, every personal ambition, even the strongest instinct in the human mind, **self-preservation is thrust aside** when the victim hears the call of duty to "the holy mother church." Then, mother love, father love, brother love—all, all, must yield to this cursed thing. This **complete mental control** that Rome exercises over its dupes whom it permits to have no more will of their own, nor resistance, than that of a cadaver. *Perinda ac cadaver* (as a corpse) to be moved here, or there, at the **will of the manipulator.**

The Roman Catholic child is thus handicapped at birth. Yes, there is a **prenatal** influence as the study of these two characters in this tragic drama will disclose. The mother, Mary E. Surratt, the intimate associate of priests, her soul deadened by the **fatal virus** of the Jesuit training, passed on to her son the terrible inheritance which made him **wax** in the black hands of the Vatican intriguers, to mold as they would.

During Surratt's theological training, he had studied St. Thomas Aquinas, who **justifies** the assassination of heretics, or any one who apostatizes from the Romish church. It was a significant and eloquent fact that the Jesuits released from time to time during the war the report that President Lincoln had been, in his infancy, baptized by Catholic priest.

On one of his visits to the White House of the Reverend Charles Chiniquy to warn President Lincoln of his danger in assassination, Mr. Lincoln is quoted by Chiniquy in his book *Fifty Years in the Church of Rome* as follows:

> "Father Chiniquy, I want your views about a thing which is exceedingly puzzling to me and you are the only one to whom I would like to speak on the subject. A great number of Democratic newspapers have been sent me lately, evidently written by Roman Catholics, publishing that I was born a Roman Catholic and baptized by a priest. They called me a renegade and apostate on account of that, and they heaped upon my head mountains of abuse. Now, **no priest of Rome has ever laid his hand on my head**. But the persistency of the Romish press to present this falsehood to their readers as gospel truth, must have a **meaning**. Please tell me, as briefly as possible, what you think about it."

This, Mr. Chiniquy answered, was done solely to incite and justify the act in the minds of some of their fanatics to assassinate the President.

It was the equivalent to a command, as it afterward proved.

From their first meeting Booth and Surratt busied themselves selecting their associates. David Herold was undoubtedly the choice of John Surratt who had known him from his college days, evidently, at Georgetown University. The testimony of Louis J. Weichmann, college chum of Surratt and the State's chief witness, at the trials of the conspirators shows that Surratt had introduced him to David Herold as one of the members of the Washington Marine Band which had serenaded the Surratt Tavern at midnight on one occasion when Weichmann was spending the week-end there. This was a year before Booth's appearance in Washington.

There is no doubt but that all the conspirators were members of the Knights of the Golden Circle; there is also no doubt that while some of them were nominal Protestants they were wholly papalized, certainly they were not Protestants. All through the testimony we see that Booth and Atzerodt were at "mass." It is morally certain that Booth himself had been secretly taken into the Roman Church when he was given the "Agnus Dei" medal which was taken from his neck. The significance of this medal is: The translation of "Agnus Dei" is "Lamb of God; it indicates sacrifice, the shedding of blood.

MICHAEL O'LOUGHLIN.
Delegated to assassinate General Grant.
Died in Dry Tortugas after serving three
years, of yellow fever epidemic.

The writer is informed by an ex-Romanist who examined the medal that it was made in Rome, probably sent direct from the Pope as was the Pope IX's letter to Jeff Davis, a distinction that would tend to flatter the vanity of John Wilkes Booth.

Michael O'Loughlin, another conspirator, was from Baltimore and was, as his name would indicate, a Roman Catholic Irishman.

Sam Arnold, it appears, had attended the same school with John Wilkes Booth in their childhood and was a nominal Protestant.

George Atzerodt was the "rough" man, that is, the uneducated and uncultured one, who was probably an Austrian Catholic, but not over-religious. He attended Mass with Louis Weichmann at the Piscataway Church and St. Patrick's church in Washington.

Lewis Payne, the athletic young giant who was delegated to murder Secretary of State Seward, and almost accomplished this deed, really showed more strength of character and less cowardice than any of the other conspirators. As far as is known, he was the son of a Protestant minister. He refused to tell anything about himself, but when he went to his death, he was courageous to a degree that astonished the newspaper correspondents and other spectators.

Edward Spangler, another conspirator, was a roustabout employee at Ford's Theatre, much given to drink. He had great admiration for John Booth and was a decided Southern sympathizer with a pronounced dislike for Abraham Lincoln, which he had often expressed.

About November 1, 1863, Mrs. Surratt and her family moved to their residence at 541 H. St., Washington, D. C, where she opened a select boarding house. Select to the extent that there were no "heretics" among her boarders. The first to come was Louis J. Weichmann, who had been for three years a classmate of John Surratt's at the Sulpician Monastery where Weichmann also was preparing for the Roman priesthood. From the very first, Weichmann and Surratt were bosom friends.

Weichmann was born in Baltimore, in 1843 and was the son of a merchant tailor who was a staunch Lutheran. The wife was a devout Roman Catholic. The family consisted of two boys and three girls, all of whom were brought up in the faith of their mother. Both boys, Louis, and the second boy, Frederick, were studying for the Roman priesthood.

With the breaking out of the Civil War, Louis Weichmann's college studies were interrupted and he came to Washington where he obtained a position as professor at Gonzaga College, when John Surratt first learned of his presence in Washington.

During the Spring vacation of 1863, young Weichmann proposed that he and Surratt pay a visit to their alma mater near Baltimore. They were received with warm cordiality by both professors and students who were eager to learn the progress of the war, etc. During this visit, according to documentary evidence to be introduced later on, both young men freely expressed their pro-Southern views. Before leaving the institution Louis Weichmann announced his intention of going to Little Texas, or Ellengown, where he had taught the parochial school for the Catholic priest there, before entering college. Reverend Denis, prefect of the Sulpician Monastery, told him that the teacher at that time in Little Texas was Henri de St. Marie, who had been a former pupil of Denis in Montreal; and that he was a fine young man who spoke French and Italian fluently. He asked Weichmann if he would hand him an Italian paper when he called upon him. On reaching Little Texas, Mr. Weichmann delivered the paper and introduced his friend Surratt to the young Canadian. This was the beginning of an acquaintance that was to end very disastrously for Surratt.

A few days before Christmas 1864, young Weichmann invited Surratt to go with him over to Pennsylvania Avenue to select some Christmas gifts for his sisters in Philadelphia. As they were nearing the Avenue on 7th Street, Weichmann said, "John, someone is calling you," and Surratt, turning, saw Dr. Mudd of Bryantown and a younger man with him, whom he introduced as John Wilkes Booth. After the introductions were over Booth invited the party up to his room at the National Hotel, where he ordered wine and cigars for the group.

From this meeting on John Booth was a constant visitor at the Surratt home on H Street, which was the rendezvous of the conspirators up to the very day of the assassination. It was also the mecca of various Roman Catholic priests, among whom were the Reverends Walters and Wiget of St. Patrick's Church, 10th and G Streets, of which the Surratts were members.

Before closing this chapter in reference to the religion of John Wilkes Booth, I might say that his family were members of the Episcopal church in Baltimore.

Edwin A. Sherman, Past Grand Registrar of the Grand Consistory of the Thirty-second of the Ancient and Accepted Scottish Rite of Freemasonry of the State of California, in his book entitled *Engineer Corps of Hell*, on page 213, had this to say:

> "It has been told to us, coming from what we believe to be true authority, that Booth, about three weeks before he committed the crime, was admitted to the Roman Catholic church, and privately received the sacraments from no less a personage than Archbishop Spaulding

himself, which he did to silence any conscientious scruples that he might have in taking Abraham Lincoln's life, and that he might have the whole influence and sympathy of persons in that faith in protecting and concealing himself when the act was done, to aid him in it. He certainly had that aid and influence in planning and accomplishing his hellish work and in making his escape, and it could not have been more cheerfully and faithfully rendered than it was, even if he had been a Jesuit priest himself. We believe the statement to be true; and it was but a short time after that Archbishop Spaulding received a donation of funds for the specific purpose which was to uniform and equip a military body in the same manner and style as the Papal Guard at Rome.

"The uniforms, muskets, cartridge boxes and belts all bearing the Papal coat of arms and consecrated by the Pope himself, were sent to Archbishop Spaulding at Baltimore; and when he died he was buried with military honors and his remains escorted by the same military bodyguard. The entire diocese of Archbishop Spaulding was rebel to the core and fierce in its hatred of Lincoln."

In a recent book written by one of Rome's apologists, we find that John Wilkes Booth was by "religion a Roman Catholic; by politics a Democrat."

VIII

The Blackest Deed In American History

And now we come to that darkest day in the history of our Republic, April 14, 1865. The April 3 surrender of General Robert E. Lee to the "Little Smoking General" Grant came like a thunderbolt out of a clear sky, and was a terrific blow to the hopes of the South, as well as an unexpected victory to the North. The people were wild with enthusiastic joy. We can get some conception of that word after four years of the most bitter civil war; we, who have the news of the Armistice still fresh in our memories in the recent World War that was several thousand miles away.

The figure of Abraham Lincoln will ever stand out on the page of our history, never to be effaced, not only in the minds of the people of his own country, but in those of the **Peoples of the World**, as the savior of the New Concept of Government!

Lincoln, that great, sad-faced man, with his shoulders drooping under the terrible burdens he had carried patiently for four long years, breathed a sigh of relief when he arose this bright balmy April morning and gazed at nature's gay spring garb.

During breakfast with his family, he had suggested to his good wife Mary, that they two **alone** should take a long drive in the country that called so strongly to this heavily laden man. Accordingly, after a few preliminary office duties were gotten out of the way, the President returned to the White House, and he and Mrs. Lincoln got into their carriage and drove out through the city over the Potomac River bridge into the country. The fruit trees were white with blossoms, the roadsides

Ford's Theatre, Washington D. C.
US Government property as it appears today.
Exterior unchanged.

House on 10th St. where President Lincoln died April 15, 1865. Now Lincoln Memorial Collection.

green, and the very birds flitting in and out through the hedges seemed to surpass themselves with their songs.

President Lincoln began to talk of their future. He confessed to her that he would welcome the day when his administration would be over, and they could return to private life, never to leave it again. "I have managed, my dear, by strict economy, to save a little nest egg out of my salary, so we will go back to Springfield to live, and I hope not have to work quite so hard. We can visit with our friends and neighbors and enjoy life a bit." Then he unfolded to her his plans to take up his law practice again and the threads of life where he had left them when he came to Washington a little over four years ago. After driving several hours and being rested by the quiet of the country and sweet breath of spring, this great **simple-hearted, plain** man and his wife returned to the White House.

I cannot but contrast that last morning on earth of Abraham Lincoln and his modest plans, with the conduct of Woodrow Wilson and his dozens of trunks, which carried the elaborate wardrobes of himself and wife to Europe. The sinful extravagance of this pedagogical upstart! It seems almost sacrilegious to mention him in the same paragraph with Lincoln.

The day began for John Wilkes Booth with his usual trip to Graves Theatre where he received his mail. This morning he had several letters, and after chatting pleasantly with the members of the cast present for rehearsal, as was his custom, he sauntered away toward the Kirkwood House, now the Raleigh, where the Vice President was stopping. He sent up the following card to Mr. Johnson, which is still, and perhaps, always will remain a mystery:

"For Mr. Andrew Johnson:
Don't wish to disturb you: are you at home?
John Wilkes Booth."

After his call at the Kirkwood House, he went to the livery barn of J. Pumphreys on C Street, in the back of the National Hotel. Here he engaged a horse to be ready that afternoon at 4:30. He had been in the habit lately of hiring his horses here after he had sold his own a few weeks previous. Upon this occasion he asked for a particular sorrel horse he preferred, but was told it was out at that time, so he took instead a small bay mare.

Booth was an expert horseman and fencer, and spent a great deal of his time horseback riding and the latter amusement, when he found a man who was skillful enough to interest him. After his arrangement for the horse was completed, he spent a large part of the day conferring with the other conspirators, who were in the city: Mrs. Surratt, John Surratt, O'Laughlin, Herold, Spangler and Atzerodt.

The evening of this same day, April 14, 1865, on which Mr. Lincoln and his wife went for their last drive in the country, the managers of Ford's Theatre featured the fact in the local press that the President and General U.S. Grant would attend the performance of *Our American Cousin* at that theatre in the evening. This would have been the first public appearance of General Grant since the surrender of Lee, and the word that the people would have an opportunity to greet their hero that night at Ford's Theatre made a rush on the box office, and the performance opened with a packed house.

The Presidential party did not arrive until 9:30. When the tall, gaunt figure of the tired-eyed President made its appearance in the flag-draped box, the house went wild with delight and the orchestra struck up "Hail to the Chief." The house arose as one body, and enthusiasm was inspiring. For several minutes, the cheering continued and the President bowed and bowed his acknowledgements.

The absence of General Grant was soon noticed, but this did not dampen the welcome for the great man who had sent out but a few days previous the most wonderful—the most extraordinary—message to a conquered enemy the world had ever heard. Namely, for them to return to their homes and help in the reconstruction of the Republic. No punishments, no criticisms, no bitterness, but just simply to return to their homes and set about rebuilding what they had tried to destroy, in a spirit of "With charity for all and malice toward none."

The President and Mrs. Lincoln, upon receiving the regrets of General Grant and wife, who had been called to the bedside of their daughter, Miss Nellie, who was ill at a private boarding school in New Jersey, had invited Mai or Rathbone, lately returned from the front, and his fiance, Miss Harris, daughter of Senator Harris, to accompany them. The party seated themselves after the long ovation given the President, and turned their whole attention to the pastoral comedy of which Mr. Lincoln was very fond.

Miss Laura Keene was playing the star lead that evening, assisted by a cast of prominent and capable actors, and the play went with a zest, the audience receiving it with a gale of laughter as one funny scene after another passed. The President chuckled quietly in his own peculiar quizzical manner. While this brilliant scene was taking place inside, a most unusual play was transpiring on the outside.

Sergeant Dye, a member of the government service, was sitting in front of the restaurant next door to the entrance of the theatre on 10th Street, talking with some other men who were enjoying the warm evening and their cigars, when a tall, young, well-dressed man stepped to the front of the theatre on the sidewalk, and in clear tones called the time. This did not attract any particular attention until he had repeated it at an interval of every fifteen minutes for the third time, at 10:15.

He disappeared and Sergeant Dye's curiosity was aroused by his strange conduct. He got up and started to walk in the direction the young stranger had taken, when wild cries and confusion within the theatre reached the street. "The President is shot!" "The President is killed!" finally was

JOHN WILKES BOOTH FIRING
THE FATAL BULLET

clearly heard. The entrance doors burst open and men, insane with fright, bolted out giving the call to those on the pavement, then rushed back in. It all happened quicker than it takes to write it.

At a moment before the last call of the time in front of the theatre, John Wilkes Booth, the popular young tragedian, stepped out of the barroom attached to the theatre on 10th Street, where he had called for several brandies, walked rapidly into the front lobby, passed the doorman at the center aisle with a genial nod, calling him familiarly by name, which was answered in the spirit which John Booth's greetings generally were.

He passed over to the side aisle and started down when his passage was barred by the arm of the head usher, who happened to be talking with friends in the aisle. Booth put his arm across the shoulder of the man who had his back to him and, peering into his face, said, "Why, you don't want to keep me out, do you, old boy?" This was in the melodious Booth voice, once heard, never to be forgotten.

The usher, swinging around said, "No, indeed, Mr. Booth. Allow me to present you to my friends." Booth acknowledged the introduction graciously and turning, sauntered down the aisle toward the box occupied by the Presidential party, intent on the most cruel, cowardly murder in all the world's history.

He passed the man on guard, who for the moment left the door of the box and was watching the play from a seat nearby.

Booth entered the box, stealthily placing the board in the socket on the inside which had been made ready that day, by Spangler, the stage carpenter.

Booth's entrance was so quiet that it attracted no attention from any of the party, all of whom had their eyes fixed upon the stage where only two people were: Laura Keene and Harry Hawks as Asa Trenchard. The lines and situation were exceedingly funny and the house was uproariously enjoying the comedy.

Booth, after securing the door from any interference from the outside, crept panther-like close to the back of the President's chair, whipped out his derringer with his right hand and a dagger with his left, placing the revolver just above the back of the chair.

There was a muffled report, a whiff of smoke, and the President's head dropped upon his breast. The intruder darted toward the railing in front of the box, but before he reached it, Major Rathbone, horror-stricken, but not really knowing just what had happened, bounded to his feet. He reached out to grab the assassin, who, dropping his revolver, slashed viciously at him, warding him off by an ugly stab that cut his sleeve from shoulder to wrist from which the blood spurted.

With the agility of the skilled athlete he was, Booth sprang over the balustrade of the box onto the stage twelve feet below, but his stirrup, for he was in riding habit, caught in the large American flag which had been draped around Stuart's Washington on the front of the box, and he fell to the stage, breaking a small bone in his leg. He bounded to his feet instantly and darted away from the stage past the petrified actors, out through the rear door, where he mounted his horse, which he had gotten the candy butcher, called "Peanuts," to hold for him just before he entered the front door a few moments previous.

Joseph B. Stewart, a man from the audience, who had taken in the situation before others in the audience had recovered from their horror, scrambled to the stage yelling "Stop that man!" and rushed after the assassin, but just as Booth darted through the alley door, someone in the dark slammed it shut before Stewart reached it and, before he could get it open, the man mounted his horse and dashed madly away in the darkness.

Spangler, the stage carpenter, the testimony developed, was the man who had slammed the door. He had been heard to promise his assistance to Booth earlier in the evening when he had dismounted from his horse. For this and disloyal statements about the President which he had been heard to make, he received a sentence of six years at the Dry Tortugas prison.

The gaunt body of the dying President was tenderly carried out of the theatre on the door of the box, which had been hastily pressed into service as a stretcher, and across the street to the three-story brick house of a man by the name of Peterson, who let his rooms furnished to the businessmen employed at the stores and nearby theatres.

The stretcher-bearers carried him to the bedroom in the rear of the hall on the first floor and into a room occupied by a returned soldier, William Clark. The bed was a single bed and the body of the President had to be laid diagonally across on account of his great height.

The pitiful scene here can scarcely be portrayed by words. The hysterical sobs of Mrs. Lincoln and her constant cry of "Oh, why did they not take me? Why did they take him?" was heart-breaking.

Captain Robert Lincoln just returned from the front a few days before, was immediately summoned from the White House, where he was entertaining a college classmate, to the bedside of his dying father. He spent the time alternately trying to comfort his mother in the front parlor and watching at the bedside of his dying father.

Soon the members of Mr. Lincoln's cabinet had gathered in the sick room and Dr. Gurley, Protestant minister, and Surgeon General Barnes, came as soon as possible from the bedside of the Secretary of State Seward, the surgeon having been called there after Mr. Seward had been stabbed by Louis Payne. Mr. Seward was now hovering between life and death. General Stanton, the cold, severe, dignified man, who had never been known to show any emotion, dropped on his knees at the foot of the President's bed, buried his face in the covering and sobbed like a child.

Charles Sumner who, perhaps, loved Lincoln with the deepest and most ardent love of them all, never stirred from his place at the bed, holding his hand, and aiding the physicians, and watching with bated breath for the slightest sign of returning consciousness. But the wounded man never for one instant recovered, and died without knowing what had occurred. From the moment the physicians first reached him and found the wound, they knew he was doomed.

The President never regained consciousness and died a few minutes after seven the next morning. Charles Sumner, as he watched the life of the great man go out, turned to those in the room and said: **"And now, he belongs to the angels!"**

At the same time that Booth assassinated the President, Louis Payne, known as the "Florida Boy," an athletic young giant who some months before joined the Conspiracy, rode up to the front of the residence of the Secretary of State, William Seward, and tied his horse to the hitching post.

Mr. Seward had been ill for three weeks, suffering from a fractured jaw, the result of the running away of his team, and was under the constant care of male nurses.

Payne rang the bell and it was answered by the colored butler. He

WILLIAM H. SEWARD
Lincoln's Secretary of State who was
stabbed by Louis Payne.

told the latter that he had been sent with some medicine which he must take to the sick room. The butler refused to allow him to enter, saying that he had orders to allow no one to go to Mr. Seward's room. The stranger, after a short struggle, knocked him down, and went bounding up the stairs. He rushed into the sick chamber, after felling each of the two sons of the Secretary, one of whom had been in the service, the blow fracturing the skull of the younger man from which he never fully recovered.

He then sprang upon the sick man and seriously stabbed him three times. By a superhuman effort the latter struggled out of the bed with his assailant who left him in a heap on the floor, bleeding from the wounds he had inflicted. After his murderous assault on Secretary Seward, the ruffian rushed down the stairs, yelling at the top of his voice, "I am mad, I am mad!"He probably was. He was entirely under the control of the hypnotic influences of the wicked people in whose power he had allowed himself to be.

It was part of the **plan** that Michael O'Laughlin one of the conspirators from Baltimore, was to have murdered General Grant that night. This was not possible, owing to the change in the General's plans.

To Atzerodt, it fell to assassinate Vice President Johnson, but he became frightened and spent the day riding into the country on a horse from the livery barn in Washington, where he was found several days after with relatives of his south of Washington. He made a written confession before he was executed that confirmed the presence of Surratt in Washington that day, a fact that nine reputable witnesses had sworn to.

Booth familiarized himself with every road leading out of Washington to the south, and had studied and planned his escape with careful attention. It is not likely that he would ever have been caught, had he not broken the small bone in his left leg in his jump. This was the providential

THE SURRATT HOUSE ON
H. STREET, APRIL 1922.

Recently sold for $10,500. Is occupied by owner. Supposed to be "haunted" by Mrs. Surratt's ghost. Stoop and steps removed by recent purchaser.

handicap that hampered not only himself and Herold, but those of his friends who were ready to assist him.

There is not the slightest doubt but that every mile of that wild ride had been planned in advance, weeks in advance.

The intense agony Booth suffered every moment from the time he first met with the accident when jumping from the box doomed his chances of escape.

The little bay mare dashed madly along under the cruel urge of his spurs as he sped over the bridge that spanned the Potomac to the Bryantown road. He passed the soldier at the bridge, after having told him his name, and was swallowed up in the blackness of the night. The moon was veiled behind a huge bank of clouds.

Presently the guard at the bridge heard the clatter of another horse's hoofs approaching and the horse and rider soon hove in sight onto the bridge. The guard stopped him and asked an account of himself before allowing him to go on. This was Herold and in explanation he gave a false name, saying that he had been in bad company that delayed him from returning home before sundown. He was permitted to pass.

He cut his spurs into his horse and sped along, finally catching up to the first rider, Booth, before they reached Surrattville. They were expected by the tenant, Lloyd, who had been visited by Mrs. Surratt that afternoon who had instructed him to "Have those shooting irons" and other things ready, as they would be needed that night.

Herold drew up to the tavern, sprang from his horse and dashed madly into the barroom, saying: "Lloyd, for God's sake, make haste and get those things."

Lloyd testified at the trials that 1. He gave the carbines, which had been left with him six weeks before to be called for later on. 2. Mrs. Surratt had been driven down by Weichmann from Washington to his house on Friday (April 14). 3. He met them on the road on his way to Washington. 4. He got out of his buggy and went over to the side of their buggy and after a few moments of conversation she told him to **"Have those shooting irons ready; that they would be called for soon."**

Weichmann also testified that he overheard this order by Mrs. Surratt.

Mrs. Surratt brought with her on this trip (the day of the assassination) a package containing Booth's field glass, to be handed out when called for. Herold took a bottle of whiskey out to Booth, who, owing to his suffering, did not come in. They only took one of the revolvers, so Lloyd testified. Herold turned as he was about to drive off and said, "I'm pretty sure that we have assassinated the President and Secretary Seward."

The two riders put their spurs into their horses and set off down the road to the little village of T.B. at full speed. The next stop was made at the residence of Dr. Samuel A. Mudd, where they arrived at 4:00 on Saturday morning. This conspirator housed them and set the bone in Booth's leg. He bound it up in splints improvised from pieces of a cigar box, after which Booth was helped upstairs to bed where he remained until the afternoon of the same day.

O'Laughlin had come to Washington on Thursday, the day before the assassination, with three of his co-religionists and prepared to make a perfectly good bullet-proof alibi for their friend O'Laughlin, which is the rule with Roman Catholic criminals. They were so solicitous in this intent that they over-reached themselves and spoiled it.

The great grievance of the Catholic church is that Mary E. Surratt was brought before a military tribunal instead of a civil court. The real basis of this complaint was, however, that there **could be no political influence brought to bear on** a military court, which the hanging of four conspirators and life sentences of the three others bears out.

As it is not within the power of the writer to present the facts in any simpler or more readable language than that used in the closing argument of the special Judge Advocate, John A. Bingham, I shall rely on excerpts from that document to give the facts.

IX

The Trials Of The Assassins By Documentary Evidence

ARGUMENT OF JOHN A. BINGHAM, Special Judge Advocate.

IN REPLY TO THE SEVERAL ARGUMENTS IN DEFENSE OF MARY E. SURRATT AND OTHERS, CHARGED WITH CONSPIRACY AND THE MURDER OF ABRAHAM LINCOLN, LATE PRESIDENT OF THE UNITED STATES, ETC.

May it please the Court: The conspiracy here charged and specified and the acts alleged to have been committed in pursuance thereof, and with the intent laid, constitute a crime, the atrocity of which has sent a shudder through the civilized world. All that was agreed upon and attempted by the alleged inciters and instigators of this crime constitutes a combination of atrocities with scarcely a parallel in the annals of the human race. Whether the prisoners at your bar are guilty of the conspiracy and the acts alleged to have been done . . . as set forth in the charge and specification, is a question, the determination of which rests solely with this honorable court, and in passing upon which, this court are the sole judges of the law and the fact.

In presenting my views upon the questions of law raised by the several counsel by the defense, and also on the testimony adduced for and against the accused, I desire to

be just to them, just to you, just to my country, and just to
my own convictions. The issue joined involves the highest
interests of the accused, and, in my judgment, the highest
interests of the whole people of the United States. . . . A
wrongful and illegal conviction, or a wrongful and illegal
acquittal upon this dread issue, would impair somewhat
the security of every man's life, and shake the stability of
the Republic.

The crime charged and specified upon your record is not
simply the crime of murdering a human being, but it is a
crime of killing and murdering on the 14th day of April, A.
D. 1865, within the Military Department of Washington
and the entrenched lines thereof, Abraham Lincoln, then
President of the United States, and Commander-in-
Chief of the Army and Navy there; and then and there
assaulting with intent to kill and murder, Wm. H. Seward,
then Secretary of State of the United States; and then and
there lying in wait to kill and murder Andrew Johnson,
the Vice President of the United States, and Ulysses S.
Grant, then Lieutenant General and in Command of the
Army of the United States, in pursuance of a treasonable
conspiracy entered into by the accused with one John
Wilkes Booth, and John H. Surratt, upon the instigation
of Jefferson Davis, Jacob Thompson, Clement C. Clay.
George N. Sanders and others, with intent thereby to aid
the existing Rebellion and subvert the Constitution and
laws of the United States.

The Government in preferring this charge, does not indict
the whole people of any State or section, but only the
alleged parties to this unnatural and atrocious crime. The
President of the United States in the discharge of his duty
as Commander-in-Chief of the Army and by virtue of the
power invested in him by the Constitution and laws of
the United States, has constituted you a military court, to
hear and determine the issue joined against the accused,
and has constituted you a court for no other purpose
whatever. To this charge and specification the defendants
have pleaded first, that this court has no jurisdiction in the

premises; and, secondly, not guilty.

After a careful covering of every point raised by the defense, embellished with numerous citations of legal authorities and court decisions as to both of the points raised by the defense, the Judge Advocate continues:

"It only remains for me to sum up the evidence and present my views of the law arising upon the facts in the case on trial. The questions of fact involved in the issue are:

First, did the accused, or any two of them, confederate and conspire together as charged?

and

Second, did the accused, or any of them, in pursuance of such conspiracy, and with the intent alleged, commit either or all of the several acts specified?

If the conspiracy be established, as laid, it results that whatever was said or done by either of the parties in the furtherance or execution of the common design is the declaration or act of all the other parties of the conspiracy; and this whether the other parties, at the time such words were uttered, or such acts done by their confederates, were present or absent—here, within the entrenched lines of your Capitol, or crouching behind the entrenched lines of Richmond, or awaiting the results of their murderous plot against their country, in Canada. . . . The same rule obtains in cases of treason. A conspiracy is rarely if ever proved by positive testimony. When a crime of high magnitude is about to be perpetrated by a combination of individuals, they do not act openly, but covertly and secretly. The purpose formed is known only to those who enter into it. . . . Unless one of the original conspirators betrays his companions and gives evidence against them, their guilt can be proved only by circumstantial evidence."

THE OLD CAPITOL PRISON, WASHINGTON, DC
Court room where conspirator trials were conducted in July, 1865.

During the course of Judge Advocate Bingham's address, the influence of the Jesuit theology showed up in his reference to Jacob Thompson, one of the conspirators referred to, who was a leader in the group of Confederates of Montreal, when he said:

> "In speaking of this assassination of the President and others, Jacob Thompson said that it was only removing them from office, that the killing of a tyrant was no murder."

Emanuel Sa, a Jesuit authority, said, "The tyrant is illegitimate; and any man whatever of the people has a right to kill him. (Uniquis - que de populo potest occidere.) But note this bit of evidence referred to by the distinguished lawyer:

> "Dr. Merritt testified further that after this meeting in Montreal he had a conversation with Clement C. Clay in Toronto about the letter from Jefferson Davis which Sanders had exhibited and in which conversation Clay gave the witness to understand that he knew the nature of the letter perfectly and remarked that he thought, **'The end would justify the means.'** The witness also testified to the presence of Booth with Sanders in Montreal last fall

and of Surratt in Toronto in February last.

The above is certainly proof positive of Jesuit influence. Continuing below record shows:

> "John Wilkes Booth having entered into this conspiracy in Canada, as has been shown, as early as October, he is next found in the City of New York on the 11th day, as I claim of November, in disguise, in conversation with another, the conversation disclosing to the witness, Mrs. Hudspeth, that they had some matter of personal interest between them; that upon one of them the lot had fallen to go to Washington . . . upon the other to go to Newbern. This witness upon being shown the photograph of Booth swears that 'the face is the same' that of one of the men, who, she says, was a young man of education and culture, as appeared by his conversation, and who had a scar like a bite near the jawbone. It is a fact proved here by the Surgeon General that Booth had such a scar on the side of his neck."

It was this witness that found the letter on the floor of the car that Booth dropped was transmitted from her to the War Department on November 17, 1864. The letter was delivered to President Lincoln who, after having read it, wrote the word "Assassination" across it, and filed it in his office where it was found after his death and was placed in evidence as a court exhibit. The letter read as follows:

> "Dear Louis:
> The time has come at last that we have all so wished for, and upon you everything depends. As it was decided, before you left, we were to cast lots, we accordingly did so, and you are to be the Charlotte Corday of the Nineteenth Century. When you remember the fearful solemn vow that was taken by us, you will feel there is no drawback. **Abe** must die, and now. You can choose your weapons, **the cup, the knife, the bullet**. The cup failed us once and might again. Johnson who will give **this** has

been like an enraged demon since the meeting, because it has not fallen to him to rid the world of a monster . . . You know where to find your **friends**. Your disguises are so perfect and complete that without one knew your face no police telegraphic despatch would catch you. The English gentleman, Harcout, must not act hastily. Remember, he has ten days. **Strike for your home; strike for your country; bide your time, but strike sure.** Get introduced; congratulate him; listen to his stories (not many more will the brute tell to earthly friends;) do anything but fail, and meet us at the appointed place within the fortnight. You will probably hear from me in Washington. Sanders is doing us no good in Canada.

Chas. Selby."

And we quote again from Judge Bingham:

"Although this letter would imply that the assassination spoken of was to take place speedily, yet the party was to **bide his time**. . . . The letter declares that Abraham Lincoln must die and **now** meaning as soon as the agents can be employed and the work done. To that end you will bide your time."
"Even Booth's co-conspirator, Payne, now on his trial . . . says Booth had just been to Canada, 'Was filled with a mighty scheme and was lying in wait for agents.' Booth asked the cooperation of the prisoner and said, 'I will give you as much money as you want; but you must swear to stick to me. It is in the oil business.' This you are told by the accused was early in March last . . . . . In the latter part of November, 1864, Booth visits Charles county, Maryland, and is in company with one of the prisoners, Dr. Samuel E. Mudd, with whom he lodged over night, and through whom he procures of Gardner one of the several horses which were at his disposal and used by him and his co-conspirator in Washington on the night of the assassination."
"Some time during December last it is in the testimony that

DAVID HEROLD
Graduate of Jesuit College at
Georgetown at which institution
he became acquainted with Surratt.

Dr. SAMUEL A. MUDD
Who met Booth at Mass in St.
Mary's Roman Church on his visit
there November 17, 1864.

the prisoner Mudd introduced Booth to John H. Surratt and the witness Weichmann; that Booth invited them to the National Hotel; that when there in the room to which Booth took them, Mudd went out into the passage, called Booth out and had a private conversation with him, leaving the witness and Surratt in the room. Upon their return to the room, Booth went out with Surratt and upon their coming in all three—Booth, Surratt and Samuel A. Mudd —went out together and had a conversation in the passage, leaving Weichmann alone. Up to the time of this interview it seems that neither the witness or Surratt had any knowledge of Booth as they were then introduced to him by Dr. Mudd. Whether Surratt had previously known Booth it is not important to inquire. Mudd deemed it necessary, perhaps a wise precaution, to introduce Surratt to Booth; he also deemed it necessary to have a private conversation with Booth shortly afterwards. Had this conversation, no part of which was heard by Weichmann been perfectly innocent, it is not to be presumed that Dr. Mudd, who was an entire stranger to the witness, would have deemed it necessary to hold the conversation secretly, nor to have volunteered to tell the witness, or rather pretend to tell him what the conversation was . . . And if it was necessary to withdraw and talk by themselves secretly, about the sale of a farm, why should they disclose the fact to the very man from whom they had concealed it?"

As a matter of fact, the above conversation about the purchase of Mudd's farm by Booth was merely a ruse to deceive Weichmann. The whole conversation was talking over the shortest and safest route for flight from the Capitol to reach their friends south of Washington.

A number of Dr. Mudd's slaves testified that he was absent from his home at this time, which corroborated Weichmann's testimony.

We quote from the summing up of the evidence at the trials by Judge Advocate Bingham referring to O'Laughlin as follows:

"Michael O'Laughlin had come to Washington on the 13th of April, 1865, the day preceding the assassination, had sought out his victim, General Grant, at the house of the Secretary of War, that he might be able with certainty to identify him, and that at the very hour when these preparations were going on, was lying in wait at Rullman's on the Avenue, keeping watch, and declaring as he did, at about ten o'clock P. M. when told that that fatal blow had been struck by Booth, 'I don't believe Booth did it.' During the day and night before he had been visiting Booth, and doubtless encouraging him, and at that very hour was in position, at a convenient distance to aid and protect him in his flight, as well as to execute his own part of this conspiracy, by inflicting death on General Grant who happily, was not at the theatre, nor in the city, having left the city that day."

"Who doubts that Booth ascertained in the course of the day that General Grant would not be present at the theatre. O'Laughlin who was to murder General Grant, instead of entering the box with Booth, was detailed to lie in wait, and watch and support him."

"His declarations of his reasons for his changing his

lodgings here and in Baltimore, so ably, and so ingeniously presented in the arguments of his learned counsel (Mr. Cox), avail nothing before the blasting fact, that he did change his lodgings and declared: 'He knew nothing of the affair whatever.' "

O'Laughlin, who said he was in the "oil business," which Booth, Surratt, Payne and Arnold, have all declared meant this conspiracy, says he "knew nothing of the affair." O'Laughlin, to whom Booth sent the despatches of the 13th and 27th of March, O'Laughlin who is named in Arnold's letter as one of the conspirators, and who searched for General Grant on Thursday night, laid in wait for him on Friday, was defeated by that Providence "which shapes our ends," and laid in wait to aid Booth and Payne, declares, he "knows nothing about the matter." Such a denial is as false and inexcusable as Peter's denial of our Lord.

While these preparations were going on, Mudd was awaiting the execution of the plot, ready to faithfully perform his part in securing the safe escape of the murderers. Arnold was at his post at Fortress Monroe, awaiting the meeting referred to in his letter of March 27, wherein he says they were not to "Meet for a month or so," which month had more than expired on the day of the murder, for his letter and testimony disclose that this month of suspensions began to run from about the first week in March. He stood ready with the arms with which Booth had furnished him, to aid the escape of the murderers by that route, and secure their communication with their employers. He had given the assurance in that letter to Booth that although the Government "suspicioned" them, and the undertaking was becoming "complicated" yet a time "more propitious would arrive," for the consummation of this conspiracy in which he "was one" with Booth, and when he "would be better prepared to again be with him."

It was upon the above evidence for which O'Laughlin and Arnold were convicted and sentenced to the Dry Tortugas.

And now I will quote from the same document the summing up of the evidence against Mary E. Surratt, for as a matter of facts tersely stated nothing could surpass that of the Judge Advocate John A. Bingham.

"That Mary E. Surratt is as guilty as her son, as having

thus conspired and combined and confederated, to do this murder, in aid of this rebellion, is clear. First, her house was the headquarters of Booth, John Surratt, Atzerodt, Payne and Herold; she is inquired for by Payne, and she is visited by Booth, and holds private conversations with him. His picture, together with the chief conspirator, Jefferson Davis, is found in her house. She sends to Booth for a carriage to take her on the 11th of April to Surrattville, for the purpose of perfecting the arrangement deemed necessary to the successful execution of the conspiracy, and especially to facilitate and protect the conspirators in their escape from justice. On that occasion. Booth, having disposed of his carriage, gives to the agent she employed (Weichmann) ten dollars with which to hire a conveyance for that purpose. And yet the pretense is made that Mrs. Surratt went on the 11th of April to Surrattville on exclusively her own private and lawful business. Can any one tell, if that be so, how it comes that she should apply to Booth for a conveyance? And how it comes that he, of his own accord, having no conveyance to furnish her, should send her ten dollars with which to procure it?"

"There is not the slightest indication that Booth was under the slightest obligation to her, or that she had any claim upon him, either for a conveyance, or for the means with which to procure one except that he was bound to contribute, being the agent of the conspirators in Canada and Richmond, whatever money might be necessary to the consummation of this infernal plot. On that day, the 11th of April, John H. Surratt had not returned from Canada with the funds furnished him by Thompson."

"Upon that journey of the 11th, the accused, Mary E. Surratt, met with the witness, John M. Lloyd at Uniontown (her tenant at Surrattville). She called him; he got out of his carriage and came to her; she whispered to him in so low a tone that her attendant could not hear her words, though Lloyd to whom they were spoken, did distinctly hear them, and testifies that she told him he should have those "shooting irons" ready, meaning the carbines, which her son, and Herold and Atzerodt had deposited with him, and added the reason, "for they would soon be called for." On the day of the assassination, she again sent for Booth, had an interview with him in her own house, and immediately again went to Surrattville, and then, about six o'clock in the afternoon, she delivered to Lloyd a field glass and told him to "Have two bottles of whiskey and the carbines ready, as they would be called for that night." Having thus perfected the arrangement, she returned to Washington to her own house at about half past eight o'clock, to await the final result. How could this woman anticipate on Friday afternoon at six o'clock, that these arms would be called for, and would be needed that night, unless she was in the conspiracy and knew the blow was to be struck, and the flight of the assassins attempted and by that route."

"Was not the private conversation with Booth held with her in her parlor on the afternoon of the 14th of April, just before she left on this business in relation to the orders she should give to have the **shooting arms ready?**"

"An endeavor is made to impeach Lloyd. But the Court will observe that no witness has been called who contradicts Lloyd's statement in any material matter; neither has his general character for truth been assailed. How, then, is he impeached? Is it claimed that his testimony shows that he was a party to the conspiracy? Then, it is conceded by those who set up any such a pretense that there was a conspiracy. A conspiracy between whom? There can be no conspiracy without the co-operation, or agreement, between two or more persons. Who were the other parties to it? Was it Mary E. Surratt? Was it John H. Surratt? Was it George Atzerodt, David Herold? Those are the only persons so far as his own testimony, or the testimony of any other witness discloses, with whom he had any communication whatever on any subject immediately or remotely touching this conspiracy before the assassination. His receipt and concealment of the arms, are unexplained evidence that he was in the conspiracy."

"The explanation is, that he depended on Mary E. Surratt; was her tenant, and his declaration, given in evidence by the accused, himself, is that: "She had ruined him and brought this trouble upon him." But because he was weak enough, or wicked enough, to become the guilty depository of these arms, and to deliver them on the order of Mary E. Surratt, to the assassins, it does not follow, that he is not to be believed on oath. It is said, that he concealed the fact that the arms had been left and called for. He so testifies himself, but he gives the reason, that he did it only from apprehension of danger to his life. If he were in the conspiracy, his general credit being unchallenged, his testimony being uncontradicted in any material matter, he is to be believed, and cannot be disbelieved if his testimony is substantially corroborated by other reliable witnesses."

"Is he not corroborated touching the deposit of arms by the fact that the arms are produced in court, one of which was found upon the person of Booth at the time he was overtaken and slain, and which is identified as the same which had been left with Lloyd, by Herold, Surratt and Atzerodt? Is he not corroborated in the fact of the first interview with Mrs. Surratt by the joint testimony of Mrs. Offut (his sister-in-law), and Louis J. Weichmann, each of whom testified, (and they are contradicted by no one) that, on Tuesday, the 11th of April, at Uniontown, Mrs. Surratt called Mr. Lloyd to come to her, which he did, and she held a secret conversation with him? Is he not corroborated as to the last conversation on the 14th of April by the testimony of Mrs. Offut, who swears that upon that evening, April 14, she saw the prisoner, Mary E. Surratt, at Lloyd's house, approach and hold conversation with him? Is he not corroborated in the fact, to which he swears that Mrs. Surratt delivered to him at that time, the field glass wrapped in paper, by the sworn statement of Weichmann, that Mrs. Surratt took with her on that occasion two packages, both of which were wrapped in paper, and one of which he describes as a small package,

SURRATT TAVERN AT SURRATTSVILLE, APRIL, 1922.
Now the residence of Mrs. William Penn who has a linen handkerchief
with "John H. Surratt" embroidered in corner, presented to an aunt of
Mrs Penn who attended school taught by him.

---

about six inches in diameter? The attempt was made, by
calling Mrs. Offut, to prove that no such package was
delivered, but it failed; she merely states, that Mrs. Surratt
delivered a package wrapped in paper to her, after her
arrival there, and before Lloyd came in, which was laid
down in the room. But whether it is the package about
which Lloyd testifies, or the other package, of the two
about which Weichmann testifies, as having been carried
there that day by Mrs. Surratt, does not appear. Neither
does this witness pretend to say that Mrs. Surratt, after she
had delivered it to her, and the witness had laid it down
in the room, did not again take it up, if it were the same,
and put it into the hands of Lloyd. She only knows that
she did not see that done; but she did see Lloyd with a
package like the one she received in the room before Mrs.
Surratt left. How it came in his possession she is not able
to state; nor that the package was that Mrs. Surratt first
handed her; nor which of the packages she afterwards saw

in the hands of Lloyd."

"But there is one other fact in this case that puts forever at rest the question of the guilty participation of the prisoner, Mrs. Surratt, in this conspiracy and murder; and that is, that Payne who had lodged four days in her house—who, during ail of that time had sat at her table, and who had often conversed with her—when the guilt of his great crime was upon him, and he knew not where else he could go so safely, to find a co-conspirator, and that he could trust none, that was not like himself, guilty, with even the knowledge of his presence, under the cover of darkness, after wandering for three days and nights, skulking before the pursuing officers, at the hour of midnight found his way to the door of Mrs. Surratt, rang the bell, was admitted, and upon being asked, "Whom do you want to see?" Replied, "Mrs. Surratt."

He was then asked by the officer Morgan, what he came at that time of night for, to which he replied, "To dig a gutter in the morning," that Mrs. Surratt had sent for him. Afterwards he said that Mrs. Surratt knew he was a poor man and **came to him**." Being asked where he last worked, he replied: "Sometimes on I street;" and where he boarded, he replied, that he had no boarding house but was a poor man who got his living with the pick, which he bore upon his shoulder, having stolen it from

the entrenchments of the Capital. Upon being pressed why he came there at that time of night to go to work, he answered that he simply called to see what time he should go to work in the morning.

Upon being told by the officer

ST. PATRICK'S ROMAN CATHOLIC CHURCH

The Surratt household were attendants of this church at 10th and G. streets.

who fortunately had preceded him to this house, that he would have to go to the Provost-Marshal's office, he moved and did not answer, whereupon Mrs. Surratt was asked to step into the hall and state whether she knew this man. Raising her right hand, she exclaimed: "Before God, sir, I have not seen that man before; I have not hired him; I do not know anything about him. The hall was brilliantly lighted."

"If not one word had been said, the mere act of Payne in flying to her house for shelter, would have borne witness against her, strong as proofs from Holy Writ. But, when she denies, after hearing his declarations that she had sent for him, or that she had never seen him, and knew nothing of him, when, in point of fact, she had seen him four consecutive days, in her own house (that same house) in the same clothing which he wore, who can resist for a moment, the conclusion that these parties, were alike, **guilty**?"

And this is the woman whom the Roman hierarchy in this country is trying to make a martyr of! Contemplate this female Jesuit, this Leopoldine, without being asked to swear to her denial, volunteered to lift her hand and in the name of her God, perjure herself in the presence of those witnesses! Do you doubt that she was a lay Jesuit? Listen. Let me quote the "Doctrine of the Jesuits" upon this point:

Under "Of Lying and False Swearing" in JUICIO TEOLOGICA, Basnedi, Jesuit authority, page 278, we find:

"If you believe in an inconvertible manner, that you are commanded to lie, then **lie**."

Again we quote from the Jesuit Father Stoz in "Of the Tribunal of the Penitent:"

"When a crime is secret, the culpability of the crime may be denied; it being understood: publicly."

Mary E. Surratt knew the command of her church at that moment, and to save it from scandal and culpability in this great crime, as well as her own life and safety, she was **dispensed to lie**, and so without any hesitancy she raised her right hand and swore to this **lie**.

Continuing, Judge Bingham said:

> "Mrs. Surratt had arrived at home from the completion of her part in the plot, about half past eight in the evening. A few minutes afterwards she was called to the parlor, and there had a private interview with someone unseen, but whose retreating footsteps were heard by the witness, Weichmann. This was doubtless the **secret**, and last visit of John H. Surratt to his mother, who had instigated and encouraged him to strike this traitorous and murderous blow at his country.
>
> "Booth proceeded to the theatre about nine o'clock in the evening, at the same time that Atzerodt and Payne and Herold were riding the streets, while Surratt, having parted with his mother at the brief interview in her parlor, from which his retreating steps were heard, was walking the Avenue (Pennsylvania) booted and spurred, and doubtless consulting with O'Laughlin. When Booth reached the rear of the theatre, he called Spangler to him and received from Spangler his pledge to help him all he could, when, with Booth, he entered the theatre by the stage door, doubtless to see that the way was clear from the box to the rear door of the theatre, and to look upon their victim, whose erect position they could study from the stage. After this view Booth passes to the street in front of the theatre, where on the pavement, with other conspirators, yet unknown, among them one described as a low-browed villain, he awaits the appointed moment. . . Presently, as the hour of ten o'clock approached, one of his guilty associates calls the time; they wait; again, as the appointed time draws nigh, he calls the time; and finally when the fatal moment arrives, he repeats in a louder tone 'Ten minutes past ten o'clock, ten minutes past ten o'clock.' . . . The hour has come when the red right hand of these murderous conspirators should strike, and the dreadful deed of assassination be done."

INTERIOR OF FORD'S THEATRE ON NIGHT OF MURDER.
JOHN WILKES BOOTH'S ESCAPE AFTER DEED.

Booth, at the appointed moment entered the theatre, ascended to the dress circle, passed to the right, paused a moment looking down, doubtless to see if Spangler was at his post, and approached the outer door of the closed passage leading to the box, occupied by the President, pressed it open, passed in, and closed the passage door behind him. Spangler's bar was in its place and was readily adjusted by Booth in the mortise, and pressed against the inner side of the door, so that he was secure from interruption from outside.

He passed on to the next door, immediately behind the President and, stopping, looks through the aperture in the door into the President's box, and deliberately observes the precise position of his victim seated in the chair, which had been prepared by the conspirators, as the altar for the sacrifice.

The president was looking calmly and quietly down upon the glad and grateful people, whom by his fidelity he had saved from the peril which had threatened the destruction of their government, and all they held dear, this side of the grave, and whom he had come, upon invitation, to greet with his presence, with the words still lingering upon his lips, which he had uttered with uncovered head and uplifted hand, before God, and his country, when on the fourth of last March, he took again the oath to preserve, protect and defend the *Constitution*, declaring that he entered upon the duties of his great office "With malice toward none and charity for all."

In a moment more, strengthened by the knowledge that his conspirators were all at their posts, at least seven of them present in the city—two of them, Mudd and Arnold, at their appointed places, watching for his coming—this hired assassin moves stealthily through the door, the fastening of which had been removed to facilitate his entrance, fires upon his victim, and the martyred spirit of Abraham Lincoln ascends to God.

> "Treason has done his worst; nor steel nor poison
> Malice domestic, foreign levy, nothing
> Can touch him further."

Now, I will let Judge Bingham pick up the thread of evidence by which Booth and Herold were left at the home of Mr. Mudd:

> ". . . They arrived early in the morning before day, and no man knows at what hour they left. Herold rode towards Bryantown with Mudd, about three o'clock that afternoon, in the vicinity of which place he parted with him, remaining in the swamp, and was afterwards seen returning the same afternoon in the direction of Mudd's house, a little before sundown, about which time Mudd returned from Bryantown towards his home. This village, at the time Mudd was in it, was thronged with soldiers in pursuit of the murderers of the President, and although great care had been taken by the defense to deny that anyone said in the presence of Dr. Mudd. Either there or elsewhere on that day, who had committed this crime, yet it is in evidence by two witnesses, whose truthfulness no man questions, that upon Mudd's return to his own house that afternoon, he stated that Booth was the murderer of the President, and Boyle, the murderer of Secretary Seward, but took care to make the further remark that Booth had brothers, and that he did not know which one of them had done the act."
>
> "When did Mr. Mudd learn that Booth had brothers? And what is still more pertinent to this inquiry, from

whom did he learn that either, John Wilkes or any of his brothers, had murdered the President?"

"It is clear that Booth remained in his house until some time in the afternoon of Saturday; that Herold left the house alone, as one of the witnesses states, being seen to pass the window; that he alone of these two assassins was in the company of Dr. Mudd on his way to Bryantown. It does not appear that Herold returned to Mudd's house. It is a confession of Dr. Mudd himself, proven by one of the witnesses that Booth left his house on crutches and went in the direction of the swamp. How long did he remain there, and what became of the horses that Booth and Herold rode to his house and which were put in his stable, are facts nowhere disclosed by the evidence. The owners testify that they have never seen the horses since."

As a matter of fact, it developed afterward, Herold and Booth skulked in the timbers near the place of Thomas Jones, not too far from the road on which they could see the soldiers and searchers riding up and down. They feared the horses might neigh and attract the attention of the riders and be betrayed, so he led the horses a safe distance away and shot them.

The late Brigadier General TM Harris, a member of the military commission that convicted the conspirators, in his great book on the Conspiracy Trials, page 80, describes Dr. Mudd as follows:

"Mudd's expression of countenance was that of a hypocrite. He had the bump of secretiveness largely developed, and it would have taken months of favorable acquaintanceship to have removed the unfavorable impression made by the first scanning of the man. He had the appearance of a natural born liar and deceiver. Mudd was a physician living on a farm. He had a considerable number of slaves at the breaking out of the Rebellion, most of whom had left him during the previous winter. His father, also living in the neighborhood, was a large land and slave holder, and Mudd's disloyalty was, no doubt, of the rabid type. His home was a place for returned Rebel soldiers and recruiting parties, and he had a place of concealment in the pines near his house, where they were sheltered and cared for, the doctor sending their food to them by his slaves; and if at any time any of these parties ventured to his house to take their meals, a slave was always placed on watch to give notice of the approach of anyone."

Mudd not only entertained Booth a weekend in November, but he was known to have made several trips to Washington that winter, and each time was in conference with both Booth and Surratt. There is no doubt that Booth's Knight of the Golden Circle signals and signs did give him entree to the Romanists in the community south of Washington, in which St. Mary's Catholic Church was the center, and to which he and Herold fled after the deed committed in Ford's Theatre.

The next damaging evidence against Dr. Mudd was, when the officers visited his house on the trail of the two fugitives, he emphatically denied he had any strange visitors.

It was not until the third visit when the officers, fortified by definite facts, informed him that they would have to search the house, that he admitted the presence of the two men, one wounded, who had been there the Saturday after the assassination. Mrs. Mudd disappeared and in a few minutes came in bringing the bootleg that Mudd had cut from Booth's boot when he bandaged his leg. On the bootleg were the initials "J. W. B." written in India ink inside.

Even then, neither Mudd nor his wife told an accurate story. Both denied they had any idea it was Booth, notwithstanding the fact they were well acquainted with him, and notwithstanding that his was a personality with voice and manner that once known could never be forgotten.

LOUIS J. WEICHMANN

Student for priesthood with John H. Surratt at Sulpician Monastery near Baltimore, MD. State's chief witness.

When Mudd was being taken to the Dry Tortugas after his conviction, he admitted to the officers who had him in charge that he recognized Booth and Herold the morning after the murder when he came to have his leg dressed.

Mudd only served three years' imprisonment and was liberated with Spangler, as was Arnold. O'Laughlin died of yellow fever in an epidemic in the prison, and Dr. Mudd rendered his professional services so efficiently that it was on this ground he received his discharge from President Johnson, who had promised he would do so before retiring from office.

The liberation of these assassins of President Lincoln by his successor, caused much sharp comment and criticism from Lincoln's friends. It seems almost unbelievable that any sort of leniency should have been shown to these criminals who were guilty not only of the murder of the most distinguished American, but of **high treason** to their government!

It may be interesting to the reader to know that in the book written by Dr. Mudd's daughter, she proudly boasts of the fact that her mother is a graduate of the Visitation Convent at Georgetown and that on graduation her diploma was presented to her class by **"Cardinal Bodini, who was the first papal Legate to the United States."**

The lady does not state—perhaps she did not know—that Cardinal Bodini, prior to his elevating to the papal **Legate**, was known all over Italy as the "BUTCHER of Bologna," because of the many Italian patriots he ordered put to death and that he gave the order that the Revolutionary priest, Ugo Bassi, who was the devoted follower of Garibaldi, **should be tortured three hours before his execution.**

She neglects also to state that this was the same **Cardinal Bodini,** who was made to leave this country between suns by the **"KNOW NOTHINGS"**—God bless them, and all their kind!

Spangler, broken in health, returned with Dr. Mudd and made his home with him until his death in 1875. He is buried in the cemetery, two miles from the Mudd residence, near St. Peter's church. Dr. Mudd lies buried in the little country graveyard connected with St. Mary's Church where he first met Booth on that bright November morning in 1864.

The body of John Wilkes Booth was given to his brother, Edwin, who had it removed from the old penitentiary in the Arsenal grounds, where it had been since the burial of the other four of his fellow conspirators, by a Baltimore undertaker, assisted by a local Washington undertaking firm, Harvey & Marr, to Baltimore, and buried in the Booth family lot at beautiful Greenmount cemetery.

The army box labeled with Booth's name at the time of the burial was somewhat decayed but the body was identified by the dentist who had filled several teeth, and who had no difficulty in identifying it as that of Booth. The skull had become detached but the jet black hair hung in long black ringlets. Edwin Booth did not view the body but remained close by until notified of the complete identification. He ordered the body placed in a casket which had been provided by him and shipped to Baltimore.

The mother of Michael O'Laughlin was given the boy of her son, which was shipped from the prison burial ground and placed in the Catholic cemetery in Baltimore.

GARRETT TOBACCO BARN, PORT ROYAL, VA.

Booth being dragged out after he fell from bullet fired by
Sergeant Boston Corbett, April 26, 1865.

X

The Trial Of The Arch Conspirator
John H. Surratt

Now, we will take up the trail of the arch-conspirator and assassin, John Harrison Surratt, the man who called the time in front of Ford's Theatre the night of the murder of President Lincoln, and track him, step by step, to the very shadow of the Vatican, whose protection he sought and received, until a formal demand was made by the United States government for his return to this country, for trial for the murder of Abraham Lincoln.

To nail the Roman church to the cross in this great treason plot, the writer asks your patience and careful reading of this subject that has lain for over a half century. It has been buried in the oblivion where the Jesuits placed it and from which we have resurrected it and pieced it together, in what we hope may prove a readable shape, to be understood and the information passed on.

It is safe to say that the escape of this tool of the Roman priesthood was one of the most spectacular in all history. It began the very night after the tragic scene in Ford's Theatre.

It will probably never be known positively by what means Surratt made good his escape from Washington that night, or early the next morning, for he has passed to his eternal accounting and did so, as far as is known, without having revealed it.

But this is certain: he succeeded in making his escape safely to Montreal, Canada, and was lodged securely in the house of the parents of the Roman priest La Pierre, who was waiting and ready to receive him, close by the papal "palace" of the Archbishop to whom he was secretary.

Then began in the United States what was one of the most extraordinary manhunts for Surratt that ever occurred, before or since, in the history of this country. The rewards by the government amounted to twenty-five thousand dollars, and every detective in the government secret service, every detective of the private agencies, and every amateur sleuth engaged in this drive to recover this nineteen-year-old boy, leader of the gang of laymen who were instigated, aided, urged and abetted by the priests of the Church of Rome, to complete the destruction of this Republic, which had recently been recovered from the awful cataclysm our foreign enemies had precipitated four years previous.

The government Secret Service, under the direction of the War Department, sent out the following letter:

"Headquarters Department of Washington,
Washington, DC, April 16th, 1865

Special Orders, No. 68,
Special officers, James A. McDevitt, George Holohan, and Louis J. Weichmann, are hereby ordered to New York on important government business, and, after executing their private orders, to return to this city and report at these headquarters. The Quartermaster's Department will furnish the necessary transportation.
By command of Major-General Augur, T. Ingraham, Colonel and Provost-Marshal-General. Defenses North of Potomac."

These officers, after leaving Washington, arrived in Montreal on April 20, and registered at the St. James Hotel. They searched the registers of the hotels in that city and found that Surratt had arrived at the St. Lawrence Hall Hotel on April 6, and checked out on the 12th of that month; that he had returned on the 18th and left a few hours later. They learned on further investigation that he had stayed at the home of a man by the name of Porterfield, a Secessionist from Tennessee who was one of the agents for the Confederacy in that city, and that Surratt had left that house with another man dressed exactly like himself, each taking a carriage and being driven in different directions. At this point, the trial ended until the government learned of his sailing on the *Peruvian*, an English steamer plying between Quebec and Liverpool.

The Secretary of State received the following code telegram from our Consul in Montreal, J. F Potter:

"No. 236.   (Mr. Potter to Mr. Seward)
                                 U. S. Consul, B. N. A. F.
                              Montreal, Oct. 27, 1865.

Sir: Have just had a personal interview with Dr. L. J. McMillan. He informs me that just before the Steamer Peruvian sailed, a person with whom he was acquainted, asked him if he was willing that a gentleman who had been somewhat compromised by the recent troubles in the United States, should pass as his friend on board on the passage out. The Doctor refused to acknowledge the person as his friend, until he should know who he was. Subsequently, the same person, accompanied by a party (Priest La Pierre—Ed.) came on board before the ship left port, whom he introduced to the surgeon as Mr. McCarthy. During the voyage McCarthy made himself known to the Doctor as John H. Surratt, and related to him many of the particulars of the conspiracy. He said he had been secreted in Montreal most of the time, with the exception of a few weeks, when he was with a Catholic priest down the river. He also stated that Porterfield of this city, formerly of Tennessee, assisted in secreting him. The Doctor also informed same that Surratt had dyed his hair, eyebrows and mustache, blackstained his face, and wore glasses. He landed in Londonderry, Ireland, fearing he might be watched and detected in Liverpool.
He told him he was obliged to remain until he could receive money from Montreal. He requested the Doctor to see his friend in this city, and bring him funds. After the return of the Peruvian, the Doctor was transferred to the Nova Scotian. When I saw him he had just had an interview with his friend who had introduced him to Surratt, as McCarthy, who told him he was expecting funds from Washington, D. C, but that they had not come yet.

The Doctor says that Surratt manifests no signs of penitence, but justifies his action, and was bold and defiant, when he speaks of the assassination of Abraham Lincoln. To illustrate this: He told me that Surratt remarked repeatedly, that he only desired to live two years longer, in which time he would serve President Johnson as Booth served Lincoln. The Doctor said he felt it his duty to give me this information for he regarded Surratt a **desperate wretch, and an enemy to society, who should be apprehended and brought to justice.**

(Signed) John F. Potter."

To this important information, our Consul received no reply from the War Department, as he had expected and the next day he followed it with a telegram, also in code, printed below:

"No. 236.   (Mr. Potter to Mr. Seward)
U. S. Consul General,
Montreal, Canada, Oct. 28th, 1865.

Sir: I sent you a telegram in cipher with information to the Department that John H. Surratt left Three Rivers, in September, for Liverpool, **where he now is**, awaiting the arrival of the Nova Scotian, which sails on Saturday, next, by which he expects to receive money from parties in this city by hand of Ship Surgeon. I have information from Dr. McMillan, Surratt intends to go to Rome. He was secreted at Three Rivers by a Catholic priest, with whom he lived, I have requested instruction in my telegram, but hearing nothing yet, I scarcely know what course to take. If an officer could proceed to England on this ship, no doubt, Surratt's arrest might be effected, and this, the last of the conspirators against the lives of the President and Secretary of State be brought to justice. If I hear nothing from Washington tomorrow, I shall go to Quebec to see further on the subject.

Respectfully, etc.
(Signed) Potter."

And now a most peculiar phase of this remarkable case presents itself to us. The US War Department, with the full knowledge of the exact whereabouts of that arch-criminal, who not only assisted, but **led** in, and actually directed the murder of the President of the United States and Secretary of State William H. Seward, refused to make the least attempt to arrest the said John H. Surratt, which the following cable to our Consul in Liverpool shows:

> "(Mr. Hunter to Mr. Wilding)
> Dept. of State, Oct. 1st, 1865.
>
> Sir: Your dispatches 541-543 inclusive have been received. In reply to your No. 538, I have to inform you, that upon consultation with the Secretary of War and Judge Advocate General, it is thought advisable that no action be taken in regard to the arrest of the supposed John H. Surratt, at present.
>
> W. H. Hunter,
> Acting Secretary"

Then, less than three weeks from that date, the following order was sent to the War Department from Andrew Johnson, President of the United States, and successor to Abraham Lincoln:

> "(General Order No. 164)
> War Department
> Adj. General's Office,
> Washington, Nov. 24, 1865.
>
> All persons claiming reward for the apprehension of John Wilkes Booth, Lewis Payne, G. A. Atzerodt, David E. Herold, and Jefferson Davis, or either of them, are notified to file their claims and their proofs with the Adj. General for final adjudication by the special commission appointed, to award and determine upon the validity of such claims before the first day of January next, after which no claims will be received.
>
> The reward for the arrest of Jacob Thompson, Beverly Tucker, George W. Sander, Wm. G. Cleary, and **John H. Surratt, are hereby revoked**.

By order of the President of the United States.

E. D. Townsend,
Ass't. Adj. General."

Naturally, with the revoking of the reward for the arrest of Surratt, his chances for his safety from expiating his crime were multiplied many fold.

On September 30, 1865, our Consulate at Liverpool, sent the following cable in Code to the Secretary of State at Washington:

"(Mr. Wilding to Mr. Seward)

No. 539.   U. S. Consulate, Liverpool,
Sept. 30, 1865.

Sir: Since my dispatch No.538, the supposed Surratt has arrived in Liverpool and is now staying at the Oratory of the Roman Catholic Church of the Holy Cross. His appearance indicates him to be about 21 years of age, rather tall and tolerably good looking. According to the reports Mrs. Surratt was a very devout Roman Catholic, and I know clergymen of that persuasion, on their way to and from America, have frequently lodged, while in Liverpool, at that same Oratory, so that the fact of this young man going there, somewhat favors the belief, that he is the real Surratt. I cannot, of course, do anything further in the matter without Mr. Adams' instructions, and a warrant. If it be Surratt, such a wretch ought not to escape.

Yours respectfully, Your obedient servant,

H. Wilding."

The Oratory of the Holy Cross was the Roman Catholic Clearing House through which the ecclesiastical agents passed between this country and the Vatican, during their activities through the Civil War.

And now, with the official correspondence to show us Surratt's moves, let me chink up the open spaces.

When Surratt left the home of Porterfield, he was taken under the wings of the French priests from under which he never departed until they had seen the ship surgeon on the Peruvian and arranged for his safe passage as we have seen. The facts brought out at the two trials of Surratt, after he had finally been returned to the United States, showed that the fugitive had gone to the little village of St. Liboire, some sixty miles out of Montreal, skirting the pine woods, and an ideal place for the purpose. The parish priest's name was La Pierre. Here he secreted Surratt for several weeks, when the hunt got too hot in Montreal, which was being combed thoroughly for him.

St. Liboire was out of the way of the general traffic, and the inhabitants, French Catholics, who worked for the most part in the lumber camps, and were by their location, as well as their lack of education, cut off from the rest of the world and its doings, as if they were people of another planet. They were **subservient to their priest**, so much so, that they would no more have thought of criticizing his acts, than they would of God Himself.

Consequently, when a strange young man appeared at the parish house nothing was thought of it, or if, perchance, some one with just a drop of rebellious blood in him, might have asked himself, "Is this another mouth to feed?" He would whisper it so softly that even his guardian angel could not hear it, and would quickly "bless" himself, for daring to criticize or find fault with what his "Bon Pierre" should take it into his head to do.

After several weeks of this life in the Canadian village, Surratt became restless, no doubt, and anxious to hear from the States, for we must remember that all his mail and the newspapers were censored by his priestly guardians, as he afterward told in his Rockville lecture. Each time the "Holy Mother Church" would step in and allay his anxiety and he received almost weekly visits from that other "Valued and trusted friend," Priest La Pierre of Montreal. Once, when he insisted, Priest La Pierre took him back to Montreal, himself in citizen's clothes, and Surratt disguised as a hunter.

You will note the solicitude of these French priests concerning this American youth who had a price of Twenty-five Thousand Dollars on his head, **"dead or alive."** Is it not an eloquent fact of, not only their personal guilt, but the guilt of their church, that they never thought of surrendering him and **receiving the reward**, notwithstanding the inordinate love of money that characterizes Rome's priests?

Do you think for one moment these **priests** in Canada, or the priests in

Washington, would have dared to have become parties in this conspiracy, thereby involving their church, without the full knowledge of the Roman hierarchy? Priests receive all their orders from the Pope through their Bishops.

Would this obscure, native-born American boy have been so carefully protected and cared for as he was by these priests, without the command of the Vatican?

You must remember that this government had sent broadcast the warning that anyone who would be found "aiding, abetting, protecting, comforting," or in any way assisting any of the conspirators, would be held as co-partners in the crime with them, and dealt with accordingly.

There is not a record that I have been able to find, wherein there is one word of criticism, one word of disapproval, one word of regret officially, or otherwise, on the part of the Roman Catholic Hierarchy for the participation of the Romanists connected with this conspiracy, which consummated in the murder of Abraham Lincoln!

THERE IS NOT IN THE LARGE COLLECTION OF OFFICIAL CONDOLENCES RECEIVED BY THIS GOVERNMENT UPON THE DEATH OF ABRAHAM LINCOLN, COMING FROM EVERY CIVILIZED COUNTRY IN THE WORLD, ONE WORD FROM THE POPE OF ROME. AND THIS IN VIEW, MARK YOU, OF THE FACT THAT THE POPE WAS KING OF THE PAPAL STATES AND HAD MORE SUBJECTS IN THIS COUNTRY THAN ANY OTHER RULER IN EUROPE!

Pius IX, by his silence at this time, made a confession of his guilt written in letters of fire—unquenchable fire—that brands him and his Jesuits with the brand of Cain in the hearts and minds of the AMERICAN PEOPLE, when they shall have been given a full knowledge of their (the Jesuits) responsibility in the CONSPIRACY OF DESTRUCTION OF THIS POPULAR GOVERNMENT ON THAT GOOD FRIDAY NIGHT IN FORD'S THEATRE, APRIL 14, 1865;

Who, among the government detectives from this country, would have thought to search the houses of the **priests** for their fugitive? How much chance would they had to secure a search warrant for such search in French Canada if they had? The Roman Catholic SYSTEM operates in safety through its institutions in this country and Canada. It is only in Catholic Mexico, where the people who have been burdened by the Papal yoke, have been progressive enough to make laws and operate them that a search warrant can be obtained with which these hellholes of the Pope of Rome in their country can be reached.

Do you realize that in Mexico a Roman priest or nun has not the right of suffrage? That they cannot vote or enjoy any of the rights or privileges that accompany the ballot box? And yet we supposedly intelligent Americans not only permit them to vote, but they are today the dominating force in politics of every large city in the United States. THINK OF IT!

All the powerful machinery of the Hierarchy of the Roman Catholic Church was set in motion from the moment after the murder of Mr. Lincoln to shield Surratt and defeat justice for his awful crime, and we have public documents with which to brand these ecclesiastical plotters. Notwithstanding the fact that the US War Department knew exactly every step taken by the young fugitive, from the day he sailed for Europe, no effort was made to arrest him.

The startling knowledge, however, came to the attention of certain members of Congress, and the matter was brought up in that body, and a committee appointed to investigate same. I herewith give the report of this committee in full:

OFFICIAL REPORT ON JOHN H. SURRATT ISSUED BY SECRETARY OF STATE FOR CONGRESSIONAL RECORD.

39th Congress House of Representatives	Report 33
2nd Session	March 2, 1867

REPORT OF JUDICIARY COMMITTEE.

That John H. Surratt sailed from Canada about September fifteenth, 1865, for Liverpool; that information was received by Secretary of State, Wm. H. Seward, from Mr. Wilding, Vice-Consul at Liverpool, by communication, dated Sept. 27th, 1865; that Surratt was at that time in Liverpool, or expected in a day or two.

By dispatch, from Wilding Sept. 30th, 1865, the supposed Surratt had arrived and was staying at the Oratory of the Roman Catholic church of the Holy Cross, and that he, Wilding, could do nothing in the matter without instructions from our Minister in England, Mr. Adams, and a warrant.

The Secretary of State received a dispatch from Mr. Potter, our Consul General at Montreal, Canada, October 25th, 1865, informing him that Surratt left Canada for Liverpool, the September previous, and was there waiting the arrival of a steamer by which he expected money, which steamer had not yet left Canada, and that he was intending to go to Rome.

Upon November 11th, 1865, Mr. Potter received a dispatch from the Department of State, that the information in his dispatch had been properly availed of, and that on the 13th day of November, the Secretary of State, requested the Attorney General of the United States, to procure indictment against Surratt, as soon as convenient, with a view to demand his surrender.

Our Minister, Mr. Rufus King, at Rome, commenced as early as April 25th, 1865, stated in his dispatch, that information of Surratt, under the name of "Watson" had enlisted in the Papal Zouaves, then stationed at Sezzes.

In a dispatch, August 8th, 1865, said he repeated information communicated to him, to Cardinal Antonelli, in regard to Surratt; that his Eminence, was greatly interested by it, and intimated that if the American government desired the surrender of the criminal, there would probably be no difficulty in the way.

REPORT OF THE COMMITTEE

"1st. That the Executive did not send any detective or agent to Liverpool to identify Surratt, or trace his movements, notwithstanding there was ample opportunity, for doing so, as appears in the communication from Potter.

2nd. That the Executive did not cause notice to be given to our Minister at Rome; that Surratt intended going there, when the government had every reason to believe, such was his intention.

3rd. That on November 4th, an order was issued from

the War Department, revoking the reward offered for the arrest of John H. Surratt.

4th. That from the reception of the communications of Mr. King, Aug. 8th, 1866, to October 16th, 1866, no steps were taken, either to identify or procure the arrest of Surratt, then known to be in the Military service of the Pope.

The testimony of the Secretary of State, Secretary of War, and others which is herewith submitted, tending to justify acts of the government in the premises, does not, in the opinion of your committee, excuse the **great delay** in arresting a person charged with complicity in the assassination of the late President Abraham Lincoln.

They are constrained from testimony to report that, in their opinion, due diligence in the arrest of John H. Surratt, was not exercised by the Executive Department of the government.

Respectfully submitted,
(signed) F. E. Woodbridge,
For Committee."

So ends the report of that splendid, fearless group of men, chosen by the House of Representatives to look into the matter.

It seems almost incredible that the memory of Abraham Lincoln, could have been so soon forgotten. That the virus of which he had such a clear knowledge should have been making its deadly inroads in the veins of his successor and the Secretary of State William H. Seward, whose life hung in the balance for days, caused by the hand of one of the assassins under the personal direction of this same Surratt!

I now call attention to the communication from our American Consul at Rome at the time, General Rufus King:

No. 33   Regarding Sainte-Marie
Ames   (Gen. Rufus King to Mr. Seward)
2nd Session

Legation IX. S., Rome
April 23rd, 1866

Sir:

On Saturday last, the 21st. Henry de Saint-Marie, called upon me for the purpose, as he said, of communicating the information that John H. Surratt, who is charged with complicity in the murder of President Lincoln, but made his escape at the time, from the United States, had recently enlisted in the Papal Zouaves, under the name of "John Watson," and is now stationed with his company at Sezze. My informant said that he had known Surratt in America; that he recognized him as soon as he saw him at Sezzes: that he called him by his proper name, and that Surratt acknowledged that he participated in the plot against Lincoln's life. . . . . . He further said that Surratt seemed to be well supplied with money, and appealed to him, Sainte Marie, not to reveal his secret. Sainte Marie, expressed an earnest desire, that if any steps were taken toward reclaiming Surratt as a criminal, that he (Sainte Marie) should not be known in the matter.

He spoke positively, in answer to my questions as to his acquaintance with Surratt, and he certainly thinks this was the man, and there seemed such an entire absence of motive for any false statements on the subject, that I could not very well doubt the truth of what he said.

I deemed it my duty, therefore, to present the circumstances to the Department, and ask instructions.

Respectfully,
(signed) RUFUS KING"

SURRATT ENTERED ENGLISH PAPAL COLLEGE AT ROME.

An affidavit from an Irish Romanist, Edward O'Conner, a book dealer there, gives this illumination upon that young criminal's movement:

"About twelve months ago Mr. Surratt came to Rome under the name of "Watson." In Canada he procured letters from several priests to friends in England. Having left England for Rome, he got betters for some people here, among others for the reverend Dr. Neane, Rector of

the English College. Being detained some days in Cevita Vecchia, and having no money to pay his expenses, he wrote the reverend Dr. Neane, from whom he received fifty francs. On his arrival here, he went to the English College, where he lived for some time; after that he entered the papal service.
Rome, Nov. 25th, 1866."

O'Connor also turned over to our Minister, which is included in the other official papers in the archives of this government, a letter received by him from Surratt as follows:

> "Edw. O'Connor, Esq.,
> Rome, Italy.
>
> Dear Sir:
>
> Will you be so kind as to send me a French and English grammar, the best method you have. I think Ollendorf's is the most in use. When I come to Rome I will settle with you. Shall be in, in the course of two or three weeks. If you should have time to reply to me, please give me all the news you can. By so doing, you will greatly oblige,
> Your friend,
> John Watson, Co. 3."

Surratt's handwriting was identified in this letter. It is perceptible that O'Connor knew the nature of the "news" wanted by his friend Watson. The statement of O'Connor shows that Surratt had evidently related to him about his letters of reference, and his pecuniary embarrassment would indicate some confidence in that gentleman.

I wonder if the non-Romanist reader gets the full import of a Roman priest in the City of Rome, at that, advancing a sum of money to a foreign youth, as the reverend Dr. Neane did? This, itself, without any of the other tremendous facts showing the aid that this young traitor received from the priests in Washington. Canada, England and Italy, was sufficient to have held them as the **actual conspirators** and to have brought them to justice by hanging them on the same scaffold with their dupes. Had this been done, it might have saved the assassination of the other Presidents of this Republic, Garfield and McKinley!

To those of us who know the coldness of the charity of the priests of

Rome, the conduct of the reverend Dr. Neane speaks volumes.

I now produce another communication in this government correspondence, which speaks for itself:

No. 43.   Mr. Seward to Mr. King
                                                    (Extracts—Confidential)
                                                    Department of State
                                            Washington, Oct. 16, 1866

Sir:

Mr. King's private letter written from Hamburg has just been received. It is accompanied by a letter from Sainte Marie of the 12th of September, to Mr. Hooker. I think it expedient that you do the following things:

1st. Employ a confidential person to visit Velletri, and ascertain by comparison with the photo sent whether the person indicated by Sainte-Marie, is really John Surratt.

2nd. Pay Sainte Marie to get his release in consideration of the information he has already communicated on the subject.

3rd. Seek an interview with Cardinal Antonelli and referring to an intimation made by him to Mr. King's letter No. 62 . . . . . Ask the Cardinal whether his Holiness would now be willing in an absence of extradition treaty, to deliver John H. Surratt upon an authentic indictment, and at the request of the Department, for complicity in the assassination of the late President Lincoln, or whether, in the event of this request being declined, his Holiness would enter into an extradition treaty with us, which would enable us to reach the surrender of Surratt.

4th. Ask as a favor of this government, that neither Sainte Marie nor Surratt be discharged from the papal army, until we have had time to communicate concerning them, after receiving a prompt reply from you to this communication. Sainte Marie should be told confidentially, that the subject of his communication to Mr. Hooker is under consideration here.

Yours respectfully,
(signed) W. H. Seward"

The following from General King gives further light:

"No. 59.   (Mr. King to Mr. Seward)
                                    Legation U. S. Rome,
                                        July 14, 1866.

Dear Sir:

Henri de Sainte Marie's deposition. In compliance with instructions heretofore received, I have obtained and herewith transmit, an additional statement, sworn and subscribed to, by Sainte Marie, touching John H. Surratt's acknowledged complicity in the assassination of the late President Lincoln.

Sainte Marie again expressed to me his great desire to return to America and give his evidence in person. He thinks his life would be in danger here, if it would be known. . . .that he betrayed Surratt's secret.

I have the honor to be with great respect,

Rufus King."

Again we hear from General King after a visit to Cardinal Antonelli. That cunning old fox, who was the **real** pope, saw that to attempt to refuse to surrender their protege would have been a dangerous move. There was, for instance, more than a billion dollars' worth of church property in the United States, and the temper of the great masses of red-blooded American people was not to be trifled with. There were thousands of priests and nuns here, and a refusal, or further protection to this young monster might precipitate such a revulsion of feeling, if the inner facts were to become known, as to jeopardize not only the property, but start a **religious war**, to which there was no question as to the outcome.

I deem this a proper place to quote again from that valuable little book, *The Roman Question* the description of Antonelli's personal appearance:

"In this year of grace, 1859, he is fifty-three years of age. He presents the appearance of a well preserved man; his frame is slight but robust; his constitution that of a mountaineer. The breadth of his forehead, the brilliancy of his eyes, his beak-like nose, and all the upper part of

GIACOMO ANTONELLI
CARDINAL AND SECRETARY OF
PAPAL STATES, PIUS IX.

Mouthpiece of the Black Pope, the General of the Society of Jesus. On death of Cardinal Antonelli, his two attractive daughters, by a court decision, were awarded his vast fortune, to the amazement and scandal of Europe.

his face, inspire a certain awe. His countenance, of almost Moorish hue, is at times lit up by flashes of intellect. But his heavy jaw, his long fang-like teeth, and his thick lips express the grossest appetites. He gives you the idea of a minister grafted on a savage. When he assists the Pope in the ceremonies of Holy Week, he is magnificently disdainful and impertinent.

He turns from time to time in the direction of the diplomatic tribune, and looks without a smile at the poor ambassadors, whom he cajoles from morning to night. You admire the actor who bullies his public.

But when at an evening party he engages in close conversation with a handsome woman, the play of his countenance shows the direction of his thoughts, and those of the imaginative observer are imperceptibly carried to a roadside in a lonely forest, in which the principal objects are prostrate postilions, an overturned carriage, trembling females, and a select party of the inhabitants of Sonnino!

He lives in the Vatican, immediately over the Pope. The Romans ask punningly, which is the uppermost, the Pope or Antonelli? All clashes of Society hate him equally. He is the only living man concerning whom an entire people is agreed . . . He wishes to restore the absolute power of the pope, in order that he may dispose of it at his ease . . . He returns to Rome and for ten years continues to reign over a timid old man and an enslaved people, opposing a passive resistance to all the counsels of diplomacy, and all the demands of Europe.

"No. 62.   Mr. King to Mr. Seward
                                                   Legation U. S., Rome
                                                      Aug. 8th, 1866.

Sir:

I availed myself of the opportunity to repeat to the Cardinal the information communicated by Henri Sainte Marie in regard to Surratt. His Eminence was greatly interested and intimated that if the American government desired the surrender of the criminal, there would probably be no difficulty in the way.

                                                   Rufus King."

                         (Mr. King to Mr. Seward)
                                (Extracts)

Sir:

. . . . . He added, that there was indeed no extradition treaty between the two countries, and that to surrender a criminal, where capital punishment was likely to ensue, was not exactly in **accordance with the spirit of the papal government**, but, that in so grave and so exceptional a case, and with the understanding that the United States under parallel conditions would do as they desired to be done by, and that he thought that the request of the United States department for Surratt*s surrender would be granted."

Do you get the entering wedge there to make Surratt's surrender on condition that would save his neck? Since when did the "spirit" of the papal government become so compassionate? The massacre of St. Bartholemew, the burning at the stake of Bruno, Savanarola, John Huss, Joan D'Arc, and thousands of others who dared to oppose the papacy, still cries to Heaven for vengeance, but with this young criminal who was **perinde ac cadaver** in the hands of Pius IX and his Jesuits, how very solicitious they are, going just as far as they dare to save him!

What cowardly and reprehensible conduct the men at the head of the United States government were guilty of in the case of Henri de Sainte Marie, who took his life in his hands when he informed General King of

John Surratt's identity. They dilly-dallied along for **months** and kept him sweating while he awaited some action, and then it took a **Congressional investigation** and a stinging rebuke and order from Congress before the proper steps were taken to bring this young scoundrel, Surratt, to time.

We have here the sequel of the communication from Mr. King from Hamburg, which the Secretary of War Seward, referred to in the letter above:

> "(Private)
> Hamburg, Sept. 23rd, 1866.
>
> My dear Governor:
>
> I enclose a letter forwarded from Rome a few days since, in which Sainte Marie related his griefs to Mr. Hooker. He thinks, of course, that too little notice has been taken to his statements about Surratt; but would be satisfied, I have no doubt, if his discharge from the Pontifical Zouaves were procured, and the means furnished him to pay his passage home to Canada, where his old mother is still living. His discharge, I could obtain without difficulty, if desirable.
>
> Faithfully yours,
> (signed) Rufus King."

The telegraph lines and mail service in the pontifical states were, of course, entirely in the hands of the prelates of the Pope, and under the strictest censorship.

It goes without saying that no state papers passed through the mails in the pontifical states from our consuls to their government that were not read by the priestly spies and reported to "His Eminence," copied and filed away for future reference, if they so desired. The following letter gives us an interesting highlight on the Jesuit **system**, and the credulity of a Protestant American's psychology.

> "Legation U. S., Rome,
> July 14, 1866.
>
> My dear Governor:
>
> As you will learn from the accompanying dispatch, the missing documents from the State Department arrived all

right today. I cannot imagine how, or where they have been delayed.

I will act forthwith upon the instructions in regard to Sainte Marie. He is willing and anxious to return to the United States, and can get his release from the Pope's army, by paying fifty dollars, or so. I should judge his parole evidence would be much more desirable than any certified statement. He would expect to have his expenses paid and some compensation for his time.

Faithfully yours,
Rufus King."

The reader will recall that Sainte Marie was cut off from any reward, which the government had offered, by a **revocation** President Johnson ordered.

President Johnson was a drunkard. He came from a disloyal State. His revocation of a reward for the arrest of John H. Surratt is conclusive proof to the mind of the writer, to say the least he was playing politics that, under the gravity of the circumstances, would make his conduct criminal.

Andrew Johnson, the drunkard, had nothing in common with Abraham Lincoln. Lincoln's pure, sober, honorable life was a rebuke to such a man as Johnson. At the first opportunity, the latter dared to take advantage of, to show his dislike, which amounted to downright disrespect to the memory of Lincoln. It was President Johnson that paralyzed the arm of the Department of State in regard to Surratt's arrest. The whole official inertness amounting to treason, it would seem, should be laid at Johnson's door.

That the Roman Catholic spirit may be truly demonstrated in the pontifical army, a perusal of the following document will be enlightening:

"No. 72.   Mr. King to Mr. Seward

Legation U. S., Rome,
Dec. 17, 1866.

Sir:

I hasten to acknowledge receipt of the dispatches Nos. **44-45-46-47**, of the State Department . . . . relative to the affair of John H. Surratt. . . . . It will give me pleasure to convey to Cardinal Antonelli, the assurance of the President's sincere satisfaction with the prompt and friendly actions of the papal court. . . Sainte Marie, who first informed me of Surratt being in the corps of Zouaves, has been discharged from the papal service, at my request. Threats had been made against him by some of his comrades, and thinking that his life might not be altogether safe, and that he might be wanted at Alexandria as a witness to identify Surratt, I put him in charge of Captain Jeffers, and he sailed on the Swatara on Friday last. His great desire seems to be to return to America, and aid in bringing Surratt to justice, I have seen, as yet, no reason to doubt his good faith, or question the truth of his statements.

Rufus King."

Surratt, one of the murderers of our great Lincoln, was the hero and Sainte Marie, the traitor! The difference in sentiment of the papal troops and the PEOPLE of Italy, the Revolutionists, who were struggling for a free and united Italy, under Garibaldi and Victor Emmanuel, can be appreciated if the reader will peruse the letters of condolence that were received by the government after they learned of the assassination of Mr. Lincoln. Every workingman's organization of Italy sent the most beautiful messages, and their intimate knowledge of the life of Lincoln astonished the writer.

The bold frankness in many of them in placing the blame on the Jesuits was most edifying. I know of nothing that will give the reader the mental attitude of the difference of sentiment, and show up the venom of the pope's silence on President Lincoln's murder, than a perusal of these messages.

After an extended diplomatic dickering that covered several months after its initiation, the order for Surratt's arrest was given by the Secretary of State Cardinal Antonelli. The official papers are exceedingly interesting and educational. We present them in full. They are all official translations of the originals, in Italian. The Lieutenant Colonel in charge at the time was an Austrian, whom the patriotic Italians greatly hated.

"Enclosure 'C' (Translation)   Kausler to Lieut. Col. Allet.

November 6, 1866

Col:—Cause the Zouave Watson to be arrested and to be conveyed under safe military escort to the military prison at Rome. It is of much importance that this order be scrupulously fulfilled.

The Gen. Pro-Minister, Kausler.

To Lieut. Col. Allet, Com. Battalion of Zouaves, Velletri."

The French Lieut. Allet acknowledges the order as follows:

"Allet to Kausler (Enclosure 'D' Translation)

Velletri, Nov. 7, 1866.

No. 463

General:—I have the honor to inform you that the Zouave Watson (John) has been arrested at Veroli, and will be conducted tomorrow morning under a good escort to Rome.

I have the honor to be General, your most humble subordinate,

Lieut. Col. Allet.

Pontifical Zouave Commander of Battalion."

And now comes the surprise, by the way of:

"(Enclosure 'E' Translation)

Presented at Velletri, Nov. 8, 1866, 8:35 A. M.

Arrived at Rome, Nov. 8, 1866, 8:50 A. M.

His Excellency, Minister of Arma, Rome.

I received the following telegram, dated 4:30 A. M. from Zambilly:

> At the moment he left the prison and while surrounded by six men as a guard, Watson threw himself into a ravine, about a hundred feet, perpendicular in depth, which defends the prison. Fifty Zouaves in pursuit of him. Zambilly.

I will transmit your Excellency the intelligence I may receive by telegram.

Allet, Lieut. Col."

It was now up to the Austrian commander to flimflam the American Consuls and State Department by giving this opera buffet the semblance of genuineness to cover the investigation they knew was sure to follow.

"Kausler to Cardinal Antonelli.
Ministry of Arms, Cabinet of the Pro-Minister
Nov. 8, 1866.

Most Reverend Eminence:

I have the honor to transmit to your most reverend Eminence, the accompanying documents on the arrest and escape of the Zouave Watson, of the 3rd Co., and I shall not fail to communicate such further information as I may receive, as the result of the pursuit of this individual. Bowing to kiss the sacred purple, I am proud to subscribe myself with profound devotion, your most Reverend Eminence's most humble and obedient servant.

His most Reverend Eminence Kausler
The Cardinal Antonelli, Secretary of State"

There you are, my dear reader. How do you like the picture? That is a glimpse of what will happen in this country if we allow the Jesuits to "Make America Catholic!"

SURRATT GIVEN WARNING BY HIS ECCLESIASTICAL PROTECTORS.

"Lieut. Col. Allet to Kausler.
My General:—Following out your Excellency's orders, I sent this morning to Veroli, Lieut. De Farnel, to make an examination of the escape of Zouave Watson. I have learned some other details of this unfortunate business. Watson, at the moment he was arrested, must have been on his guard, having obtained knowledge of a letter addressed ..... which concerned him probably. This letter was sent by mistake to a trumpeter named . . . . was opened by him and shown to Watson, because it was written in English. I have sent it to your Eminence, with a report from Captain Zambilly.

I am assured that the escape of Watson savors of a prodigy.

He leapt from a height of 23 feet on a narrow rock, beyond which is a precipice. The filth from the barracks accumulated on the rocks, and in this manner the fall of Watson was broken. Had he leaped a little further he would have fallen in an abyss.

I am, etc, etc."

We have below a description of the arrest of Surratt given in the report from Lieut. Col Allet.

". . . . Then, the prisoner was awakened, who arose and put on his gaiters and took his coffee with the calmness and phlegm quite English. The gate of the prison opens on a platform which overlooks the country, situated at least thirty feet below the windows of the prison.
Beside the gate of the prison are the privies of the barracks. Watson asked permission to halt there. Corp. Warrin who had six men with him as guards, allowed him to stop, very naturally, not doubting, neither he, nor the Zouaves, present, that the prisoner was going to try to escape at a place which seemed quite impossible to us, is quite clear. In fact, Watson who seemed quiet, seized the ballustrade, made a leap, and cast himself into the void, falling on the uneven rocks where he might have broken his bones a thousand times, and gained the depth of the valley below. Patrols were immediately organized, but in vain! We saw a peasant who told us he had seen an unarmed Zouave going towards Commari which is the way to Piedmont. . . Lieut. Mosley and I have been to examine the localities, and we asked ourselves how one could make such a leap without breaking arms and legs?

DeZambilly, Com. of Detachment."

That Surratt was given his warning by some emissary of the pope's government is beyond a doubt. Do you think for one moment if Surratt's crime, for instance, had been **the murder of a priest**, he would have escaped?

This government, through General King, demanded a report of the affair, and his request was complied with by Cardinal Antonelli and the above translations were made and sent to Washington where they are now with the data pertaining to the affairs of Surratt. Mr. King sent the following letter to Mr. Marsh, our Consul at Florence, Italy, by courier:

> "Mr. King to Mr. Marsh.
> (Enclosure 'A' Confidential)
>
> Dear Sir:—I send to you under very peculiar circumstances and as bearer of these dispatches, my friend, Mr. Robert McPherson. He will tell you the story which the accompanying dispatches will help to illustrate.
>
> Rufus King
>
> On November 13th."

The dispatches referred to above are the ones given here, pertaining to the arrest and "escape" of Surratt. We see now the pontifical government maneuvered to permit Surratt to be taken on condition that he be not condemned to death; we see by some friendly advance information he was prepared for his arrest and took it with perfect calmness and nonchalance, notwithstanding the fact he was aroused from his sleep and that "he put on his gaiters and took his coffee, with a calmness that was quite English."

We see that his arrest was a farce and that he was permitted to escape. We see Antonelli assuring our Consul that he had undoubtedly "made good his escape" and was in Italian territory.

After the order of Cardinal Antonelli for the arrest of Surratt from the Papal Guard had been given the official wires of this country were busy. The following orders were telegraphed to the officers of our Fleet in the Mediterranean:

> "Rome, Nov. 16, 1866, 11:50 A. M.
>
> His Excellency, Mr. Harvey, American Minister, Lisbon Inform Adm. Goldsborough that very important matters renders the immediate presence of one of our ships-of-war necessary at Vecchia.
>
> Rufus King."

Mr. Harvey's reply was:

"As Rear Adm. Goldsborough is not now in port, I sent immediately for Commodore Steedman, who arrived here some days ago, and who is now the superior officer present, in order to consult as to the proper measures to be adopted. The U. S. Steamer Swatara, left here yesterday for Tangier, Gibraltar, and other ports in the Mediterranean, and if the Rear Admiral who is believed to have left Cherbourg for Lisbon, within the last few days, does not appear as soon as expected. Commodore Steedman will intercept and order the Swatara by telegram to proceed to Civiti Vecchia.

Harvey"

On November 17, 1866, a telegram from Minister Harvey announced that the *Swatara* had been ordered to Civiti Vecchia, which arrived in due time, but Surratt had made his escape on a steamer that left Naples for Egypt, and Henri de Sainte Marie was placed on board the *Swatara*, and held awaiting word from our Consul at Alexandria.

The vessel upon which Surratt sailed put in at Malta. Our American Minister there who had been notified to be on the alert for that young fugitive, found that he was on board and cabled our Consul at Rome. This message was sent on to our Minister at Alexandria, Egypt, so that when the ship arrived at that port, it found Mr. Hale, the US Consul General, waiting for him. I will let the official wire to the United States War Department describe his arrival.

"(Extract)
It was easy to distinguish him, (Surratt) from among the seventy-eight third-class passengers by his Zouave uniform and scarcely less easy, by his almost unmistakable American type of countenance. I said at once to him: "You are the man I want; you are an American?" He said "Yes sir." I said, "You doubtless know why I want you? What is your name?" He said, promptly, "Walters." I said, "I believe your name is Surratt," and in arresting him I mentioned my official position as United States Consul-General.
The Director of Quarantine speedily arranged sufficient escort of soldiers, by whom the prisoner was conducted

to a safe place within the Quarantine walls. Although the walk occupied several minutes, the prisoner close at my side, made no remark whatever, displaying neither surprise nor irritation.

Arrived at the place prepared, I gave him the usual magisterial caution, that he was not obliged to say anything, and that anything he did say would be taken down in writing. He said, "I have nothing to say. I want nothing but what is right." He declared he had neither transportation nor luggage, nor money, except six francs. His companions confirmed his statement. They said he came to Naples, a deserter from the Papal army at Rome. I find he has no papers, no clothes but those he is wearing. The appearance of the prisoner answers very well the description given by witness Weichmann on page 116 of Pittman's Report, sent me by the government.

Hale."

Here, again, we see Surratt, under the most trying circumstances under which an innocent man would have broken, taking his arrest with amazing coolness. The same, in fact, he displayed previously when he was taken at Velletri, although, so far as is known, that was the first time he had ever been arrested. He was beyond doubt, fortified by the assurance that under the protection of the Vatican, and he had, like all Jesuits, a clear understanding of all that fact guaranteed. He was clever enough to realize that with his inner knowledge of this whole sordid, treasonable transaction, his "holy church" would be compelled to continue its protection, as their interests were inseparable.

His confidence must have been further intensified by the fact that he would not have to face a military tribunal, as had his mother, and the rest of his co-conspirators, who were executed, and that the political influence of the Jesuit machine already had reached the presidential chair, so recently occupied by his victim, Abraham Lincoln.

Taking stock of the above facts, the young monster had good and sufficient reason to be philosophical about his present condition. He was probably rather relieved when he found himself a manacled prisoner, with his face turned homeward to the country of his nativity, to the country he had so miserably and wickedly betrayed. He knew many staunch friends awaited him, friends who, like himself, hated the government.

JOHN HARRISON SURRATT, IN PAPAL UNIFORM AT TIME OF HIS ARREST AND RETURN TO THE UNITED STATES.

The above is reproduced from the only photo taken at the time, which is the property of Col. OH Oldroyd of Washington, DC who kindly gave permission to reprint it here. It is taken from Oldroyd's Lincoln Memorial Collection. Col. Oldroyd is himself author of an interesting book on Lincoln's Assassination.

Before going further, we present another official communication of this matter that throws added light upon the situation in Italy when the POPE WAS KING.

"Mr. Marsh to Mr. Seward.
Legation of U. S. Florence, Italy, Nov. 18, 1866.

Sir:—On my arrival from Venice on Tuesday morning, I found the papers, copies and translations, of which marked respectively, A B C D and E, are hereto annexed. Mr. McPherson introduced by a letter, marked A, had gone to Leghorn, and I had no other information on the subject of his mission, than such as the papers referred to above have furnished.

I lost no time in seeing the Secretary of the Minister of Foreign Affairs. I stated to him such facts as I was possessed of, and enquired whether he thought his government would surrender Surratt to the United States for trial, if he should be found in Italian territory. He replied, he thought the accused man would be surrendered on proper demand and proof, but probably, only on stipulation on our part, that the punishment of death, should not be inflicted on him.

Having no instruction on the subject, and knowing nothing of those Mr. King might have received, and at that time having no reason to suppose that Surratt had escaped into the territory of the King, I did not pursue the discussion farther. . . . I doubt whether in case of surrender of Surratt, a formal stipulation to exempt him from punishment by death, will be insisted upon.

In the famous LaGala escape, Mr. Viscount Venosto, then, as now, Minister of Foreign Affairs, refused to enter into such a stipulation, on the extradition of the offenders, but nevertheless, the government yielded to the intercession of the Emperor of France, and the sentences of those atrocious criminals, though convicted of numerous murders, robberies and even cannibalism, were commuted, and I suppose the government of Italy, would strongly oppose capital punishment and recommend Surratt to mercy, if he surrendered to us.

The public sentiment of all classes in Italy, is decidedly averse to the infliction of capital punishment, and I shall not go too far, if I add, to any severe or adequate punishment for grave offenses.

Marsh."

There is a psychological reason for the innate enmity in the hearts of Romanists for severe punishment. It is traceable to the long dark centuries of unjust, atrocious cruelties of the misrule the Italians endured, under the reigns of the popes of Rome. Suppression of any peoples continued for ages, will react and have a strong tendency to make government of any sort resented and distasteful to them.

Surratt did not overestimate the protection of his church, for from the moment he landed in this country, he was greeted and sustained by the priests of that church. When his trial began in Washington on June 10, 1867, the presence of Roman priests and the students from the Jesuit University at Georgetown and the Sulpician Monastery where he had studied three years for the priesthood, were the most noticeable features of the sessions.

Although he declared himself a bankrupt, he was furnished the services of the best lawyers. When it became necessary to furnish bail for his final release, it was immediately presented by an Irish woman he did not even know, to the amount of thirty thousand dollars. According to press reports, this stood there until his death in 1916. That is some friendship, is it not?

AFFIDAVIT OF HENRI DE SAINTE MARIE.

Aims report, House of Representatives, 39th session Congress, Page 15, Ex. Document No. 9.
Rome, July 10, 1866.

"I, Henri de Ste Marie, a native of Canada, British America, age 33, do swear and declare under oath, that about six months previous to the assassination of Abraham Lincoln, I was living in Maryland, at a small village called Ellangowan, or Little Texas, about 25 or 30 miles from Baltimore, where I was engaged as a teacher for a period of about 5 months. I there and then got acquainted with Louis J. Weichmann and John H Surratt, who came to that locality to pay a visit to the parish priest. At that first interview a great deal was said about the war and slavery, the sentiment expressed by the two individuals being more than strongly secessionist. In the course of the conversation I remember Surratt to have said that President Lincoln would certainly pay for the men that were slain during the war. About a month afterward I removed to Washington at the instigation of Weichmann and got a situation as tutor at Gonzaga College where he was himself engaged. Surratt visited us weekly, and once he offered to send me South, but I declined.

I did not remain more than a month at Washington, not being able to agree with Weichmann and enlisted in the army of the North as stated in my first statement in writing to General King.

I have met Surratt here in Italy at a small town called Velletri. He is now known under the name of "John Watson." I recognized him before he made himself known to me and told him privately, "You are John Surratt, the person I have known in Maryland. He acknowledged he was and begged me to keep the thing secret. After some conversation we spoke of the unfortunate affair, of the assassination of President Lincoln, and these were his words: 'Damn the Yankees, they have killed my mother; but I have done them as much harm as I could. We have killed Lincoln, the nigger's friend.' He then said, speaking of his mother, 'Had it not been for me and that coward Weichmann, my mother would be living yet. It was fear made him speak. Had he kept his tongue, there was no danger for him; but if I ever return to America or meet him elsewhere I shall kill him."

He then said he was in the secret service of the South. And Weichmann, who was in some department there, used to steal copies of the dispatches and forward them to him and thence to Richmond. Speaking of the murder he said, they had acted under the orders of men who were not yet known, some of whom are still in New York and others in London.

I am aware that money is sent to him yet—from London. 'When I left Canada,' he said, 'I had but little money, but I had a letter from a party in London. I was in disguise, with dyed hair and false beard; that party sent me to a hotel, where he told me to remain until I heard from him. After a few weeks he came to me and proposed to me to go to Spain, but I declined, and he asked me to go to Paris. He gave me seventy pounds with a letter of introduction to a party there who sent me here to Rome where I joined the Zouaves.'

He says he can get money in Rome any time. **I believe he is protected by the clergy and that the murder is the result of a deep laid plot, not only against the life of President Lincoln but against the existence of the republic, as we are aware that priesthood and royalty are and always have been opposed to liberty.**

"That such men as Surratt, Booth, Weichmann and others of their own accord planned and executed the infernal plot which resulted in the death of President Lincoln is impossible. There are others behind the curtain who have pulled the strings to make these scoundrels act. . . . .

"He says he does not regret what has taken place and he will visit New York in a year or two, as there is a heavy shipping firm there that had much to do with the South, and he is surprised that they have not been suspected.

This is the exact truth of what I know about Surratt. More I could not learn, being afraid to awaken his suspicion and further I do not say."

Sworn and subscribed before me at the American Legation in Rome, this tenth day of July, 1866, as witness my hand and seal.

Signed: Henri de Ste Marie
Rufus King, Minister Resident."

XI

The Trial Of John H. Surratt

From the very moment the *Swatara*, the specially chartered warship, reached this country with John H. Surratt, bound hand and foot on board, all the wheels of the Roman Catholic political machine were set in motion for his certain release. The intense excitement that had enveloped the trials of the conspirators two years previous had naturally subsided perceptibly. This, of course, being an advantage to the prisoner, and the smallest details were looked after by the array of high-priced lawyers who fought the two legal battles for this penniless young traitor and assassin.

His attorneys, Messrs. Merrick, Bradley and Bradley were Romanized, the former professed a Catholic, and the other two, by strong sympathy, left no stone unturned in the building of his defense, although his alibi, so carefully planned and presented, was soon shattered by a number of reputable witnesses who could not be shaken by the unprofessional tactics these lawyers resorted to.

The first step in the proceedings was a motion filed by the State's lawyers from which we quote in part:

IN THE SUPREME COURT OF THE DISTRICT
OF COLUMBIA, UNITED STATES AGAINST
JOHN H. SURRATT, INDICTMENT: MURDER.

"And now, as this day, to-wit, on the 10th day of June, A.D., 1867, come the United States and the said John H.

Surratt, by their respective attorneys and the jurors of the jury, impanelled and summoned also come; and hereupon the said United States by their attorney challenge the array of the said panel, because he saith, that the said jurors comprising the said panel, were not drawn according to the law, and that the names from which said jurors were drawn, were not selected according to law, wherefore, he prays judgment, and that the said panel may be quashed. This motion, if your Honor please, is sustained by an affidavit which I hold in my hand, and which, with the permission of your Honor I will now proceed to read. We think after this affidavit shall have been read it will not be found necessary to introduce any oral testimony."

The reader will note that the two charges made were that the names were not **drawn** according to law; and that they were not **selected** according to law.

The law required that the registrar of the City of Washington should make out a list of four hundred names on or before the first day of February; the City Clerk of Georgetown was to make out a list of eighty names to be selected; and the Clerk of the Levy Court of the County of Washington was to make out a list of forty names to me selected; and that such lists should be preserved, and any names that had not been drawn for service during the year, might be transferred to the lists made up for the subsequent year.

After this had been done, the officers should meet and **jointly** select their respective lists of the number specified; the names being written by each officer on a separate paper, folded or rolled up, so that no one could see the name, and then deposited in a box provided for that purpose. The box was then to be thoroughly shaken and officially sealed, and then by these three officers, given into the custody of the clerk of the County Court of Washington City for safe keeping.

These same officers were to meet in the City Hall, Washington City at least ten days before the commencement of each term of the Circuit Court, or Criminal Court, and there the Clerk of the Circuit Court was to publicly, and in their presence, break the seal of the box and proceed to draw out the number of names required. If it were a Grand Jury Court, the next twenty-six names drawn were to constitute the petit jury for that term. This having been done, the box was to be sealed and returned to the clerk for safe keeping.

The clerk of the circuit court at that time was a Samuel E. Douglas, registrar of the City of Washington. His examination showed that no such lists had been made out as required; that no joint action had been had by these three officials, but that each one had written his own required list, and deposited it in the box independently of the others.

It was also brought to the attention of the court that these officers had not sealed the box as required, but had delivered it to the clerk to be sealed by him. It was also shown that the names had been drawn, not by the clerk of the circuit court, but by the clerk of the City of Georgetown.

There was nothing to prevent the Georgetown clerk from carrying any of the names of the jurors whom he might have seen fit, and who might have been "fixed" in his hand, and when he put his hand into the box, which was a perfectly illegal act, to have withdrawn the very names he held in his hand.

The whole procedure was so infamously bold and irregular that the Court said: "My order is that the marshal summon twenty-six talesmen. This occupied several days. After the jury had been selected. Surratt's attorneys filed the following to be made the basis of carrying the case up on a writ of error:

"IN THE SUPREME COURT OF THE DISTRICT OF COLUMBIA, THE UNITED STATES VS. JOHN H. SURRATT, IN THE CRIMINAL COURT MARCH TERM 101, 1867.

And the said Marshal of the District of Columbia, in obedience to the order of the Court, made in this case on the 12th of June, this day makes return that he hath summoned, and now hath in court here, twenty-six jurors, talesmen, as a panel, from which to form a jury to try the said case, and the names of the twenty-six jurors, so retained being called by the clerk of said court, and they having answered to their names as they were called, the said John H. Surratt, by his attorneys, doth challenge the array of the said panel, because, he saith, it doth plainly appear by the records and the proceedings of the court in this case, that no jurors have ever been summoned according to law, to serve during the present term of this court, and no names of jurors, duly and lawfully summoned, have been placed in the box, provided for in the fourth section of the Act of Congress, entitled: "An act providing for the selection of jurors to serve in the several courts of the District" approved, sixteenth day of June, 1862, on or before the first day of February, 1867, to serve for the ensuing year; wherefore, he prays judgment, that the panel now returned by the said Marshal, and now in the court here, be quashed,

Merrick, Bradley & Bradley,
Attorneys for Surratt"

It is a notable fact that there were sixteen Romanists out of the twenty-six in the first panel drawn in that irregular manner.

The answer filed in the motion of Surratt's attorneys was the first step in this bitterly contested case and while the prisoner was, according to his own statement, absolutely penniless, he was represented by an expensive array of legal talent and where the money came from reimbursing them remains a mystery today.

Georgetown—Jesuitized Georgetown— was constantly in evidence at the trial. The priests from the Jesuit college were there, and the students who were just dismissed for their vacations, were on hand and would always make it a particular point to greet Surratt who had been a student of that institution for two years, most cordially, and he was scarcely ever without a priest at his side. It is small wonder that the priests of Rome gave every assistance to the prisoner at the bar. Their interests were inseparable.

The interest of the Roman church in this country was deeply involved and no one appreciated this more than Surratt. He was confident and defiant all through the weeks, of what would have been to most young men an unendurable ordeal, stimulated by the knowledge that all of the powerful machinery of his church was being used in his defense and that his liberty was guaranteed.

John Surratt was a bold, cold-blooded, unscrupulous, unrepentant criminal, who had been steeped in the immoral teachings of the Doctrines of the Jesuits from his earliest childhood when his misguided mother had placed him under the guidance of priest Wiget at the Boys' Preparatory school at Gonzaga College, a fact which was testified to by that gentleman at Surratt's trial.

Surratt's lawyers presented the following petition at the beginning of the trial:

> "To the Honorable, the Justice of the Supreme Court of the District of Columbia, holding the Criminal Court in March Term, 1867.
>
> The petition of John H. Surratt shows that he has been put upon his trial in a capital case in this court; that he has exhausted all his means, and such further means as have been furnished him by the liberality of his friends, in preparing for his defense, and he is now unable to procure the attendance of his witnesses. He therefore prays your Honor for an order that process may issue to summon his witnesses, and to compel their attendance at the cost of the government of the United States, according to the statute in such cases made and provided."

This petition was granted by the court.

From the very beginning, duplicity and innuendo were used, and **unprofessional** conduct of the most flagrant character was resorted to. The States' witnesses were badgered, abused and bulldozed, so much so mat the Judge had to interfere more than once. Especially was this the tact in the case of Dr. McMillen, the ship surgeon of the *Peruvian*, to whom priest La Pierre introduced Surratt under the name of "McCarthy." The physician made a splendid witness and refused to be confused, but the attorney for the defendant was so abusive that the witness gave an angry response in pure self-defense.

The papal venom showed itself all through the trials of Surratt in the never-ceasing effort of his attorneys to stab the memory of Lincoln and through their contention that the Military Court that had convicted Surratt's mother, had been an usurpation of power by President Johnson, and the act of a tyrant. When one reads the records of those trials, one marvels that in so short a time after the passing out of that great man, these tools of the **ecclesiastical murderers** would **dare** to venture so far out in the open, with their treasonable utterances.

When court was called to order in the John H. Surratt trial, Judge Fisher, presiding, said: "Gentlemen, this is the day assigned for the trial of John H. Surratt, indicted for the murder of Abraham Lincoln, late President of the United States. Are you ready to proceed?"

Surratt's lawyer, Bradley, answered: "The prisoner is ready, sir, and has been from the first."

This unnecessary falsehood was a beginning quite in keeping with the life and action of the prisoner, and his Jesuit attorney brazenly tried to implant in the minds of the jury the innocence of his client who had fled to Canada, then put the Atlantic ocean between him and his pursuers and when arrested at Velletri, Italy, dashed himself down an unscalable precipice to evade being returned to his native land!

Nothing less than Roman effrontery could have proffered such an answer to that question, "Are you ready?" DESPERATE FLIGHT HAS NEVER BEEN USED AS AN ARGUMENT FOR READINESS BEFORE, I will wager, and it gives the keynote of the conduct of the defense. This is just a sample of one of those little Jesuit jokes.

No doubt his attorney had a mental reservation when he assured the court that his client had "been ready from the first," to skip again, if the slightest opportunity offered itself.

Mental reservation is one of the **ethics** of the Jesuit theology.

The Roman Catholic religion was first dragged in by Surratt's own lawyer, RT Merrick, when they called attention to a telegraph dispatch to the *New York Herald*, in which the fact that the State had demanded a new jury impanelled because there were sixteen Romanists out of the twenty-six jurors called in the first panel.

The district attorney interrupted by showing that the news came from Washington and as afterward proved that it was but one of many press dispatches, which were instigated by the defense to prejudice the public in Surratt's favor. If there were no other signs to indicate that the hand of Rome was the guiding one in the trials of Surratt, this alone would be sufficient to the esoteric.

A most convincing presentation of the charges against the prisoner was made by assistant district attorney Nathaniel Nelson who made the opening address. It ran in part as follows:

"May it please your Honor, and gentlemen of the jury, you are doubtless aware that it is customary in criminal cases, for the prosecution at the beginning of the trial, to inform the jury of the nature of the offense to be inquired into, and of the proof that will be offered in support of the charges of the indictment.

"The Grand Jury of the District of Columbia has indicted the prisoner at the bar, John H. Surratt, as one of the murderers of Abraham Lincoln. It has become your duty to judge whether he is guilty or innocent of that charge,—a duty, than which more solemn or momentous, was never committed to human intelligence. You are to turn back the leaves of history, to that red page, on which is recorded in letters of blood the awful incidents of that April night on which the assassins' work was done on the body of the chief Magistrate of the American Republic,—a night, on which for the first time in our existence as a nation, a blow was struck with the fell purpose, not only to destroy a human life, but the life of the nation, the life of LIBERTY itself.

"Though more than two years have passed by since then, you scarcely need witnesses to describe to you the scene at Ford's Theatre, as it was visible in the last hour of the President's life. . . . Persons who were present will tell you that about twenty minutes past ten o'clock, the 14th of April, 1865, on that night, John Wilkes Booth, armed with pistol and knife, passed rapidly from the front door of the theatre, ascended to the dress circle, and entered the President's box. By the discharge of a pistol he inflicted a death wound, then leaped upon the stage, and passing rapidly across it, disappeared into the darkness of the night.

"We shall prove to your entire satisfaction, by competent and credible witnesses, that at that time, the prisoner at the bar was then present, aiding and abetting that murder; and that at ten minutes past ten o'clock that night, he was in front of the theatre in the company of Booth. You shall hear what he then said and did. You shall know that his cool and calculating malice was the director of the bullet that pierced the brain of the President, and the knife that fell upon the venerable Secretary of State. You shall know that the prisoner at the bar was the contriver of that villainy, and that from the presence of the prisoner, Booth, drunk with theatric passion and traitorous hate, rushed directly to the execution of their mutual will. We shall further prove to you, that their companionship upon that occasion was not an accidental or unexpected one, but that the butchery that ensued was the ripe result of a long premeditated plot, in which the prisoner was the chief conspirator.

"It will be proved to you that he is a traitor to the government that protected him: a spy in the employ of the enemies of his country in the years 1864-65; he passed repeatedly from Richmond to Washington, from Washington to Canada, weaving the web of his nefarious scheme, plotting the overthrow of this government, the defeat of its armies, and the slaughter of his countrymen; and as showing the venom of his intent, as showing a mind insensible to every moral obligation and fatally bent on mischief—we shall prove his gleeful boasts, that during these journeys he had shot down in cold blood, weak, unarmed soldiers, fleeing from rebel prisons.

"It will be proved to you that he made his home in this city, the rendezvous for the tools and agents in what he called his "bloody work" and that his hand deposited at Surrattville, in a convenient place, the very weapons obtained by Booth while escaping, one of which fell, or was wrenched from Booth's death grip, at the moment of his capture.

"While in Montreal, Canada, where he had gone from Richmond on the 10th day of April, on the Monday before the assassination, Surratt received a summons from his co-conspirator, Booth, requiring his immediate presence in this city. In obedience to that pre-concerted signal, he at once left Canada and arrived here on the 14th. By numerous. I had almost said a multitude of witnesses, we shall make the proof to be clear as the noonday sun. . . . that he was here during the day of that fatal Friday, as well as present at the theatre that night. . . . We shall show him to you on Pennsylvania Avenue, booted and spurred, awaiting the arrival of the fatal moment.

"We shall show him in conference with Herold in the evening; we shall show him purchasing a contrivance for disguise an hour or two before the murder. When the last blow had been struck, when he had done his utmost to bring anarchy and desolation upon his native land, he turned his back upon the abomination he had wrought, he turned his back upon his home and kindred and commenced a shuddering flight. We shall trace that flight, because in law, flight is the criminal's inarticulate confession, and because it happened in this case, as it always happens. . . . that in some moment of fear or elation, or of fancied security, he too, to others, confessed his guilty deeds. He fled to Canada. We will prove to you the hour of his arrival there and the route he took. . . He found there safe concealment and remained there several months. . . In the following September, he took his flight. . . . . Still in the disguise and with painted face, painted hair, painted hand, he took ship to cross the Atlantic. In mid-ocean he revealed himself and related his exploits, and spoke freely of his connection with Booth in the conspiracy relating to the President. He rejoiced in the death of the President, he lifted his impious hands to heaven, and expressed a wish that the might live to return to America and serve Andrew Johnson as Abraham Lincoln had been served. He was hidden for a time in England, and received there sympathy and hospitality. . . . From England he went to Rome and hid himself in the ranks of the papal army in the guise of a private soldier. Having placed almost the diameter of the globe between himself and the dead body of his victim, he might well fancy that pursuit was baffled. . . but he was discovered by an acquaintance of his boyhood. When denial would not avail, he admitted his identity and avowed his guilt in these words: 'I have done the Yankees as much harm as I could. We have killed Lincoln, the niggers' friend!'

"The man to whom Surratt made this statement did as was

his high duty to do—he made known his discovery to the American Minister. . . Having him arrested, he escaped from his guards by a leap down a precipice. . . He made his way to Naples and then took passage on a steamer that carried him across the Mediterranean Sea to Alexandria, Egypt. . . . The inexorable lightning thrilled along the wires that stretch through the wasted waters which roll between the shores of Italy and Egypt and spake in his ear its word of terrible command; from Alexandria. . . manacled, he was made to turn his face towards the land he had polluted by the curse of murder. He is here at last to be tried for his crime."

In his closing argument attorney Carrington for the Prosecution referring to Surratt's mother in connection with him said:

"Now, gentlemen of the jury, let us view the connection of Mrs. Surratt with this assassination. I feel the delicacy of the ground upon which I stand. I know the situation. I know that you dislike to consider this question which has been forced upon you. I do not want to do it. My duty is to prosecute the prisoner, but one of the counsel has said she was murdered, and another that she was butchered, and it becomes my duty to trace her connection with this crime, and then leave it to you, to say whether she was guilty . . . of the crime for which she suffered.
"First, I call your attention to the fact to which we have already adverted; that her house, 541 H Street, was the rendezvous for these conspirators. Now, gentlemen, will you pause for a moment and reconcile that with innocence? You remember the law, that it is not how much a party did, but whether she had anything to do with it. Can you, I say, reconcile it with innocence that this woman's house should have been the rendezvous of Booth. Lewis Payne, Atzerodt, Herold and John Surratt? Would you not know by intuition? Would you not know by their conversation? Would not your judgment and your hearts tell you who they were and what they contemplated?

"Secondly, who furnished the arms with which this bloody deed was done? . . . According to the testimony of John M. Lloyd, this is shown. Do you believe him, or disbelieve him? My friend, Mr. Bradley, said he was a common drunkard; but, mark you, he was an attendant and friend of Mrs. Surratt."

(Mr. Bradley) "Who says so?"

(District Attorney) "I will prove it. When I was examining that witness and proposed to ask him certain questions in reference to Mrs. Mary E. Surratt, he said, 'Mr. Carrington,' for he knew me personally, 'I do not wish to talk about Mrs. Surratt, for she is not on trial.' I said 'Go on, Mr. Lloyd.' I applied to the court and he said it was his duty to answer. He saw her continually. He lived in her house; he drank her liquor. Why, this evidence shows that John H. Surratt, Herold and John M. Lloyd played cards and drank together. But, says the friend and companion (Lloyd) of the prisoner at the bar, (Surratt) unwilling to testify against her, when put on solemn oath. . . . he says certain arms were furnished him by the prisoner at the bar who showed him where they could be safely concealed. . . . he (Lloyd) protesting that it might get him into personal difficulty. The mother knew about the transaction, for on the 11th of April we have Lloyd's own testimony that she asked him where those shooting arms were, and said that they might be needed soon. I say, first her house is the rendezvous: secondly, she furnished arms or knows of their being furnished.

"On the night of the 14th of April, Booth and Herold are leaving Washington in flight for their lives. At Surrattville they call for whiskey from the agent (Lloyd) and friend of the prisoner and his mother. She gives them a home, gives them arms, gives them whiskey, not to nerve them, but to refresh them after the commission of the horrid crime.

"But Booth, in making his escape, needs something more

than whiskey and arms. . . . He needs a field glass, and has it delivered for him by his friend, Mrs. Surratt. With the defense, no witness told the truth whose testimony went to convict their client, whilst the stories of the most infamous men, self-confessed scoundrels and accomplices, after the fact, if not before the fact, such as Fathers Boucher and Cameron, must be taken as gospel truth!"
(See testimony of Father Boucher, trial of Surratt, page 859. Also Kev. Stephen Cameron, page 793.)

There were some eight or nine reputable witnesses who testified to having seen John Surratt in Washington on the day of the murder. Sergeant Dye positively identified him as the young man who called the time before Ford's Theatre on the evening of the murder. A colored cook who had been engaged by Mrs. Surratt during John's absence testified that Mrs. Surratt had ordered her on the day of the assassination to bring a pot of tea and some toast into the dining room for John. While serving it to him, Mrs. Surratt said, "This is my son John. Don't you think he looks like his sister Anna?"

I am herewith giving the testimony of David C. Reed, a tailor who had known John Surratt since he was 14 years old, whose evidence could not be questioned. His professional critical eye was naturally more attracted to the up-to-date cut of Surratt's clothing.

TESTIMONY OF DAVID C. REED, JUNE 3, 1867.

"The last time I saw John H. Surratt was about half past two o'clock on the day of the assassination, April 14th last. I was standing on the stoop of Hunt and Goodwin's military store. Mr. Surratt was going past the National Hotel. I noticed his hair was cut very singularly, rounding away down on his coat collar. I did not notice whether he had whiskers or a mustache as I was more attracted by the clothing he had on. His appearance was very genteel, remarkably so. He did not look like a person from a long journey. I cannot say I ever had any connection with Mr. Surratt since he was quite a child. I knew him by sight and we had just bowing acquaintance. (Surratt Trial)

TESTIMONY OF SHIP SURGEON
DR. L. J. McMILLEN, THE *PERUVIAN*.
Washington, DC, Tuesday, June, 1867

Question. Did you know John H. Surratt?
If so state where and under what circumstances.

Answer: "I became acquainted with John H. Surratt in the month of September, 1865. I did not know him under the name of Surratt. He was introduced to me under the name of 'McCarthy' by a gentleman in Montreal who kept him in secrecy after the assassination of Mr. Lincoln. I was then ship surgeon of the Steamship Peruvian plying between Quebec and Liverpool. He came on board on September 11, 1865. I never suspected who he was until after we left. One day he inquired of me, 'Who is that gentleman?' pointing to a passenger. He said he believed he was an American detective and that he was after himself. 'But,' said he, 'if he is (he put his hand in his pocket and drew out a revolver) that will settle him.' Then I began to suspect—not that he was Surratt but that he had been connected with the Rebellion here in some way. After that he would be continually with me every day, because I was the only person on board he knew, having been introduced to him by my friend, and he seemed not to care for being in the company of any one else. He used to come to me when I was alone and ask me to walk with him on deck; and he would always talk about what happened here during the war. He told me that he had been from the beginning in the Confederate State's service, carrying dispatches between here and Richmond, and also as far as Montreal; that he and Booth had planned at first the abduction of President Lincoln; that, however, they could not succeed in that way and they thought it necessary to change their plan. After this, before the assassination, Surratt was in Montreal when he received a letter from

Booth ordering him immediately to Washington; that it was necessary to act and act promptly and he was to leave Montreal immediately for Washington. He did not tell me he came here, but he told me he came as far as Elmira, N. Y. and from that place telegraphed to New York to find out whether Booth had already left for Washington and was answered that he had. He did not tell me that he had gone any farther than Elmira. The next place he spoke to me was St. Albans, Vermont, where he said he arrived early one morning about breakfast time and went to a hotel there for breakfast. When he was sitting at the table he heard several talking about the assassination and he inquired, 'What was up?' They asked if he did not know President Lincoln had been assassinated. He said, 'I do not believe it, because the story is too good to be true.' On that a gentleman pulled out a newspaper and handed it to him. He opened it and saw his own name as one of the assassins. He said this unnerved him so much that the paper fell out of his hands and he immediately left the room. As he was going out through the house he heard another party say, that Surratt must have been or was at the time in St. Albans, because such a person (mentioning that person's name) had found a handkerchief on the street with Surratt's name on it. He told me he actually looked in his pocket and found that he had lost his handkerchief. From that place he went to Canada and was concealed there from April to September.

"There were a great many things he told me that I had forgotten, or at least are not fresh in my memory. At the time I paid particular attention to what he said, and when I first made a deposition in Liverpool, everything was fresh in my memory.

"The first time I was sure he was Surratt was on the day he was talking about his mother having been hung. He did not call her Mrs. Surratt or by any other name, but just spoke about his mother having been hung; of course I knew well enough that there was only one woman that had been hung in connection with the assassination so I was pretty certain he was her son. He also asked me who did I believe he was. I was not sure who were the parties that escaped so I answered that I believed he was either Surratt or Payne. He gave me no reply but only laughed. But the last day he was on board he called me aside and began to talk of the assassination. It was in the evening and we were alone together and he took out his revolver which was always kept in his pocket, pointed it at the heavens and said, 'I hope and wish to live just a few years more—two will do me—and then I shall go back to the United States and I shall serve Andy Johnson as Abraham Lincoln has been served.' I asked him why? 'Because he has been the cause of my mother being hung.' I then said, 'Now who are you?' I was pretty sure then who he was but still he had not given me his name himself. He looked around to see whether any one was near us and said: 'I am Surratt.'

"I made this affidavit September 25th in Liverpool. Next day would be Wednesday the 26th. I told Mr. Wilding, United States Counsel, he would be in Liverpool in a

SCAFFOLD AND EXECUTION OF FOUR CONSPIRATORS.
"Davy" Herold, Louis Payne, Atzerodt and Mary E. Surratt, July, 1865.

day or two. On Wednesday the 26th, Surratt came to my boarding house but I was absent. . . .

"He returned in the evening and wanted me to go with him to a place he had been recommended to go, but he could not find the place, so I went with him. Mr. Wilding, I think, had sent a detective to watch us, for I saw a man follow us from the time we left my house until I left Surratt and he went to that house to which he had been recommended (Oratory of the Holy Cross Church). He promised to see me next day but didn't. I got a short note stating he intended to go to London but when he got to the station there were several Americans there and he was afraid of being recognized, and did not go any farther. In a few days again I saw him and he gave me a letter to bring back to the party who had taken care of him in Montreal. He expected some money because when he got to Liverpool he had very little money. . . . He told me he expected a remittance from Washington but it would come through his friend in Montreal, and that I would very likely be charged with it when I returned.

TESTIMONY OF FL SMOOT, JUNE 2.

(Conversation with Mr. Joseph T. Nott occurred in the barroom of the Surratt Tavern at Surrattsville on April 15.)

Mr. Nott said: "He reckoned John was in New York by this time." I asked him why he thought so and he said, "My God! John knows all about this murder. Do you suppose he is going to stay in Washington and let them catch him?" I pretended to be much surprised and said, "Is that so?" He replied, "It is, by God! I could have told you that this thing was coming to pass six months ago." Then, putting his hand on my shoulder, "Keep that in your own skin, my boy. Don't mention it; if you do, it will ruin me forever."

(See Surratt trial)

Joseph T. Nott was Lloyd's bartender at the Surratt Tavern. General Harris, in his *Assassination of Lincoln,* on page 280, says:

"Mr. Merrick then went on to meet the argument that Surratt had confessed his guilt by flight, by declaring that the mad passions of the hour and **tyrannical usurpations of the government** in its methods of dealing with those charged with this crime, by sending them before a military court instead of a civil court for trial, **justified** him in his flight. He (Merrick) then went on to vindicate the Catholic Church, which he claimed had been assailed in this matter. The only reference to the Catholic church in connection with this trial had been made in the public press. The prosecution had carefully abstained from any assault on that church, and had tried to exclude religious prejudices from the minds of the jurors. Mr. Merrick, however, seized the occasion to pass a eulogium on that church, in which he showed as much disregard for facts of history, as he did for the proven facts in this case. Perhaps, he felt this vindication to be called for from the fact **that most of the conspirators were Catholics in religion, and the further fact that the friends who waited and watched for the return of his client, to Montreal, after the assassination**, and who on his return, spirited him away (priests La Pierre and Boucher) and kept him secreted five months, and then helped him off to Italy, where he was found in the ranks of the Pope's army, and who voluntarily came before the court on his trial to testify, and to procure testimony in his behalf, **were priests of that church.**"

Continuing, General Harris comments:

"In his eulogium on that church, he forgot to mention the fact that the pope, during the progress of the war, acknowledged the Southern Confederacy, and wrote a sympathizing letter to Jefferson Davis, in which he called him 'his dear son,' and by implication denounced President Lincoln as a tyrant.

"He could have scarcely forgotten that the pope of Rome had sought to take advantage of the arduous struggle in which our government was engaged for the preservation of its life, to establish a **Catholic empire in Mexico**, and had sent Maximilian, a Catholic prince, to reign over at the time, unhappy people under the protection of the **arms** of France, lent to the furtherance of this un-holy purpose, by the last loyal son of the church that ever occupied a throne in Europe."

"Perhaps, he did not realize that it was God who frustrated the last grasp of the drowning man at a straw that eluded his grasp, by preparing for his holiness, the pope, and for Louis Napoleon, just at that moment, the Franco-Prussian War, which resulted in **the final loss of his temporal power to the pope**, and with it, his grip on the world and his empire and crown, to the last servile supporter of his temporal pretensions—Napoleon III!"

"To proclaim for that church, as Mr. Merrick did, friendship to civil liberty, respect for the rights of conscience and of private judgment, and love for our republican institutions, is to ignore or set at naught, all the dogmas of that church on the above questions and all the claims of the papacy. Mr. Merrick manifestly thought that the attitude of the Catholic clergy toward the assassination of the President could be hidden from public view, by his fulsome eulogy."

"The appeals made by the eminent counsel for the prisoner, to the political and religious prejudices of jurors, was ably seconded, all through the trial by the Jesuit priesthood of Washington City and the vicinity. It will be recalled by scores of people who attended the trial that not a day passed, but that some of these were in the court room as the most interested spectators. That they were not idle spectators may be inferred from the fact that, whenever it seemed necessary to the prisoner's counsel to find witnesses to contradict any testimony, that was particularly damaging to their cause, they were always promptly found, and were almost always uniformly Catholics in religion, as shown by their own testimony upon cross-examination."

"It was a remarkable fact also, that these witnesses were scarcely ever able to come from under the fire of Judge Pierrepont's searching cross-examination, uncrippled, and also, that when they took the risk of bringing two witnesses in rebuttal, of the same testimony, their witnesses uniformly killed each other off, before they got through the ordeal, that tests the truthfulness of witnesses—cross-examination."

"Other outside influences were brought to bear on the jurors, such as these: Father J. B. Menu, from St. Charles College, (Sulpician Monastery) spent the day in the courtroom, sitting beside the prisoner all day, thus saying to the jury: 'You see which side I am on.' A great many of the students from the same college also visited the trial, it being vacation, and they uniformly took great pains to show their sympathy with the prisoner by shaking hands with him."

"The press also was prostituted almost daily by publishing cunningly devised paragraphs impugning the motives of the government in the prosecution and management of the case. Thus were the prejudices of the jurors annealed to and efforts also made to pervert public opinion."

The above, from General Harris, who was present at the trials of Surratt. He was also one of the Military Commission that tried and convicted Mrs. Surratt and the other three conspirators, recommending the death penalty, and sentences to the Dry Tortugas to four others. In his testimony, he gives the reader a concise picture that correctly photographs the "fine Italian hand" that directed Surratt's attorneys in their line of action. Nothing could be more clear.

And now permit us to quote from the closing address of Judge Pierrepont, which is a masterpiece from a legal standpoint and a classic in pure English, superb in its logic, impregnable in its TRUTH:

"May it please your honor, and gentlemen of the jury, I have not in the progress of this long and tedious case, had the opportunity as yet of addressing to you one word. My time has now arrived. Yea, all that a man hath, will he give for his life! When the book of Job was written, this was true, and it is just as true today. A man, in order to save his life, will give his property, will give his liberty, will sacrifice his good name, and will desert his father, his mother, his sister. He will lift up his hand before Almighty God, and swear that he is innocent of the crime with which he is charged.

"He will bring perjury upon his soul, giving all that he hath in the world, and be ready to take the chances and jump the life to come and so far as counsel place themselves in the situation of their client, and just to the degree that they absorb his feelings, his terror and his purposes, just so far will counsel do the same.

"I am well aware, gentlemen, of the difficulties under which I labor in addressing you. The other counsel have all told you that they know you, and that you know them. They know you in social life, and they know you in political affairs. They know your sympathies, your habits, your modes of thought, your prejudices, even. They know how to address you, and how to awaken your sympathies, whilst I come before you a total stranger. There is not a face in those seats that I have ever beheld until this trial commenced, and yet, I have a kind of feeling pervading me, that we are not strangers.

"I feel as though, we had a common origin, a common country, and a common religion, and that on many grounds we must have a common sympathy. I feel as though, if hereafter, I should meet you in my native city, or a foreign land, I should meet you not as strangers, but as friends. It was not a pleasant thing for me to come into this case. They had, perhaps, the right to ask, and so asking, I give you the answer. I was called into it at a time ill-suited in every respect. I had just taken my seat in the convention called for the purpose of forming a new constitution for my State, and I was a member of the judiciary committee. The convention is now sitting, and I am absent, where I ought to be present. I feel however, that I had no right to shirk this duty.

"The counsel asked whether I represented the Attorney General in this case . . . and so asking, I will give my answer. There is no mystery about the matter. The District Attorney, feeling the magnitude of this case, felt that he ought to apply to the Attorney General for assistance in the prosecution of it, and he accordingly made the application. I have known the Attorney General for more than twenty years. Our relations have been most friendly, both in social and professional point of view. The Attorney General conferred with the Secretary of State, who is, as you know, from my own State, and they determined to ask me to assist in the prosecution of this cause. . . This is the way I happened to be engaged in this case. . . .

"When the President of the United States was assassinated, I was one of the committee sent on by the citizens of New York, to attend his funeral. When standing, as I did stand, in the East room by the side of that coffin, if some citizen sympathizing with the enemies of my country had, because my tears were falling in sorrow over the murder of the President, there insulted me and I had at that time repelled the insult with insult. I think my fellow citizens would have said to me, that my act was deserving of condemnation; that I had no right in that solemn, holy hour, to let my petty passions or my personal resentments disturb the sanctity of the scene. To my mind, the sanctity of this trial is far above that funeral occasion, solemn and holy as it was, and I should forever deem myself disgraced, if I should ever allow any passion of mine, or personal resentment of any kind, to bring me here into any petty quarrel over the murder of the President of the United States. I have tried to refrain from anything like that, and God helping me, I shall so endeavor to the end.

"To me, gentlemen, this prisoner at the bar is a pure abstraction. I have no feeling toward him whatever. I never saw him until I saw him in this room, and then it was under circumstances calculated to awaken only my sympathy. . . . To me he is a stranger. Toward him I have no hostility, and I shall not utter one word of vituperation against him. I came to try one of the assassins of the President of the United States, indicted before you . . . so far as I am concerned, gentlemen, I believe that what you wish to know in this case is the truth. . . . My duty is to aid you in coming to a just conclusion. I believe that it is your honest desire to find out whether the accused was engaged in this plot to overthrow this government, and assassinate the President of the United States. When this evidence is reviewed, and when it is honestly and fairly presented, when passions are laid aside, and when other people who have nothing whatever to do with the trial are kept out of this case, you will discover that in the whole history of jurisprudence, no murder was ever proved with the demonstration with which this has been proven before you. The facts, the proofs, the circumstances, all tend to one point, and all prove the case, not only beyond a reasonable doubt, but beyond any doubt.

"This has been, as I have already stated, a very protracted case. The evidence is scattered. It has come in, link by link, and as we could not have witnesses here in their order when you might have seen it in its logical bearings, we were obliged to take it as it came. I shall not attempt, gentlemen, to convince you by bold assertions of my own. I fancy I could make them as loudly and as confidently as the counsel for the other side, but I am not here for that purpose. The counsel are not witnesses in the case. We have come here for the purpose of ascertaining whether, under the law, and on the evidence presented, this man arraigned before you, is guilty as charged. . . . My business is to prove to you from the evidence that this prisoner is guilty. If I do that, I shall ask your verdict. If I do not do that, I shall neither expect nor hope for it.

"I listened to the two counsels who have addressed you for several days without one word of interruption. I listened to them respectfully and attentively. I know their earnestness, and I know the poetry that was brought into the case, and the feeling and the passion, that was attempted to be excited in your breasts, by bringing before you the ghost trailing her calico dress and making it rustle against these chairs. I have none of these powers which the gentlemen seem to possess, nor shall I attempt to invoke them. I have come to you for the purpose of proving that this party accused here was engaged in this conspiracy to overthrow this government, which conspiracy resulted in the death of Abraham Lincoln, by a shot from a pistol in the hand of John Wilkes Booth. That is all there is to be proven in this case.

I have not come here for the purpose of proving that Mrs. Surratt was guilty or that she was innocent, and I do not understand why that subject was lugged into this case in the mode that it has been; nor do I understand why the counsel denounced the Military Commission which tried her, and thus indirectly censored in the severest manner, the President of the United States. The counsel certainly knew, when they were talking about that tribunal, and when they were thus denouncing it, that President Johnson, the President of the United States, ordered it with his own hand; that President Johnson, President of the United States, signed the warrant that directed the execution; that President Johnson, President of the United States, when that record was presented to him, laid it before his Cabinet, and that every single member voted to confirm the sentence, and that the President with his own hand, wrote his confirmation of it, and with his own hand signed the warrant. I hold in my hand the original record, and no other man, as it appears from that paper, ordered it. No other one has touched this paper; and when it was suggested by some of the members of the Commission, that in consequence of the age, and the sex, of Mrs. Surratt, it might possibly be well to change her sentence to imprisonment for life, he signed the warrant for her death with the paper right before his eyes—and there it is (handing it to Mr. Merrick). My friend can read it for himself.

"My friends on the other side have undertaken to arraign the government of the United States against the prisoner.

They have talked very loudly and eloquently about this great government of twenty-five or thirty millions of people, being engaged in trying to bring to conviction, one poor young man, and have treated it as though it was a hostile act, as though two parties were litigants before you, the one trying to beat the other.

"Is it possible that it has come to this, that, in the City of Washington, where the President has been murdered, that when under the form of law, and before a court and jury of twelve men, an investigation is made, to ascertain whether the prisoner is guilty of this great crime, that the government is to be charged as seeking his blood, and its officers as lapping their tongues in the blood of the innocent? I quote the language exactly. It is a shocking thing to hear. What is the purpose of a government? What is the business of a government?

"According to the gentlemen's notion, when a murder is committed the government should not do anything towards ascertaining who perpetrated the murder, and if the government did undertake to investigate the matter and endeavor to find out whether the man charged with the crime is guilty, or not . . . the government and all connected with it, must be expected to be assailed as 'bloodhounds of the law,' and as seeking to 'lap their tongues in the blood of the innocent.' Is that the business of the government, and is it the business of the counsel, under any circumstances, thus to charge the government? What is government for? It is instituted for your protection and my protection, for the protection of us all. What could we do without it? Tell me, my learned and eloquent counsel on the other side, what would you do without government? What would you do in this city?"

Have you ever heard, my dear reader, a more direct, explicit analysis of Roman Catholic anarchy portrayed than the above presentation of Judge Pierrepont?

There were 85 witnesses and 96 in rebuttal called by the government, and Surratt called 98 witnesses in chief and 23 in rebuttal.

The hearing began June 17, 1867 and closed July 26, 1867. The arguments of the attorneys covered twelve days. The case went to the jury August 7, three days later. The jury brought in a report that they stood about even for conviction and acquittal, with no prospect of reaching an agreement.

Surratt was remanded to jail.

His attorneys asked that he be released on bail, which was refused by the court. The following September, the case was *nolle prosequi*. He was then indicted on the charge of engaging in rebellion. He was admitted to bail on this charge in the amount of $20,000, which still stands.

A second indictment was found against him, but the district attorney entered a *nolle prosequi* on this. The prisoner was finally released and permitted to go free on a technicality—an omission of the three words in the indictment, viz.: "Was a fugitive."

All of the above proceedings in the face of the burning facts brought out by his two trials, and that every charge of his guilt of the murder of Abraham Lincoln was proven beyond the peradventure of a doubt.

XII

Summing It All Up: Two And Two

The aim of the Jesuits in this country is to ultimately extricate the Roman Church from its responsibility in the murder of Lincoln by exonerating Mary E. Surratt and her son John, by placing the whole blame on John Wilkes Booth—the man falsely labeled a Protestant.

The recent activity in this direction of these Leopoldines—the Knights of Columbus—is most significant and interesting to observe. Wide publicity was recently given through the official press of the Knights of Columbus of an offer of $5,000 to "anyone who can prove that John Wilkes Booth was a Roman Catholic" is one move in the **plan**.

The Surratts must be whitewashed before the Catholic Church can clear its skirts. The documentary evidence pertaining to this tragedy has been so carefully and completely removed from the public eye that they feel it safe now to openly refer to the death of Lincoln. But for years his name never passed the lips of either the priests or the press of Rome!

With a desire to get at the **truth**, we have made a study of these two characters.

There is much to convince the fair-minded investigator that John Wilkes Booth had been a pervert to the Roman Church. The evidence in both the trials of the conspirators and John H. Surratt shows that Booth was frequently at "Mass" in various Roman Churches. The fact that he wore an "Agnus Dei" bronze medal at the time of his death, which was taken from his neck by Surgeon General Barnes as his body lay on the Montauk, which had become corroded from the moisture of his body showed long wear. Only three weeks prior to the murder, as Rear Admiral Baird tells us, he met Booth coming out of a Vesper Service at a Roman Church in Washington. This alone, of course, would not be conclusive, but taken together with other evidence strengthens the conclusion, that he was not only a professed Romanist, but that he was a **devout one**.

The close associates of Booth from his arrival in Washington from Montreal the middle of November 17, 1864, until his flight after the murder, were fanatical Romanists. His first visit the next day after he registered at the National Hotel was to the little Roman Church at St. Mary's near Bryantown. He had attended "Mass" and presented his credentials to the Roman Catholics, Drs. Queen and Mudd. He also was entertained by them and enquired for the whereabouts of John Surratt on that occasion, whom he met shortly afterward in Washington and became a constant, almost daily, visitor at the Surratt home on H street which was the meeting place of the Romish priests of Washington and vicinity.

The complete confidence that existed between Booth and the Surratts, in the mind of the writer, is sufficient evidence that these schemers were taking no chances on any "**Heretic**." The fact that every member of this household was a Romanist, and undoubtedly a **member of the Knights of the Golden Circle** further confirms this belief. Having absorbed the Jesuit psychology during my early girlhood training, and understanding the **peculiar** tie that binds all devout Romanists together, there is not the slightest doubt in my mind that John Booth was a full-fledged **pape**.

Add to this the fact that Booth himself had taken the Jesuitized oath of the Order of the Knights of the Golden Circle, given in full in this book, which no honorable or sincere Protestant's conscience would permit him to blacken his soul with, and we have another link in the chain of circumstantial evidence. He was under the influence of the small group of Confederate leaders in Montreal, who in turn were the most abject tools and associates of the French priests in that city. Considering these and other things we will be justified in concluding that if John Wilkes Booth was not a professed Romanist, he might as well have been and most certainly **he was nothing else**.

There is no professed Catholic assassin in all history, within the writer's knowledge, who was a more effectual dupe of the priests of Rome and their lay agents than this once brilliant, carefree, talented young man whose most distinguishing characteristic, barring his kindly courtesy, was his reverence and devotion to his mother.

Without wishing to excuse or condone the cruel, cowardly act that snatched Abraham Lincoln away from us at the moment when his great wisdom, kindliness, and broad charity would have guided the reconstruction as no other could, but the aim is to call attention to the instigators, higher up—**the priests of Rome** who were accessories both before and after the fact, and who have always escaped without even censor or suspicion, leaving their tools to pay the price!

Booth was chosen for this bloody deed with keen discernment and fine discrimination by these ecclesiastical plotters against this government. That he was a young man without much depth of character is to be conceded, for they do not seek strong characters to execute these wicked and dangerous deeds. No doubt the Jesuits followed Booth for months, studying him, finding his most vulnerable point, delving into his very soul, before they decided to cast on him the leading role.

There were many advantages in his selection. His profession and the well known loyalty of the Booth family to the Government, placed him almost above suspicion. His knowledge of changing his appearance, his expertness in the use of firearms, horsemanship, fencing, etc., his pronounced personal magnetism and easy graceful manner and above all his childlike vanity without egotism, all tended to, from their standpoint, make him an ideal victim of their subtle **influence**.

One other point. Booth, even if he had no previous idea of the responsibility or knowledge of the **oath** he was to take when he entered the Golden Circle, must have fully realized after, that had he failed to carry out instructions after he had drawn the fatal blank, **it meant his own certain death**.

Geniuses are usually so absorbed in the line of work in which their gift inclines them, that they are often easy victims of stronger designing or unscrupulous minds, and the dramatic instinct in this unfortunate young man would tend to make him particularly susceptible to the weird ceremonies, garbs, etc. of the Roman Church and its psychology.

Booth, by several authors, is charged with entering this conspiracy of murder and destruction from a monetary object. The value of a dollar does not go hand in hand with talent nor genius. If so, it is the **exception** to the rule and John Wilkes Booth was not an exception. Actors make their money easily and quickly and the rule is that they let it go as easily; their improvidence is proverbial. I believe it is unjust to attribute Booth's part in this affair to a mercenary motive and am inclined to think that he very probably used much of his own money during his operations. The several genuine oil speculations in which he was the loser, shows him to have been short on business qualifications and the EZ mark in that respect that characterized the member of the profession in his day.

That John H. Surratt, on the contrary, was mercenary and that money held a high place in his estimation is plentifully evidenced. He talked about the large sums of money he expected to get and repeatedly boasted to Weichmann and displayed the large bills and twenty-dollar gold pieces in his possession while carrying on the Secret Service work in his trips between Richmond, Washington and Canada.

He began to dress expensively and it was because of his ultra-fashionable appearance that the attention of the tailor. Reed, was attracted to him on the fatal Good Friday as he walked down Pennsylvania Avenue from the National Hotel.

It was his habit to show his money and talk of it to his friends in a boastful way. The testimony of St. Marie shows that he was still given to this while a member of the Pope's Army.

The difference in the filial devotion and the lack of it is very pronounced between these two young men. Surratt's immediate flight to Canada the morning after the tragedy at Ford's theatre, where he had directed and "**called the time**," where he remained in safety under the care of the Roman priests La Pierre and Boucher, during his mother's arrest, trial, conviction and execution; his heartless desertion of his mother and only sister, is unparalleled as the most concentrated selfishness and base ingratitude and the only charitable thing to be said, is that it was due greatly to his theological training—or it might have been owing to the **espionage** of his priestly "protectors."

GENERAL THOMAS M. HARRIS "NAILS" PRIEST WALTERS' ATTEMPT TO WHITEWASH MRS. SURRATT.

The review of the trial of John H. Surratt made by Gen. T. M. Harris who was a member of the Military Court Martial that tried and convicted the four conspirators and sentenced four others to the Dry Tortugas, was written in response to the charges of Mrs. Surratt's confessor, the pastor of St. Patrick's Roman Church, Washington, DC, who had dared to raise his voice in defense of this woman **27 years** after her execution. General Harris, whose book, the only one of its kind, has so effectually and completely "nailed" the ecclesiastical liar, that it has been removed from most of the public libraries throughout the country on account of its contents. Because it has gone out of print and because it is not accessible to the readers, I am incorporating the whole chapter on "FATHER WALTER" page 204, for the benefit of my readers, below:

"From the time of the trial of the conspirators by a military commission, and of the execution of Mrs. Surratt by the order of President Johnson, Father Walter, a secular priest of Washington City, has made himself conspicuous by his efforts to pervert public opinion on the result of the trial of the conspirators by the Commission. Whilst rebel lawyers, editors and politicians have boldly assailed the lawfulness of the Commission and have denounced it as an unconstitutional tribunal, and have characterized the trial as a 'star chamber' trial, as a contrivance for taking human life under a mockery of a judicial procedure, with no purpose of securing the ends of justice, Father Walter and other priests whose sympathies were with the Southern Confederacy have earnestly seconded their efforts by the invention and circulation of cunningly devised falsehoods.

"Father Walter has every now and then bobbed up with the assertion of Mrs. Surratt's entire innocence. **Knowing that not one in a thousand of our people has ever read the testimony on which she was convicted,** he feels that he can boldly assert, 'There was not enough evidence against her to hang a cat.' He has also become bold enough to state as facts what the evidence shows to be falsehoods. As an example of this: In an article in the *Catholic Review* he asserts in regard to Mrs. Surratt's trip to Surrattville on the afternoon of the day of the assassination that she had ordered her carriage for the trip, which was purely on private business, on the forenoon of that day, and before it was known that the President would go to the theatre. Why, if this was true was it not proven in her defense? There was no such testimony produced. The testimony on this point against her was that shortly after

SURRATT HOUSE,
541 H STREET,
WASHINGTON, D. C, 1865.

"The Nest where the Egg was hatched." President Johnson's reply, when he was asked to commute her sentence to life imprisonment because of her age (46) and sex."

2 o'clock on that afternoon she went upstairs to Weichmann's room, tapped at the door, and when it was opened she said to Mr. Weichmann. 'I have just received a letter from Mr. Calvert that makes it necessary for me to go to Surrattville today and see Mr. Nothey. Would you be so good as to get a conveyance and drive me down?' Upon Weichmann's consenting to do so, she handed him a ten dollar bill with which to procure a conveyance. Surely, there is no evidence here that a carriage had been ordered already, as Weichmann was left free to procure a conveyance where he might see fit. Weichmann went downstairs, and as he opened the front door he saw John Wilkes Booth, who was in the act, as it were, of pulling the front door bell. Booth entered the house.

"When young Weichmann returned, after having procured the buggy, he went up to his own room after some necessary articles of clothing, and as he again descended the stairs and passed by the parlor doors he observed that Booth was in the parlor conversing with Mrs. Surratt. In a little while Booth came down to the front door steps and waved his hand in token of adieu to Weichmann, who was standing at the curb.

"When Mrs. Surratt came and was in the act of getting into the buggy, she remembered she had forgotten something, and said, 'Wait a moment, until I go and get those things of Mr. Booth's.' She returned from the parlor with a package which was done up in brown paper, the contents of which the witness did not see, but which was afterwards shown to have been the field glass which Booth carried with him in his flight. This glass Booth sent to Lloyd by Mrs. Surratt, with a message to have it, with the two carbines and two bottles of whiskey, where they would be handy, as they would be called for that night. Lloyd swore that this was the message delivered to him by Mrs. Surratt in the private interview she sought with him in his backyard on his return home that evening, and that in accordance with these instructions he delivered them to Booth and Herold about midnight that night.

"Now, let us see about the private business on which she professed to be going, and on which she claimed at her trial that she went. The letter from Mr. Calvert was a demand for money that she owed him, and was written at Bladensburg on the 12th of April. On the afternoon of the fourteenth she presented herself to Weichmann and claimed that she had just received it. It would seem very strange that it took this letter two days to reach her at a distance of only six miles. She claimed that she must go and see Mr. Nothey who owed her and get money from him to pay her debt to Mr. Calvert. Mr. Nothey lived five miles below Surrattsville, and as she claimed that she had just received Mr. Calvert's letter, it was impossible that she could have made any arrangement with Nothey to meet her at Surrattsville that day. She did not meet him there, neither did she go to his house to see him. When she arrived at Surrattsville she took Weichmann into the parlor at the hotel and asked him to write a letter for her to Mr. Nothey, which he did at her dictation; and this she sent to Mr. Nothey by Mr. Bennett Gwinn, a neighbor of his who happened to be passing down.

"Now, in view of all these facts, can anyone see how her private business was in any way subserved by her trip to Surrattsville on that afternoon? She could as easily have written to Mr. Nothey from Washington as from

Surrattsville. A postage stamp, a sheet of paper and an envelope would have saved her six dollars, the cost of her trip, and would have served her business just as well. The truth is that this talk of going on private business of her own was all a fabrication, first to deceive Mr. Weichmann as to the object of her trip, and then to be used, should it become necessary, in her defense. We have already seen what her real business was.

"Father Walter falsifies again in the article referred to saying that she did not see Lloyd on that afternoon, but delivered the things to his sister-in-law, Mrs. Offutt. Both Lloyd and his sister-in-law testified to her interview with him in his backyard, and Lloyd testified as to what passed between them on that occasion."

(See testimony of John M. Lloyd, Trial Conspirators, PP. 85-86 and Testimony Mrs. E. Offutt and Trial of Surratt, P. 281.)

It would seem that Father Walter is going on the theory that we have gotten so far past the time, and that the testimony has been so far forgotten that he can foist upon the public any statement that he may please to fabricate. We would kindly remind the reverend Father that no ultimate gain can be derived from an effort to suppress the truth. Neither can it be obliterated by our prejudices. We may misconstrue facts, but we cannot wipe them out by a mere stroke of a pen, and a fact once made can never be recalled.

But I am not done yet with this Father. He prefaces this article in the *Review* with the statement that he heard Mrs. Surratt's last confession and that while his priestly vows do not permit him to reveal the secrets of the confessional, yet from knowledge in his possession he is prepared to assert her entire innocence of this most atrocious crime. He means that we shall understand that were he at liberty to give her last confession to the world, he would say that she then and there asserted her entire innocence.

Will Father Walter deny that, under the teachings of the Roman Catholic Church, he had an absolute right, with her consent, to make her confession public on this point? Nay, moreover, could not Mrs. Surratt have compelled him to do so in vindication of her good name, and of the honor of the church of which she was a member? And having this consent, was it not his most solemn duty to proclaim her confessed innocence in every public way through the press and even from the very steps of the gallows?

Why was not that confession made public?

Why was it not reduced to writing and signed with her own hand?

Why has it not, in its entirety, been given to the world?

Why must the public wait twenty-seven years, and instead of having the full confession, be required to content itself, in so great a case, with a mere assertion from the reverend Father, based on his alleged knowledge? Aye, just there's the rub!

That confession of Mrs. Surratt's would have proved very interesting reading, and might have let in a flood of light on some of the places that are now very dark; it would, indeed, have shown how far Mrs. Surratt was involved in the abduction and assassination plots and to what degree she was the willing or unwilling tool of her son, and of John Wilkes Booth.

That confession would have shown the object of Booth's visit to her on the very day and eve of the murder. It would have explained what she had in her mind when she carried Booth's field glass into the country and told Lloyd to have the "shooting-irons" and two bottles of whiskey ready on that fatal night of 14 April. And if she did not explain satisfactorily every item of testimony which bore so heavily against her, then her last confession was worth nothing.

Father Walter never had at any time Mrs. Surratt's consent to make her confession public, and he dare not do so now after 27 years have elapsed since he shrove his unfortunate penitent.

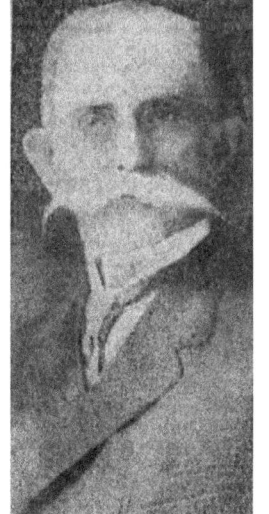

Why did Father Walter not do this? He was interesting himself very much in her behalf in trying to get her a reprieve.

Why did he not use this as an argument with the President in her behalf, that in her final confession

---

JOHN H. SURRATT at 72.

This is the last picture taken of John H. Surratt who died in Baltimore, MD, April 23, 1916, surrounded by his wife and grown family. At his request he was buried in the Surratt lot at Mt. Olivet, Washington, DC at left side of his mother's grave. He was auditor of a large corporation until his death.

she asserted her innocence?

Why did he wait until the sentence had been confirmed by the President and a full Cabinet without a dissenting voice, and then had been carried into execution, before he put into circulation the story of her confessed innocence?

And why does he refer to his priestly vows as his excuse for this conduct, when he knows full well that, having gained Mrs. Surratt's consent to make her confession public as an entirety, these vows imposed upon him no such restrictions?

In vindication of the Commission and also the Court of Review— the President and his Cabinet—we submit that the evidence shows her to have been guilty, no matter what she might have said, in her final confession.

Perhaps she had been led to believe that President Lincoln was an execrable tyrant, and that his death was no more than that of the "meanest nigger in the army." Her remarks to her daughter the night her house was searched indicate the views she took of the subject. "Anna, come what will, I am resigned. I think that Booth was only an instrument in the hands of the Almighty to punish this wicked and licentious people."

To one who could have taken this view of the case, Booth's act could not have been regarded as a crime, and she who rendered him all the aid she could would feel no guilt. They were only cooperating with the Almighty in the execution of vengeance. On the trial of John H. Surratt, Mr. Merrick brought Father Walter on the stand and asked him if he heard the last confession of Mrs. Surratt, to which the Father answered, "I did. I gave her communion on Friday and prepared her for death."

Mr. Merrick in his argument before the jury said, "I asked him, 'Did she tell you as she was marching to the scaffold that she was an innocent woman?' I told him not to answer that question before I desired him to. He nodded his head, but did not answer that question, because he had no right, as the other side objected."

Now, what was the object of all this?

Mr. Merrick brought the Father on to the stand and asked him a question that had not the slightest relevancy to any issue before that jury. He knew, of course, that the prosecution would object, and that the question could not be answered. It was a direct question and could have been answered by "She did" or "She did not."

Why does not the Father answer at once?

He had been cautioned not to do so until desired, and so he waits for the prosecution to object and stop him from answering the question.

Mr. Merrick, however, in his argument, assumes that the Father stood ready to say that: "She solemnly declared her innocence to me in her last confession," and throws the responsibility on the other side for not getting this answer. The argument was this: "You see that Father Walter stood ready to testify to this fact, but the prosecution objected, and so he could not do it."

Now, what has become of the Father's priestly vows, behind which he has always been hiding? Or was all this a mere piece of acting, to give the counsel a point from which to denounce the government, the Commission, and all who were concerned in visiting justice upon the assassins?

We believe it to be true that the laws of his church do not forbid him to make public, with her consent or command, her last confession on this point, and that the Father in making the statements he does at this late day is simply practicing sleight of hand upon the public. It is a very strange circumstance, too, that while Payne, Arnold, O'Laughlin, Atzerodt, and even John H. Surratt admitted their connection with one or the other of the conspiracy plots, Mrs. Surratt has not left one word or line after her to explain away the incriminating evidence brought against her. The reason is plain; she could not have explained anything without involving herself and her son and giving away the whole case.

For twenty-six years Father Walter and his rebel coadjutors have kept a paragraph going the rounds of the papers, stating as a fact that all the members of the Commission but one are dead, and that they died miserable deaths that marked them as the subjects of heaven's vengeance and that some of them perished from the violence of their own hands, being crazed with remorse.

The truth is that, at this writing, in April 1892, all the members of the Commission are alive except General Hunter and General Ekin. General Hunter lived to over four score years and General Ekin to 73. The present writer is nearly 79 and is still able to vindicate the truth in the interest of a true history of this period.

> "Is it not high time that the American people should be
> fully informed as to this most important episode in their
> history, in order that they may not be misled by men who
> were not the friends, but the enemies, of our government

in its struggle for its preservation and perpetuation." (See page 204)

The above statement of facts is sufficient to refute the lying priest Walter and block the Roman Church's mad efforts to subvert this damning evidence of its own participation in Lincoln's murder.

OTHER TESTIMONY OF THE SURRATTS' CATHOLIC FRIENDS.

TESTIMONY OF MISS ANNA WARD, FOR THE DEFENSE, JUNE 3.

"I reside at the Catholic Female Seminary on Tenth Street, Washington. I have been acquainted with Mrs. Surratt six or eight years. I have not been very intimate with Mrs. Surratt. She always bore the character of a perfect lady and a christian, as far as my acquaintance with her extends.
"I received two letters from John H. Surratt postmarked Montreal, Canada for his mother. I received the second the day of the assassination. . . . I answered his letters to me, and left them with his mother as I supposed that she would be glad to hear from him. I have not seen him since." (See *Conspirators Trial*, page 134.)

This Miss Ward, by the way, was twice brought into the trial sufficient participation it might seem to involve her in conspiracy. Mr. Weichmann testified that, in March 1865, Surratt invited him to accompany him to the Herndon Hotel to see about securing a room. When they arrived, Surratt called for the housekeeper, a Mrs. May Murray, and asked her to have the room ready for the man, not mentioning the name, whom Miss Ward a few days previous, had spoken to her about. The housekeeper seemed not to remember until Surratt further reminded her that it was "For a delicate gentleman" who was to have his meals served in his room. With this refreshing, she remembered. Surratt then told her that the gentleman would occupy the room on the following Monday. Later on, Weichmann met Atzerodt coming along 7th Street, who told him in answer to his question as to where he was going, that he was going to the Herndon House.

Weichmann then said "Is that Payne that is at the Herndon House?" Atzerodt answered, "Yes."

Then Miss Ward, this Catholic school teacher, was the one who prior to the crime, had been delegated to establish an alibi for John H. Surratt by calling at the Surratt house on the day of the assassination with a letter which she had purported to have received that day from John Surratt in Canada. She proffered this information to Lonis Weichmann, who happened to be at home. Weichmann did not read the letter which disappeared and was never introduced into the evidence.

Surely, it was a fact worth noting from the amount of evidence that Mrs. Surratt, a woman impoverished by the war with no special social standing, should have had the **privilege** of intimate acquaintance with so many priests. I give below the verbatim testimony of these reverend gentlemen as the records show:

REV. B. F. WIGET FOR DEFENSE, MAY 25th.

"I am president of Gonzaga College, F Street between Tenth and Eleventh.

"It is about ten or eleven years since I became acquainted with Mrs. Mary E. Surratt. I know her very well, and I have always heard everyone speak very highly of her character as a lady and as a christian. During all this acquaintance nothing has come to my knowledge respecting her character that could be called un-christian.

"I have a personal knowledge of her character as a christian, but not as to her character for loyalty. My visits were all short and political affairs were never discussed; I was not her pastor. I first became acquainted with Mrs. Surratt from having her two sons with me. I have seen her perhaps once in six weeks. I cannot say that I remember hearing her utter a disloyal sentiment, nor do I remember hearing anyone talk about her being notoriously disloyal before her arrest." (See page 135.)

REV. FRANCIS E BOYLE, FOR THE DEFENSE, MAY 25

"I am a Catholic priest. My residence is St. Peter's Church. I made the acquaintance of Mrs. Mary E. Surratt eight or ten years ago. . . . Have always heard her well spoken of as an estimable lady. I do not undertake to say what her reputation for loyalty is." (See page 136.)

REV. CHARLES H. STONESTREET, FOR THE DEFENSE, May 26

"I am pastor of Aloysius Church in this city. I first became acquainted with Mrs. Mary E. Surratt twenty years ago. I have only seen her occasionally since. At the time of his acquaintance there was no question of her loyalty." (page 136.)

By the bye, on a recent trip the author took through the Jesuit University at Georgetown in the cloister of one of the buildings, there are a number of paintings of Jesuit priests connected with the institution, among whom I noted one labeled. Rev. Chas. H. Stonestreet. The reverend gentleman testified that at the time of his acquaintance there was no question about the lady's loyalty. Certainly not. The question of loyalty had not arisen 20 years before the war. Evidently, this is an example of "Mental reservation" of a Jesuit priest. All of them could have said, "I never questioned her loyalty." ("Mental reservation," to the Holy Mother Church)

REV. PETER LANIHAN, DEFENSE, MAY 26.

"I am a Catholic priest. I reside near Beantown, Charles County, MD. I have been acquainted with Mrs. Surratt, prisoner at the bar, for about thirteen years; **intimately so**, for about nine years, in my estimation she is a good christian woman and highly honorable. Have never on any occasion heard her express disloyal sentiments. **I have been very familiar with her, staying at her house.**" (page 136.)

In *The Doctrine of the Jesuits* by Father Jean Pierre Gury, in the Eighth Precept of the Decalogue, pages 156, 442-1, "Is it not permitted to make use of the purely and properly mental restriction?" pages 443-2. "It is sometimes permitted to make use of the restriction largely; that is to say, improperly mental, and also of equivocal words, when the meaning of the speaker can be understood. . . . Besides, the good of society demands that there should be a means to lawfully hide a secret; now there is no other way than by equivocation or restriction, ... One is permitted to use this restriction even under oath. . . page 444: A culprit interrogated judicially, or not lawfully, by the judge, may answer that he has done nothing, meaning: "About which you have the right to question me."

The canon law of the Roman Church does not concede the right of any civil authority to question or cross-question a priest. Not only so, but the canon law of the Roman Church automatically excommunicates any Catholic layman who would bring a priest into a civil court. Consequently none of these priests' testimony was worth the paper it was written on in the matter of truth, and they were at perfect liberty to swear to anything they chose, or to whatever would seem best for the interest of the prisoner and their church.

Gury, in a footnote, quotes Bessius, a Jesuit authority as follows:

> "If a judge interrogates on an action, which must have been committed without sin, at least a mortal one, the witness and the culprit are not obliged to answer according to the judge's intention."

REV. N. D. YOUNG, DEFENSE, MAY 26.

> "I am a Catholic priest. I reside at the pastoral home of St. Dominick's church on the Island and Sixth Street, Washington City. I became acquainted with Mrs. Mary E. Surratt eight or ten years ago. My acquaintance has not been very intimate. I have occasionally seen her and visited with her. I had to pass her house about once a month, and I generally called there, sometimes stayed an hour. I have heard her spoken of with great praise. She never uttered any disloyal sentiments to me."

Certainly the above testimony makes the position of Mrs. Surratt and her church beyond question, but to say that any one of these priests did not know that she was DISLOYAL TO THE UNION and entertained a deep hatred for President Lincoln, to whom she, like many others, attributed the loss of her wealth, might be acceptable to non-Romanists who do not understand the relation of such a woman to her priest, but certainly no ex-Romanist could be deceived by it.

TESTIMONY OF THE REVEREND B. F. WIGET
Washington, DC, February 28, 1867

Question: "State your residence and profession."
Answer: "I am connected with the Gonzaga College on F. Street. Washington, between Ninth and Tenth."
Question: "How long have you resided in Washington?"
Answer: "With an interruption of four months I have resided here four years."
Question: "Look at this photo (marked exhibit G) and state whether you have known this person from whom it was taken."
Answer: "John H. Surratt, I should think."
Question: "Have you known Surratt many years?
Answer: Many, many years, yes, sir. I knew him when he was about 12 years old. He was one or two years under my tuition."

EXTRACTS FROM THE TESTIMONY OF
LOUIS J. WEICHMANN

"Mrs. Surratt and her family are Catholics. John H. Surratt is a Catholic and was a student of divinity at the same college as myself. I met the prisoner, David E. Herold, at Mrs. Surratt's house on one occasion. I also met him when we visited the theatre when Booth played Pescara; I met him at Mrs. Surratt's in the country in the spring of 1863 when I first made his acquaintance.
"I met him (Herold) in the summer of 1864 at the Piscataway (Roman Catholic) church. These are the only

**MONUMENT OF
PRIEST JACOB WALTER**

Pastor of St. Patrick's Church, Washington, D. C, friend and confessor of Mrs. Surratt, who, as such must have been fully cognizant of the woman's knowledge and participation in the conspiracy and murder. After General Thomas M. Harris brought Walter to time by his book, he ceased to "break into print."

times to my recollection I ever met him. . . . I generally accompanied Mrs. Surratt to church on Sunday.

"Surratt never intimated to me nor to anyone else to my knowledge that there was a purpose to assassinate the President. He stated to me in the presence of his sister shortly after he made the acquaintance of Booth that he was going to Europe on a cotton speculation. That three thousand dollars had been advanced to him by an elderly gentleman whose name he did not mention, residing somewhere in the neighborhood, that he would go to Liverpool and remain there probably two weeks to transact his business; then he would go to Nassau and from Nassau to Matamoras, Mexico and find his brother Isaac . . . His character at St. Charles College, Maryland, was excellent. On leaving college, he shed tears and the president approaching him told him not to weep, that his conduct had been excellent during the three years he had been there, and that he would always be remembered by those in charge of the institution . . . I had been a companion of John H. Surratt for seven years (in answer to a question) No, I did not consider that I forfeited my friendship to him in mentioning my suspicions to Capt. Gleason. He forfeited his friendship to me by placing me in the position in which I now stand, testifying against him. I think I was more of a friend to him than he was to me. He knew I had permitted the blockade runner at the house without informing upon him, because I was his friend, but I hesitated for three days; still when my suspicions of danger to the government were aroused, I preferred the government to John Surratt. My remark to Captain Gleason about the possibility of the capture of the President was merely a casual remark. He laughed at the idea that such a thing could happen in a city guarded as Washington was.

"Mr. Weichmann also testified that on the night of the arrest he answered the doorbell when the detectives rang it for the purpose of demanding admittance so that they might search the house. He rapped at Mrs. Surratt's door and informed her who was at the door and what they had come for. Her answer was: 'For God's sake, let them come in; I have been expecting them.' " (See page 394, Trial of Surratt; also supplemental affidavit of L. J. Weichmann.)

Other comments by General Thomas H. Harris are as follows:

"When they inquired for her son, she said, 'He is not here; I have not seen him for two weeks.' This was a sufficient answer, but her guilty conscience would not let her stop here, she had to add, 'There are a great many mothers who do not know where their sons are.' Let us ask ourselves at this point, how many mothers in Washington City at that hour of that eventful night were lying awake expecting their houses to be searched by detectives? Our inner consciousness will unerringly dictate the answer, 'Not one who was innocent of crime.' It is only necessary to say further, in regard to this defense set up of an alibi that although there is no more common defense resorted to by criminals, because there is none more easy of establishment, there was never perhaps in ail the history of jurisprudence a weaker and more unsuccessful effort made to establish it, than in this defense.

"Probably no witness had ever been subjected to the

severe grilling which Louis Weichmann received during these trials, his testimony at John H. Surratt's trial being precisely the same, and he could not be shaken by the badgering which the defense's lawyers resorted to. A lifelong persecution followed in consequence.

"During a recent interview, the writer had with a relative of his who was with him during his last illness said: 'No one will ever know the sadness of Lou's life nor dream of how he was persecuted for simply telling the truth. The day before he died he motioned for a pencil and paper and before a witness wrote: 'To All Lovers of Truth, I, Louis J. Weichmann, being of sound mind and memory do declare that everything that I testified to at the trials of Mary E. Surratt and John H. Surratt, was the truth, the whole truth and nothing but the truth, so help me God. (Signed) Louis J. Weichmann.' He died the next day."

The "persecution" was that they accused him of swearing away the life of an innocent woman who had been a kind friend to him. For many years, Mr. Weichmann was under the protection of the government where he held a public position in Philadelphia. He was practically excommunicated from the church, although he in later years attended. On the other hand ,John H. Surratt, conspirator and assassin, was protected and helped by the priests up until his death April 22, 1916.

After Surratt's release from prison on a technicality, he went to Rockville, MD where he delivered a lecture which he prepared with the ostensible purpose of going on the lecture platform. He only delivered it once. The public sentiment, even in the South, was strong against him. He then secured a position in the public school at Montrose, near Rockville, where he taught several years.

The writer, in making the picture of the Surratt house produced here, had a talk with the present tenant, a Mrs. William Penn, whose stepmother was a pupil of John Surratt's while he taught at Montrose. Mrs. Penn has a linen pocket handkerchief, hemstitched, with the name "Surratt" embroidered in large script letters across the corner of it, which her step-mother, a Mrs. A. M. Higgins, was given by the owner, John H. Surratt.

Some years later, he secured a lucrative position with a Baltimore

"MRS. SURRATT"

The small headstone with but two words on it, "Mrs. Surratt" which marks the lonely grave in the outskirt of Mt. Olivet Catholic Cemetery, Washington, D.C. That the body lies in "consecrated" ground is significant.

steamship company where he remained until just a short time before his death. He left a widow and several grown children, one of whom, William, is an attorney in the "Monumental" city.

On looking up the death notices some months ago when the writer was in Baltimore for that purpose, the protection of the Catholic church was shown by the information that a High Requiem Mass was to be said for the deceased and that the funeral would be private, interment would be at Bonnie Brae. As a matter of fact, the body was brought quietly to Washington and buried in the family lot at the left side of his mother.

The significance of this probably is that some day in the future the Roman Catholic church plans to erect a memorial to John Surratt and his "Martyred" mother. In a talk with the superintendent of Mt. Olivet Cemetery as we stood by the graves, he proffered this information, he being himself a Catholic. "The hanging of this woman was one of the greatest crimes ever committed. We would erect a monument to her in a minute, if we could."

I asked him why they did not do it. He said: "We wouldn't dare now. The feeling for Lincoln is too strong." On pressing the matter further with him, I found that he had no personal knowledge of the case and knew nothing but what he had been told by his church.

Before closing this chapter, I cannot but call your attention to God's "wondrous ways" of just retribution. Contemplate the small lonely headstone, labeled merely: "Mrs. Surratt" on the outskirst of the Roman Catholic Cemetery in Washington, the scene of her wicked work and within a gunshot the magnificent white marble **Lincoln Memorial** as it stands overlooking the Potomac River. The Memorial was erected to the memory of the great American whom she and **her priestly sponsors** had tried so energetically to destroy because he was the living **type of the triumph of Popular Government** and every act of his beautiful, clean, upright public life was a stinging rebuke to the tyrannical, corrupt **System**, of which Mary E. Surratt, her son and the other papal assassins were legitimate products!

EXECUTING THE SECRET TREATY OF VERONA

Reverting to the Secret Treaty of Verona, we recall that:

> "The **high contracting parties**, on being convinced that the system of representative government is . . . incompatible with monarchial principles . . . engage mutually, in the most solemn manner, to use all their efforts to put an end to the system of representative government . . . and to prevent it from being introduced in those countries where it is not yet known.
>
> Article 2. As it cannot be doubted that the liberty of the press is the most powerful means used by the pretended supporters of the rights of nations . . . the high contracting parties promise reciprocally to adopt all proper measures to **suppress** it . . . "

The process of destruction has gone on steadily from the assassination of the five presidents in the United States, which begun in 1841, and has continued at intervals, which finds us without a semblance of a free press.

After sixty years of activity by these foreign enemies within our borders what do we find?

We find a subversion of free speech; a subversion of a free press; we find a denial of the right of the American people to peaceable assemblage; we find the complete separation of Church and State the very basis of our form of government being a dead letter; we find the freedom of conscience being attacked; we find our great IDEA of public education being viciously undermined and sapped by a great system of parochial schools wherein are taught the principles of the old concept of monarchial institutions.

And by whom is this concerted plan of destruction being carried on, principally?

By the priests and lay members of the Roman Catholic Church. Upon what authority is this work of subversion being operated? By the ex-cathedra mandates of the Popes of Rome, conveyed to their "subjects" in this country through Encyclical Letters. We find that the Roman Catholics who comprise **less than one sixth** of the population, have been the dominating power in our political affairs and of late years have headed almost every national, state and municipal office from the president down to the dog catcher.

During the Wilson administrations, the Army, the Navy, the Treasury, the Secret Service, the Post Office, the Emergency Fleet, Transports, Printing, Aircraft and dozens of others were presided over by Fourth Degree Knights of Columbus!

The PLUNDERS of Hog Island and the Emergency Fleet under E. N. Hurley are matters of Congressional Record, which mounted up into the millions.

Mr. Hurley is a Roman Catholic and Knight of Columbus.

The "Aircraft Scandal" under the supervision of John M. Ryan, ardent Roman Catholic and Fourth Degree Knight of Columbus ran into the billions and was also subject of investigation.

Admiral Benson, who was advanced in a most **unusual** and peculiar way by his sponsor Woodrow Wilson, is a Fourth Degree Knight of Columbus and violated the spirit and the letter of this Republican Government by accepting a foreign title from the Pope of Rome. Admiral Benson is a member of the "Household" of this alien ruler, who never has ceased to claim his right to temporal power for one moment since he was forced to relinquish it by the Italian People, Sept. 20, 1870.

This disloyal act has never been rebuked by the American people whom Admiral Benson is supposed to represent. "Knighthood" is not a spiritual acquisition, nor was it bestowed as such. **It is a foreign title** given in recognition of his service to the Pope of Rome **who claims temporal sovereignity and allegiance from his subjects in every country**. One of the aims of the Knights of Columbus is to restore the temporal power of the Pope.

The presence of these laymen of the Romish Church in our public offices is not accidental or incidental. They are there by the express command of their Pope, whom they are obliged to Obey as God Himself." (See *The Great Encyclical Letters of Pope Leo XIII*, page 192)

Roman Catholics are serving under a **Citizenship** diametrically opposed to American citizenship, which is based upon the contention that the only authority to rule must come from the consent of the governed. Roman Catholic citizenship is based upon the negation of this. Pope Leo XIII has this to say:

> "The sovereignty of the people, however . . . is held to reside in the multitude; which is doubtless a doctrine exceedingly well calculated to flatter and inflame the many passions, but which lacks all reasonable proof, and all power of insuring public safety and preserving order." (page 123)

LIBERTY OF SPEECH AND PRESS

So too, the liberty of thinking, and of publishing whatsoever each one likes, without hindrance . . . is the fountainhead and origin of many evils. (page 123)

The unrestrained freedom of thinking and openly making known ones thoughts is not inherent in the rights of citizens, **and is by no means reckoned worthy of favor or support**. (page 126)

We must now consider briefly liberty of speech, and liberty of the press. It is hardly necessary to say that there can be no such right as this. . . . (page 151)

If unbridled license of speech and writing be granted to all, nothing will remain sacred and inviolate. (page 152)

So you see the Pope denies today the right to **think**. The Romanists of this country are obliged to obey and inculcate these treasonable principles. It is because of this citizenship that the Roman Church has established its gigantic parochial school system.

ATTEMPTING TO DESTROY THE FREE PRESS
FITZGERALD BILL (H. R. 6468)

On December 17, 1915, Roman Catholic Representative John J. Fitzgerald, Knight of Columbus, of Greater New York, introduced the following Bill:

"Be it enacted by the Senate and House of Representatives of the United States of America, in Congress assembled. That whenever it shall be established to the satisfaction of the Postmaster General that any person is engaged, or represents himself as engaged the business of publishing any obscene or immoral books, pamphlets, pictures, prints, engravings, lithographs, photographs, or other publications, matter, or thing of an indecent, immoral, or scurrilous character, and if such person shall, in the opinion of the Postmaster General, endeavor to use the post office for the promotion of such business, it is hereby declared that no letter, packet, parcel, newspaper, book, or other things sent or sought to be sent through the Post office, or by or on behalf, of or to, or on behalf of such person, shall be deemed mailable matter, and the Postmaster General shall make the necessary rules and regulations to exclude such non-mailable matter from the mails."

The Record shows that Holy Names Societies of the Roman Catholic Church immediately became active and sent to their Representatives many petitions urging the enactment of these measures into laws.

"Liberty, then, as we have said, belongs only to those who have the gift of reason or intelligence." (*The Great Encyclical Letters of Pope Leo XIII*, page 137).

And the priests claim the right to be the judge of those who would have the "gift of reason or intelligence."

Roman Catholic citizenship is inimical to American citizenship. Roman Catholic citizenship is represented by the confessional box. American citizenship is represented by the BALLOT BOX.

GALLIVAN BILL (H. R. 13778)

On March 27, 1916, Roman Catholic Representative James A. Gallivan of Boston, introduced the following:

"Be it enacted by the Senate and House of Representatives of the United States of America, in Congress assembled, that the Postmaster General shall make the necessary rules and regulations to exclude from the mails those publications, the avowed and deliberate purpose of which is to attack a recognized religion, held by the citizens of the United States or any religious order to which citizens of the United States belong."

In January, 1915, Representatives Fitzgerald and Gallivan had each introduced a Bill substantially identical with the Fitzgerald Bill hereinbefore set out. At the hearing on those Bills before the House Committee on the Post Office and Post Roads, Roman Catholic Representative James P. Maher, of Greater New York, stated frankly that the Bills had been introduced to shield sixteen million Roman Catholics and twenty thousand Roman Catholic priests from public criticism, by excluding *The Menace*, the *Yellow Jacket* and similar publications from the mails.

The above un-American citizens sponsored these Bills on the explicit instructions of their Church. Pope Leo XIII commands them thus:

> "Furthermore, it is in general fitting and salutary that Catholics should extend their efforts beyond this restricted sphere (Municipal politics) and give their attention to national politics . . . While if they hold aloof . . . this would tend to the injury of the Catholic religion, forasmuch, as **those would come into power who are badly disposed towards the Church**, and those who are willing to befriend her would be deprived of all influence." (page 131)

These laymen, tools of the Romish Church, would strangle our Press to prevent criticism of their religion and 20,000 bachelor fathers!

POPE LEO XIII ON LIBERTY OF CONSCIENCE

> Another **liberty** is widely advocated, namely the **liberty of conscience**. If by this is meant that every one may, as he chooses, worship God or not, it is sufficiently refuted by the arguments already adduced. (page 155)

> Hence follows the fatal theory of the need of separation of Church and State. (page 148)

HON. JOHN J. FITZGERALD
Who introduced one of the
postal bills.

HON. JAMES A. GALLIVAN
Who introduced two of the
postal bills.

From this teaching, as from its source and principle flows
that fatal principle of the separation of Church and State.
(page 159)

From what has been said, it follows, that it is **quite
unlawful** to demand, **to defend, or to grant** unconditional
freedom of thought, of speech, of writing, or of worship.
(page 161)

And now let us see how well the Roman Catholic Church requires its
members to observe and accept the above concentrated treason to our
POPULAR GOVERNMENT.

The strangulation of a Free Press in this country is to be completed
through legislation. We call your attention to the three Bills the Knights
of Columbus have been trying to engineer through for the past seven
years under the photographs of the Pope's Catholic Citizens, Messrs,
Fitzgerald and Gallivan and the papalized Hebrew, one, Isaac Siegal.

PEACEABLE ASSEMBLAGES DENIED IN THE UNITED STATES BY ROMAN CATHOLIC MOB RULE

That the right of peaceable assemblage is almost a thing of the past in this country is proven by the numerous mobs instigated and led by the priests and Knights of Columbus and their hoodlums in the various cities from coast to coast.

The reader has seen from the foregoing quotations from *The Great Encyclical Letters of Pope Leo XIII* that the right to think and to speak and liberty of conscience is absolutely prohibitive in CATHOLIC citizenship.

To prove to you the existence of this divine right citizenship; and to prove to you that the members of the Roman Catholic church cannot and do not grant liberty of conscience to Romanists who have left the church, I call your attention to the following table of mobs and riots carried on by them:

June 12, 1913, the Protestant people of Oelwein, Iowa, invited Jeremiah J. Crowley, ex-priest and author of the *Parochial School; A Curse to the Church and a Menace to the Nation*, to address them in the theatre of that town on the subject of the public school question. At the instigation of the Roman Catholic priest of that city, who delivered his sermon the Sunday before the Crowley lecture, some two thousand Romanists, led by the Knights of Columbus and their hoodlums, mobbed Mr. Crowley as he was leaving the theatre with some of his friends, and beat him severely.

April 14th, 1914, the Rev. Otis Spurgeon of Iowa, who had been called to deliver a course of lectures by Protestant Americans at Denver, Colorado, was kidnapped from the Pierce Hotel in that city at eight o'clock in the evening, bound hand and foot, gagged and a strap placed around his neck, was thrown into an automobile, parked in front of the hotel, whisked out into the country and beaten into unconsciousness. En route, his captors told him they were Knights of Columbus and repeatedly during the trip, when he refused to answer or did not answer as they wished, he was choked by the strap ("Strangulation cord").

The Rev. Spurgeon was finally rescued, taken to a hospital where he was found to have sustained internal injuries and lay very ill for three weeks. According to the Roman Church, Rev. Spurgeon was a "heretic" and a "Mason."

On *February 4, 1915*, Rev. William Black, ex-priest, at that time a

Congregational minister, was delivering a course of lectures en route to the California Coast, where he was to have testified that while he was a Roman priest and a Knight of Columbus he had taken the Jesuit oath on the Congressional Record . . . cited heretofore. The reverend Black had reached Marshall, Texas, where he was to deliver two lectures. He gave his first lecture on the public school question in the auditorium of the City Hall at Marshall, February 3. About five o'clock in the evening on Feb. 4th, Mr. Black and his body guard, a Mr. J. A. Hall, ex-soldier and expert shot whom he took with him on his trip, were returning from a walk about the city.

On reaching his door, four men standing at the end of the corridor nearby approached him. They asked if he was Mr. Black and then asked permission to come in and speak with him a few minutes. The Rev. Black opened the door and invited them in.

The visitors informed him that they were members of the Knights of Columbus Council of Marshall, and that they understood that he intended to deliver another lecture "against their church" that night. Mr. Black assured them that they were correct.

Then the spokesman, a prominent attorney, Ryan by name, said, "No you won't. We will give you just 15 minutes to pack your suitcase and get out of town."

Mr. Black coolly informed them that he intended to deliver his lecture, and that he would relinquish his American constitutional rights for no man.

On rising from a shoe-blacking case where he had been sitting, John Rogers, a leading architect of that vicinity who had drawn up plans of the hotel in which they now were, sprang toward him, pinioned his arms and in shorter time than it takes to tell it: Black's body was riddled with bullets, and in the melee John Rogers' body fell across that of Black's, being also instantly killed.

Copeland, a leading banker the third Knight of Columbus and Catholic citizen, received a wound from which he will never fully recover and promptly received the consolations of his church in the corridor, outside the room where they carried him.

It may be of interest to know that the priest was in the lobby of the hotel when Black and Hall entered to go to their room. Through political influence, these surviving Knights of Columbus participants in this cowardly assassination went free.

April 6th, 1915, the Reverend Dr. Joseph and Mary Slattery, ex-priest and ex-nun, of Boston, MA were called by Protestant Americans to deliver some lectures in Chicago, IL. They were lecturing in a Masonic hall on the south side of the city. In the early part of Dr. Slattery's talk, a mob of Roman Catholic hoodlums and members of the Knights of Columbus left their hall just across the street, entered the Slattery meeting, and proceeded to start a riot in true Roman style, by calling Dr. Slattery "a liar." At a signal from a man wearing a Roman collar, from which he drew a handkerchief which had concealed it, the riot started in earnest.

Chairs and furniture were smashed, men and women were beaten indiscriminately and disfigured by the use of brass knucks and blackjacks. The telephone wires in the hall and even the nearby drugstores had been cut and it was fully three-quarters of an hour before they had any response from the Fourth Degree Knights of Columbus policemen.

The speaker and his wife made a miraculous escape. The windows of the automobile in which they were driven were shattered by bullets. These Roman thugs entered street cars, attacked the passengers who had not been at the lecture and knew nothing about the riot. They pulled the trolleys off the wires and derailed and demolished several cars. So much for Roman Catholic citizenship in the great city of Chicago.

In Haverhill, Mass., *April 4th, 1916*, these Knights of Columbus and their hoodlums, being summoned for the occasion from neighboring cities and towns, forced their way into the City Hall where a meeting was being held by Thomas E. Levden, who was speaking upon the political activities of the Roman Church in American politics. I will quote the headlines from some of the Massachusetts papers:

Boston Post,

BIG RIOT RAGES IN HAVERHILL

MANY BEATEN MILITIA IS CALLED

CITY HALL STORMED BY ANGRY MOBS

WHILE REV. THOS. E. LEYDEN WAS HIDDEN IN THE ALDERMAN'S CHAMBER

10,000 IN WILD HAVERHILL RIOTS—MILITIA
CALLED OUT TO SUPPRESS MOB THAT GETS
BEYOND POLICE

———————

City Hall and Police Station Attacked With Missiles
Torn from Streets. National Club Wrecked and Officer
and Civilian Badly Beaten

———————

EDITORIAL FROM THE CHRISTIAN SCIENCE
JOURNAL, BOSTON, APRIL 21, 1916

———————

MOB LAW

The question of free speech is one of such fundamental importance to humanity that it is easy to understand the commotion it has caused in the State of Massachusetts by the recent riots in Haverhill. The contention that a mob, with or without cause, is at liberty to usurp the prerogatives of the courts and to substitute lynch law for official justice, constitutes, indeed, a precedent destructive of all popular liberty. The history of liberty is very largely the effort of authority to restrain license. When the human passions are roused, license is always apt to come to the top.

There is no rhyme or reason in the attack of a mob. It is just as willing to smash a great invention like the spinning-jenny, for fear of the displacement of labor, as it is to stuff the mouth of a Foulon with straw. It is just this that makes the case of the mob in Haverhill so important. If its action is overlooked, if it is connived at, worse still if it is justified today, there is no length to which it may not go tomorrow, and the example set, in Haverhill, may be repeated elsewhere at the expense of the very views the Haverhill exhibition was intended to support.

The simple fact is that the Haverhill mob outraged in the frankest and most indefensible way the common right of free speech. It is not of the slightest importance who Mr. Leyden was, what he was going to say, or what the effect of his words might be. He was entitled to speak, or he was not entitled to speak. If he was entitled to speak, no mob had any right to prevent him. If he was not entitled to speak, no mob had any right to decide the question and to enforce its own decision.

In each event, it outraged entirely the rights of free speech, the only difference is that in one case it outraged it rather worse than in the other.

RESOLUTIONS OF BAPTIST MINISTRY

The Protestant clergy of greater Boston have registered their protest against the outrage in no uncertain tones. Perhaps the most notable of these were the resolutions adopted by the Baptist ministers of greater Boston on April 10th. They were read by Professor F. L. Anderson of Newton Theological Seminary and were, in part, as follows:

"The plain, significant and undisputed fact is that an American citizen was denied the right of free speech, guaranteed by the constitution of Massachusetts, and that the authorities failed to protect him. That the mob was the result of a premeditated plan appears clear from the fact that the lecturer was not permitted even to begin.

"We want to know whether this sort of thing is to continue, whether it is possible that we are entering upon an era of Catholic tyranny in this state, whether henceforth in this state criticism of one church, and only one, is to be indulged in only at the risk of life and limb. We demand of the cardinal that he publicly state his attitude and enforce his authority in such a manner as shall make Catholic mobs impossible in this state. If the cardinal fails to accede to our demand, we shall know how to interpret his continued silence and shall act accordingly.

"We demand that the public authorities bring to justice the leaders of the mob and that the courts Impose suitable punishment. A failure here will prove the constitution and laws of Massachusetts mere scraps of paper, and will forever debar our state, the nursery of liberty, from criticising those Commonwealths where lynching goes unavenged. We say this advisedly, for, according to the beliefs of both our fathers and ourselves, liberty of speech is more precious than life.

"But more than this is required. The only adequate reparation which can be made for this public outrage is a public atonement. This, to our mind, should take the form of an arrangement with Mr Leyden by the citizens of Haverhill, by which he shall speak in Haverhill on the topic already advertised, and shall be protected in his rights by the city and state at any cost. If he then transgresses the laws against slander or incendiary speech, let him be proceeded against by due process of law."

PROTESTANT MINISTERS SPEAK

The entire body of the Protestant clergy of Haverhill, 13 in number, appeared before Mayor Bartlett and Commissioner Hoyt, on April 7, to protest against the outrage, the inefficiency of the police and the equally disgraceful failure of the department of justice to ferret out, arrest and punish the ringleaders of the mob.

The Rev. Nicholas Van der Pyl acted as spokesman for the ministerial body. In the course of his address, he thus voiced the sentiments of the united Protestant ministry of Haverhill:

"I speak in behalf and by the authority of the entire Protestant clergy of the city of Haverhill.

"We deplore, and we feel indignant about the lawlessness which overran this city last Monday night. Our city has been disgraced before the country, and only the people of this city can remove the disgrace which is ours today.

"We are not bigots. We have the highest charity for all who worship God in their own way and according to the dictates of their own conscience.

"But we are also American citizens, and we are the accredited representatives of the morals and religious interests of this city. We hold inviolable the great principles of freedom of speech and freedom of the press, subject to the laws of libel and incendiarism, after the fact, which have been established by all the people, and which only the people can abrogate.

"A mob has overrun our city. Churches have been broken into and desecrated by that mob. The homes of unoffending and innocent citizens have been stoned. In some cases lives have been threatened and placed in jeopardy. We cannot forget so long as the mob is permitted to be victorious, and its leaders glowing in the fact that they have trampled under their feet the most sacred rights of all our people. We will not forget until the principle of free speech has been impressively vindicated by the law-abiding element of this community itself."

In point of fact, the condition is this, that no ex-Romanist now in the field in this conflict in this country is granted his or her constitutional rights by the priests and prelates of the Roman Catholic church. There is not an ex-Catholic lecturer in the field today who does not take his or her life in their own hands every time they appear before an audience. Speaking from personal experience, the writer has had several mobs, one of which was in the Pioneer Congregational Church in Chicago, where the following subjects were advertised:

"The Enemy within our borders."
"The Public vs. Parochial schools."
"The Suppressed Truth about the Assassination of Abraham Lincoln."

The church early in the evening was surrounded by a mob of about 2,000 Catholics some of whom forced their way in and filled up the auditorium. After listening for about three quarters of an hour, at a whistle from the leader of the mob which was the signal to begin, windows were broken, chairs were smashed, literature torn and scattered all over the hall. In response to a riot call from the downtown station (police at that precinct there would not respond), two wagon loads of officers stepped out, all of whom but one were Knights of Columbus. I know this because they admitted it to me. Such wide publicity has been given by the local and anti-Roman press of Knights of Columbus mobs in San Francisco, Sept. 22 and Sept. 26, 1921, that it is not necessary to dwell on them.

Only a few weeks ago, we read of the mobs of the meetings of the Baptist minister, ex-Monk Eli M. Erickson in Chicago, who speaks upon his conversion from Romanism to Protestantism. But again the priests of Rome denied Rev. Erickson his American rights.

This mobbing is not confined to ex-Romanists. That splendid patriotic worker and eloquent lecturer, William Lloyd Clark of Milan, IL, has, in spite of Rome's vicious mobs, time without number, held the torch of American patriotism up for the last thirty-five years. For the most part, he was almost single handed and alone. Mr. Clark has been rotten-egged, shot at, arrested and jailed, all dozens of times, but he has never ceased to batter at these assassins of Liberty.

In closing, I will leave it to my reader to decide whether I have proven my contention in the beginning of this book that the assassination of Abraham Lincoln and four other presidents is but a part of the great conspiracy, outlined in the Secret Treaty of Verona, to destroy this Republic . . .

That the execution of this conspiracy in Lincoln's case was delegated by the Pope of Rome to the Jesuits in the United States and their lay agents, the Leopoldines . . .

That instead of the use of bullets and bayonets, their method has been and is to destroy from within by the subversion of all of the free institutions upon which this Republic is based . . .

That the Church of Rome has established a separate citizenship to promote its teachings and by its enormous wealth a large proportion of which has been obtained by unconstitutional and illegal appropriations from public funds; that with this wealth (over two and a half billion dollars' worth of church and other religious property, for the most part exempt from taxation) it has by a system of intimidation and bribery corrupted our free press and is in control of every avenue of publicity, so that the American people remain in almost total ignorance of its pernicious activities, which, if not curbed, will succeed in accomplishing its object in these United States.

For the further information of the reader, allow me to impress it upon you, that the present Pope, Pius XI, is the Cardinal Ratti whom the late Pope sent to Poland on the express mission of inducing the makers of the new constitution to **restore the Roman church as the State church**, a feat that the gentleman covered himself with papal glory by accomplishing, an act no doubt, that earned him the **Pontifical throne**. Also remember that Pius XI stands for just what all Popes have stood.

Purchase Our Books

Our books can be purchased on
Amazon stores worldwide
AdagioPress.com
WilliamDeanAGarner.com
RioRamirez.com
SeanMaclarenBooks.com
VADisabilityClaimBook.com
BarnesandNoble.com and
Apple iTunes Bookstore.

Please enjoy browsing our selection. . . .

Burke McCarty

The Suppressed Truth About The Assassination of *Abraham Lincoln*

The Suppressed Truth About the Assassination of Abraham Lincoln

Ex-Catholic Burke McCarty spent years researching the details surrounding the murder of President Abraham Lincoln, who was one of the few American politicians who openly acknowledged that the Jesuits were a menace to our society, but he felt powerless to do anything about the threat.

This hidden gem should be read by every person who calls himself or herself an American, as it uncovers an ongoing sinister plot to overthrow the liberties of our beloved nation and her people.

You owe it to yourself to read the well-carved thoughts of this brave woman who risked her own life to present the facts that most others continue to ignore, even 150 years after the murder of President Lincoln.

Paperback available from Amazon.com and other retail outlets
eBook available from WilliamDeanAGarner.com and
AdagioPress.com

THE PRINCE

Machiavelli's *The Prince* has become a classic over the centuries since it first appeared around 1510, not because of its elegance or style but because of its subversive content about the true nature of power. Mainstream historians and academics have labelled it a "political treatise," but this is only a small part of the picture.

The Prince isn't just for princes who thirst for, or are forcibly thrown into, advancement.

It is a raw and bloody field manual for upper- and mid-level managers on predatorial ethics and power: what it is, how to obtain it, and what to do with it once you have found, stumbled across, or been granted it.

Paperback available from Amazon.com and other retail outlets

eBook available from WilliamDeanAGarner.com and AdagioPress.com

ROMANIC DEPRESSION
How the Jesuits Designed,
Built and Destroyed America

Sean Mclaren has carefully researched and written the two sequels to *Who Really Owns Your Gold,* which was an introductory historical perspective about the Jesuits and their malevolent actions and behaviors over the past 100-plus years in America. In this ground-breaking volume, he analyzes and examines 40 sectors of American society, and demonstrate how the Jesuits have designed and built, and manipulated and corrupted each one, then marketed and advertised something decidedly contrary.

The book's Reference section contains more than 200 books about the Jesuits. If you take the time to read even a few of them, your heart, mind and soul will expand immensely, and you will begin to understand what others have known for centuries: this brood of snakes and vipers has done, and continues to do, great harm to humanity. . . .

Paperback available from Amazon.com and other retail outlets
eBook available from WilliamDeanAGarner.com,
AdagioPress.com and SeanMaclarenBooks.com

ARCANUM
A critical analysis of the original 36 sermons of Jmmanuel, the man known to the world as Jesus Christ

ARCANUM by Sean Maclaren is one of two sequels to *Who Really Owns Your Gold*, which was an introductory historical perspective about the Jesuits and their malevolent actions and behaviors over the past 100-plus years in America.

The 410-page sequel is a highly detailed and provocative two-part essay:

Part One is an unsparing, meticulous and diligent analysis and evaluation of each of the original 36 sermons of Jmmanuel Sananda, the half-extraterrestrial/half-human known to the world as Jesus Christ.

Part Two is an actual full English translation and new edit (for clarity and readability) of the 36 extant sermons of Jmmanuel Sananda, the man known to the world as Jesus Christ.

Paperback available from Amazon.com and other retail outlets
eBook available from WilliamDeanAGarner.com, AdagioPress.com and SeanMaclarenBooks.com

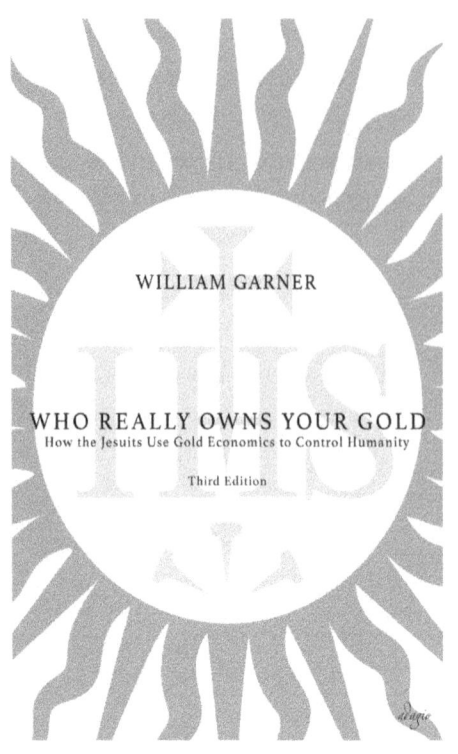

***Who Really Owns Your Gold
How The Jesuits Use Gold
Economics To Control
Humanity,*** **Third Edition**

The power that controls your gold, your assets and your life is a dynastic group of men in Rome, and it's not the Vatican. They control every government on the planet and, using celestiophysics, manipulate to their advantage all actions and behaviors in law, politics, economics and finance, business, law enforcement, military and defense affairs, science and high-tech, entertainment, medicine and healthcare, education, etc.

New York Times bestselling ghostwriter and editor William Dean A. Garner takes you on a journey into a labyrinth where up is down, black is white, yes is no . . . and nothing is what it seems.

This revelation is for everyone, not just those who "own" gold or precious metals.

Paperback available from Amazon.com and other retail outlets
eBook available from WilliamDeanAGarner.com and
AdagioPress.com

Sun Tzu *The Art of War*
Ancient Wisdom . . . Modern Twist

Edited by William Garner
New York Times bestselling ghostwriter/editor

"Dean Garner's version of *The Art of War* confirms for us that for the past 2,000 years the fundamental principles of special operations in battle have not only remained true, but they apply equally to today's boardrooms and bedrooms. When on the hunt or holding ground, success can only be had by the precise application of disguise, deception and diversion, and a genuine appreciation for angles, inches, and seconds. Ranger Garner masterfully shows us how."
—Dalton Fury
New York Times bestselling author of *Tier One Wild* and *Kill Bin Laden*

New York Times bestselling author Dalton Fury has this to say about William Dean A. Garner's updated version of *The Art of War*: "Dean Garner's version of *The Art of War* confirms for us that for the past 2,000 years the fundamental principles of special operations in battle have not only remained true, but they apply equally to today's boardrooms and bedrooms. When on the hunt or holding ground, success can only be had by the precise application of disguise, deception and diversion, and a genuine appreciation for angles, inches, and seconds. Ranger Garner masterfully shows us how."

Paperback available from Amazon.com and other retail outlets

eBook available from WilliamDeanAGarner.com and AdagioPress.com

How To Write Your First Book
A Simple & Practical Method
For Anyone Who Can Tell a Story

This gem is much more than just a book about writing. It reveals metaphysically how our subconscious functions during the creative process to produce the finished product, and how we grow spiritually as this process evolves before us to create our first book.

Garner employs a simple, step-by-step method we have used all our lives, and includes easy-to-follow examples and exercises, plus anecdotes from his work as a ghostwriter/editor on some very sexy novels and books.

Paperback available from Amazon.com and other retail outlets
eBook available from AdagioPress.com

Lightning Source UK Ltd.
Milton Keynes UK
UKHW012352290121
377923UK00003B/947